Utz Schäffer

Management Accounting & Control Scales Handbook

GABLER EDITION WISSENSCHAFT

Research in Management Accounting & Control

Herausgegeben von Professor Dr. Utz Schäffer
WHU – Otto Beisheim School of Management, Vallendar

Die Schriftenreihe präsentiert Ergebnisse betriebswirtschaftlicher Forschung im Bereich Controlling. Sie basiert auf einer akteursorientierten Sicht des Controlling, in der die Rationalitätssicherung der Führung einen für die Theorie und Praxis zentralen Stellenwert einnimmt.

The series presents research results in the field of management accounting and control. It is based on a behavioral view of management accounting where the assurance of management rationality is of central importance for both theory and practice.

Utz Schäffer

Management Accounting & Control Scales Handbook

With the collaboration of Dr. Markus Eckey, Nico Rose
and Dr. Karin Schermelleh-Engel

Deutscher Universitäts-Verlag

Bibliographic information published by Die Deutsche Nationalbibliothek
Die Deutsche Nationalbibliothek lists this publication in the Deutsche Nationalbibliografie; detailed bibliographic data is available in the Internet at <http://dnb.d-nb.de>.

1st Edition October 2007

Readers: Frauke Schindler / Anita Wilke

Deutscher Universitäts-Verlag is a company of Springer Science+Business Media.
www.duv.de

Cover design: Regine Zimmer, Dipl.-Designerin, Frankfurt/Main
Printed on acid-free paper
Printed in Germany

ISBN 978-3-8350-0525-9

Preface

I owe the idea of creating this scales handbook to Klaus Brockhoff. At the Vallendarer Controlling-Tagung 2002 and with reference to German-language controlling research, he rightly pointed out that methodological approaches aim – among other things – at establishing the intersubjective comparability of research questions. Therefore, differing, unrelated definitions of latent constructs do a disservice to comparative research and cumulative discovery processes.

This is where scales handbooks offer a concrete benefit: a quick and concise overview of the relevant constructs and their use in previous studies. Not surprisingly, scales handbooks have existed for quite some time in marketing and other disciplines. Most controlling researchers, however, have traditionally been rather hesitant to engage in rigorous empirical research and to connect to the international scientific community in management accounting. As a consequence, a handbook of management accounting and control-related constructs does not yet exist. However, we were able to build on a smaller compilation of scales which was collected and published by Jürgen Weber, Bianca Willauer and myself in 2003.

Against this background, the collection of scales in this book aims at promoting empirical research in controlling by giving researchers a quick and – to the extent possible – concise overview of relevant constructs and their use in previous studies. A significant number of the constructs presented in this collection are based on data sampled in Germany, and have not been translated into English. However, the names of constructs, their descriptions and all the goodness-of-fit measures are given in English.

Dr. Markus Eckey, Nico Rose, Dr. Karin Schermelleh-Engel and Anita Wilke contributed significantly to developing this scales handbook, for which I would like to express my heartfelt thanks to them.

Utz Schäffer

Table of Contents

I Introduction to Construct Measurement

Scales concisely show how a theoretical construct has been empirically measured. Their reliability and validity ratios give a notion of the quality of the scale. Since most scales are developed by the respective authors and are therefore in a first version, they can be used as a basis for supplementation and further development.
A multilevel procedure was applied to develop and evaluate these scales, as described below. The calculation of the reliability and validity ratios and their necessary ranges for high-quality designs is also presented.
The chosen approach is mainly based on Homburg's[1] guidelines and Homburg/Giering's[2] concept for conceptualizing and operationalizing complex constructs.
Many empirical studies examine relations between complex constructs and latent variables that cannot be measured directly.[3] As these constructs cannot be measured directly they have to be measured indirectly using indicator variables. Indicators are observed variables that are operationalizations of the latent variables and are therefore formally associated with the constructs. In order to perform a causal analysis with data from an empirical survey, the latent variables are first conceptualized and then operationalized. Conceptualization is the formulation of the relevant construct dimensions. In the subsequent process of operationalization, the measurement instrument in question is developed with its indicator variables.[4]
After conceptualization and operationalization, it is necessary to assess on the basis of empirical data whether or not the developed measurement instruments or scales fulfill the psychometric requirements of reliability and validity.[5]
Reliability refers to consistency of scores on a particular measurement instrument or scale. Methods that assess the reliability of a measurement instrument are in most cases based on classical test theory.[6] According to classical test theory each item *i* can be decomposed into a linear combination of a true score (common to all items) and a random error:

$$X_i = T + E_i$$

The random error is assumed to be uncorrelated with the true score. Additionally, researchers generally assume that the measurement error is not correlated with measurement errors of the other items. The total score is the sum of all *k* indicators or items that constitute the measurement instrument or scale:

$$X = X_1 + X_2 + \ldots + X_k$$

---

[1] Homburg (2000).
[2] Homburg/Giering (1996).
[3] Bagozzi/Phillips (1982), p. 465; Long (1983), p. 11.
[4] Churchill Jr. (1979), p. 66; Bagozzi/Baumgartner (1994), p. 388.
[5] Carmines/Zeller (1979), pp. 11-13.
[6] Lord/Novick (1968).

The reliability of the scale is the ratio of the true score variance to the total variance:

$$Rel(X) = \frac{\sigma_T^2}{\sigma_X^2} = \frac{\sigma_T^2}{\sigma_T^2 + \sigma_E^2}$$

The higher the reliability of an instrument, the closer the true scores will be to the total scores for that instrument. In case of high reliability only a minor proportion of shared variance of different measurements (indicators, items) can be attributed to an incorrect measurement process.[7] The association with the underlying constructs can instead explain an important amount of shared variance of the indicators.

Conceptually, reliability is consistency. Reliability is therefore frequently assessed in terms of internal consistency of a measure using Cronbach's alpha. Other methods for the assessment of an instrument's reliability are retest reliability and parallel test reliability.[8]

Construct validity is one of the most central concepts in psychometrics. Researchers typically establish construct validity by estimating correlations between a measure of a construct and other measures that should be associated with it (convergent validity) or vary independently of it (discriminant validity)[9]. A measurement instrument is valid if it is as free of random errors as possible and additionally conceptually correct.[10] This is why the reliability of a measurement is a necessary prerequisite for its validity.[11] The validity concept, however, goes beyond the reliability concept because it includes conceptual accuracy.[12] A measurement instrument is valid if it measures what it is supposed to measure. Various quantitative methods are used to verify that measurement models comply with the criteria of reliability and validity. Fornell (1982) differentiates between 1st generation and 2nd generation methods.[13]

1st generation criteria for reliability and validity derive from psychometrics and are based on classical test theory. Among the 1st generation criteria described in the construct part of this book are item-to-total correlations, Cronbach's alpha and exploratory factor analysis.[14]

2nd generation criteria for reliability and validity are based on modern test theory, i.e. structural equation modeling using confirmatory factor analyses (CFA). Another measurement theory that assesses reliability and validity in a different manner is item response theory.[15] In various respects, evaluation methods based on modern test theories are more powerful than 1st generation criteria.[16] The advantages of CFA models include estimates of reliability and validity as well as an overall test of the fit of the model to the data.

---

[7] Churchill Jr. (1991), p. 495.
[8] Moosbrugger (in press); Schermelleh-Engel/Werner (in press).
[9] Westen/Rosenthal (2003).
[10] Churchill Jr. (1979), p. 65.
[11] Peter (1979), pp. 6-10.
[12] Homburg/Baumgartner (1995).
[13] Fornell (1982), p. 217.
[14] Anderson/Gerbing (1988).
[15] Van der Linden/Hambleton (1997).
[16] Long (1983), pp. 11-19.

Evaluation of model fit in structural equation modeling is not as straightforward as it is in statistical approaches based on variables measured without error. As there is no single statistical significance test that identifies a correct model given the sample data, it is necessary to take multiple criteria into consideration and to evaluate model fit on the basis of various measures simultaneously.[17]

There is a consensus that one should avoid reporting all fit indices that have been developed within the framework of structural equation modeling, but there is a certain disagreement on just which fit indices to report. As the only overall test – the χ^2 test – is sensitive not only to sample size but also to the violation of the assumption of multivariate normality, it should not serve as the sole basis for judging model fit[18]. Bollen and Long (1993) recommend evaluating several indices simultaneously which represent different classes of goodness-of-fit criteria.[19]

Gradual application of these criteria of goodness-of-fit improves the measurement model by excluding single indicators from measurement if they do not fulfill certain criteria of goodness-of-fit. Only constructs whose criteria of goodness-of-fit fulfill certain commonly accepted threshold values are considered as useable for further research and utilized for hypothesis testing. However, for an acceptable measurement not all criteria of goodness-of-fit have to be fulfilled simultaneously.[20]

In the following the 1st generation and 2nd generation criteria of goodness-of-fit will be described further. The description is limited to a short summary and explanation of the measurements used in the scales shown below. For further explanation of the 1st generation and 2nd generation criteria please refer to the respective literature.

II Evaluation of Reliability using 1st Generation Criteria

In the following three 1st generation criteria for evaluation of the goodness-of-fit of a scale will be described: item-to-total correlation, Cronbach's alpha, and the explained variance within the scope of exploratory factor analysis.

The item-to-total correlation is defined as the correlation of an indicator (=item) with the sum of all indicators (= total score) which is assigned to the same factor (single item-to-total correlation). The corrected item-to-total correlation is the correlation of an indicator with the sum of the remaining indicators after removing the considered indicator.[21] In general, item-to-total correlations should be as high as possible. High values for all indicators of a factor designate convergence validity. Single indicators with low item-to-total correlations can be eliminated in order to increase reliability.[22]

---

[17] Schermelleh-Engel/Moosbrugger/Müller (2003), p. 31.
[18] Hu/Bentler/Kano (1992).
[19] Bollen/Long (1993).
[20] Homburg/Giering (1996), p. 20.
[21] Norušis (1993), p. 146.
[22] Churchill Jr. (1979), p. 68.

While the item-to-total correlation is calculated separately for each examined indicator, Cronbach's alpha[23] is a criterion of goodness-of-fit that evaluates a scale as a total. Cronbach's alpha is one of the most frequently used criteria of goodness-of-fit for reliability measurement.[24] It is an internal consistency estimate that requires only a single administration of a scale. The assumptions underlying coefficient alpha are that errors among items are uncorrelated, that the error scores for an item are uncorrelated with the true scores, and that the error scores for each item are uncorrelated with the error scores for all other items.[25]
Cronbach's alpha is calculated as follows:

$$\alpha = \left(\frac{q}{q-1}\right) \cdot \left(1 - \frac{\sum_{i=1}^{q} \sigma_i^2}{\sigma_t^2}\right)$$

where q is the number of items in the scale, σ_i^2 is the variance of item i and σ_t^2 is the variance of the scale. In general, Cronbach's alpha can take on values varying between zero and one with higher values indicating higher reliability. A Cronbach's alpha of .70 is commonly considered as acceptable.[26] Cronbach's alpha is affected by several problems, such as item heterogeneity, multidimensionality, and negatively worded items.[27] Furthermore, Cronbach's alpha is positively correlated with the number of indicators.[28] Consequently, a high number of indicators can lead to a high value for Cronbach's alpha although the internal consistency is not satisfactory. Since the measurement of complex constructs requires a sufficient number of indicators, a large number of indicators is arguably necessary for complex constructs.
Exploratory factor analysis is used to determine the factorial validity of indicators measuring one or more factors. In contrast to confirmatory factor analysis, the factorial structure underlying the indicators is not defined ex ante.[29] The objective of exploratory factor analysis is to reduce the indicators to as few factors as possible, which represent the totality of indicators sufficiently well.[30] This aggregation of indicators to a lower number of underlying factors is reached by eliminating those indicators which do not sufficiently load on a single factor.[31] The allocation of an indicator to a factor is non-ambiguous if the indicators load sufficiently (.40) on one factor. In the case of a multi-factorial structure the indicators of one factor must additionally load clearly lower on the other factors.[32] The number of factors to be extracted is derived from the Kaiser criterion that refers to the eigenvalues of the correlation

---

[23] Cronbach, L. J. (1951).
[24] Peterson (1994).
[25] Lord/Novick (1968), p. 87-90.
[26] Nunnally/Bernstein (1994), pp. 264f.
[27] Schermelleh-Engel/Werner (in press).
[28] Malhotra/Birks (2003), p. 314.
[29] Anderson/Gerbing (1988), p. 189.
[30] Hartung/Elpelt (1992), p. 505.
[31] Backhaus et al. (2003), p. 266.
[32] Homburg/Giering (1996), p. 8

matrix.[33] The eigenvalue is the sum of the squared factor loadings of a factor for all indicators and describes the variance contribution of a factor regarding the variance of all variables. Since the variance of a (standardized) variable is one, a factor with an eigenvalue of less than one can explain less variance than a single variable.[34] Therefore, according to the Kaiser criterion, only those factors with an eigenvalue of greater than one are considered.[35] Another method to determine the number of factors is parallel analysis, where the empirically derived eigenvalues are compared with randomly generated ones. Parallel analysis is often recommended as the best method for assessing the true number of factors[36]. The measurement of a single extracted factor can be evaluated with the variance share of the indicators that this factor explains. A single factor should amount to at least 50% of the variance of the corresponding indicators.[37]

1st generation criteria are criticized for being based on very restrictive assumptions,[38] mainly rules of thumb,[39] and therefore offering no possibility for the explicit estimation of errors of measurement.[40] 2nd generation criteria can overcome these shortcomings.

III Evaluation of Reliability and Validity using 2nd Generation Criteria

2nd generation criteria are based on confirmatory factor analysis. This is a method for the formal description of the measurement of complex constructs through indicators and for the simultaneous evaluation of the goodness-of-fit of this measurement.[41] Confirmatory factor analysis describes the measurement of a construct through multiple indicators. In contrast to exploratory factor analysis, the allocation of single observed indicators to underlying factors is performed a priori, i.e. before conducting the actual analysis through specification of a measurement model.

In the following such a measurement model will be presented using the notation of the LISREL method.[42] The confirmatory factor analysis can be described by the vector equation

$$x = \Lambda \cdot \xi + \delta$$

where x is the vector of the indicator variables, Λ is the matrix of the factor loadings, ξ is the vector of the latent variables and δ is the vector of the measurement errors.

The population covariance matrix Σ can under certain assumptions be expressed by the parameter matrices Λ, Φ and Θ_δ. The corresponding equation is

$$\Sigma = \Lambda \Phi \Lambda' + \Theta_\delta$$

[33] Kaiser (1974).
[34] Backhaus et al. (2003), pp. 295f.
[35] Kaiser (1974).
[36] Moosbrugger/Schermelleh-Engel (in press).
[37] Homburg/Giering (1996), p. 12.
[38] Anderson/Gerbing (1988).
[39] Bagozzi/Yi/Phillips (1991), p. 428.
[40] Homburg/Giering (1996), p. 9.
[41] Jöreskog/Sörbom (2001), p. 1.
[42] Jöreskog/Sörbom (2001), p. 1.

where Λ' is the transposed matrix to Λ, Φ is the covariance matrix of the latent variables, and Θ_δ is the covariance matrix of the measurement errors. The objective of confirmatory factor analysis is to determine if the number of factors, the factor intercorrelations and the factor loadings of the indicator variables conform to the expectations on the basis of pre-established theory. In order to estimate the model's parameter, the maximum likelihood (ML) method is most often used. The ML estimator assumes that the variables in the model are multivariate normal, i.e., the joint distribution of the variables is a multivariate normal distribution. This method leads to parameter estimates that maximize the likelihood that the empirical covariance matrix S is drawn from a population for which the model-implied covariance matrix $\hat{\Sigma}$ is valid. The model-implied covariance matrix is estimated by

$$\hat{\Sigma} = \Sigma\left(\hat{\Lambda}, \hat{\Phi}, \hat{\Theta}_\delta\right).$$

Following parameter estimation the model fit is evaluated using various criteria of goodness-of-fit.[43] Generally, goodness-of-fit criteria of a confirmatory factor model indicate to what extent the specified model fits the empirical data. Model evaluation can be assessed inferentially by the χ^2 test or descriptively by applying several other criteria.[44] Although there are no well-established guidelines for what minimal conditions constitute an adequate fit, it is generally accepted to establish that the model is identified, that the estimation method converges, that all parameter estimates are within the range of permissible values, and that the size of the standard errors of the parameter estimates are reasonable.[45]

The χ^2 test statistic is used for hypothesis testing to evaluate the appropriateness of a confirmatory factor model. The following null hypothesis is tested: The model is correct and the empirical covariance matrix S is consequently equal to the covariance matrix $\hat{\Sigma}$ generated by the model. The χ^2 value

$$\chi^2 = (N-1) \cdot F\left(S, \hat{\Sigma}\right)$$

is calculated with

$$df = \frac{1}{2} \cdot q(q+1) - t$$

degrees of freedom where N is the sample size, q is the number of indicator variables and t is the number of parameters to be estimated. As the researcher is interested in obtaining a nonsignificant χ^2 value with associated degrees of freedom, the p-value associated with the χ^2 value should be larger than .05. In this case the test states that the model fits the data. But there are several shortcomings associated with the χ^2 test statistic.[46] One disadvantage of the χ^2 value is that it decreases when parameters are added to the model. Thus, the χ^2 value of complex models tend to be smaller than for simpler models. Another disadvantage is that the

---

[43] Sharma (1996).
[44] Schermelleh-Engel/Moosbrugger/Müller (2003), p. 31.
[45] Marsh/Grayson (1995).
[46] Schermelleh-Engel/Moosbrugger/Müller (2003), p. 32.

χ^2 value increases with increasing sample size and a constant number of degrees of freedom. This leads to the problem that correct models might be rejected based on a significant χ^2 statistic even though the discrepancy between the sample and the model-implied covariance matrix may be small.

An essential problem of the χ^2 goodness-of-fit test is that the absolute correctness of a model is examined. However, since models can only be approximations to reality, the χ^2 test is only partly suited for the evaluation of the goodness-of-fit of constructs.[47]

The quotient between the χ^2 value and the model's number of degrees of freedom is used as a descriptive measure for evaluating goodness-of-fit.[48] For a good model fit, the ratio χ^2/df should be small. As there are no absolute standards, a ratio between 2 and 3 is said to be indicative of a „good" or an „acceptable" data-model fit. Therefore a maximum value of three is required.[49] Because of the drawbacks of the χ^2 test statistic, numerous descriptive fit indices have been developed.

In contrast to the χ^2 goodness-of-fit test the RMSEA (root mean squared error of approximation) assesses whether the model fits the population sufficiently well. The RMSEA is estimated by the discrepancy due to approximation per degrees of freedom:

$$\text{RMSEA} = \sqrt{\max\left\{\left(\frac{F(\mathbf{S},\boldsymbol{\Sigma}(\hat{\theta}))}{df} - \frac{1}{N-1}\right), 0\right\}},$$

where max is the maximum of the argument, $F(\mathbf{S},\boldsymbol{\Sigma}(\hat{\theta}))$ is the minimum of the fit function, df is the number of degrees of freedom, and N is the sample size. RMSEA values below .05 are generally considered as a good model fit, values between .05 and .08 as an adequate fit, and values between .08 and .10 as a mediocre fit, while values > .10 are not acceptable. [50]

A further commonly used goodness-of-fit measure is the GFI (goodness-of-fit index). It is calculated as follows:

$$\text{GFI} = 1 - \frac{tr\left[\left(\hat{\Sigma}^{-1}S - I\right)^2\right]}{tr\left[\left(\hat{\Sigma}^{-1}S\right)^2\right]}$$

where tr is the sum of the diagonal elements of the matrix (trace) and I the identity matrix. A GFI of one is observed in the case of a perfectly fitting model. The usual rule of thumb for this index is that .95 is indicative of a good fit, while values greater than .90 are typically interpreted as indicating an acceptable fit. [51]

---

[47] Cudeck/Browne (1983).
[48] Bagozzi/Baumgartner (1994).
[49] Homburg (2000), p. 90.
[50] Cudeck/Browne (1983).
[51] Homburg/Baumgartner (1995), p. 168.

However, the goodness-of-fit of the construct measurement depends not only on the fit of the model to the data but also on the number of parameters to be estimated. Since the degrees of freedom of the model are not considered when calculating the GFI, the goodness-of-fit of the model is automatically improved by adding a model parameter to be estimated. The AGFI adjusts for the model's degrees of freedom relative to the number of observed variables and therefore rewards less complex models with fewer parameters:

$$\text{AGFI} = 1 - \frac{q \cdot (q+1)}{2df}(1 - \text{GFI})$$

Similar to the GFI the AGFI has an upper limit of one indicating a perfect fit of the model to the data set. A rule of thumb for this index is that .90 is indicative of good fit relative to the baseline model, while values greater than .85 may be considered as an acceptable fit.[52] But there are also shortcomings associated with this index. Simulation studies suggest that GFI and AGFI are not independent of sample size.[53] Furthermore, both indices favor complex over parsimonious models as they decrease with increasing model complexity, especially for smaller sample sizes (Anderson & Gerbing, 1984).[54]

An additional goodness-of-fit measure is the CFI (comparative fit index). This ratio evaluates the goodness-of-fit of a relevant model in comparison to a baseline, the independence model. The CFI is calculated by the following equation; degrees of freedom are considered in the same way as in the AGFI:

$$\text{CFI} = 1 - \frac{\max\left(\chi_r^2 - df_r; 0\right)}{\max\left(\chi_b^2 - df_b; \chi_r^2 - df_r; 0\right)}$$

where χ_r^2 designates the χ^2 value of the examined model and χ_b^2 is the χ^2 value of the baseline model; df_r and df_b are the degrees of freedom of the examined model and the baseline model. A rule of thumb for this index is that .97 is indicative of good fit relative to the baseline model, while values greater than .95 may be interpreted as an acceptable fit. A value of .97 seems to be more reasonable as an indication of a good model fit than the often stated cutoff value of .95 when variables are highly correlated.[55]

Apart from the global goodness-of-fit measures presented so far that serve to evaluate the consistency of the total model with the empirical data structure, there are other local goodness-of-fit measures as well. Local criteria allow the evaluation of single model parts as for example single indicators or a factor.

On the level of single indicators the indicator reliability is described. It is a measure for the variance of an indicator explained by the underlying factor. The range of values is from zero

---

52 Homburg/Baumgartner (1995), p. 172.
53 Hu/Bentler (1998).
54 Anderson/Gerbing (1984).
55 Schermelleh-Engel/Moosbrugger/Müller (2003), p. 42.

to one; usually a minimum value of 0.4 is demanded.[56] The share of variance of the indicator not explained by the factor is based upon influences from measurement errors. The indicator reliability is calculated as follows:

$$\mathrm{IR}(x_i)=\frac{\lambda_{ij}^2\phi_{jj}}{\lambda_{ij}^2\phi_{jj}+\theta_{ii}}$$

where λ_{ij} is the estimated factor loading, ϕ_{jj} is the estimated variance of the latent variable ξ_j and θ_{ii} is the estimated variance of the measurement errors δ_i.

Additionally, the *t*-statistic (the quotient of the estimated factor loading divided by its standard error) is used to check whether the factor loading of an indicator is significantly different from zero. This is the case if the *t*-statistic is higher than or equal to 1.645 (one-tailed test on a 5% significance level).[57]

On the level of latent variables conclusions regarding the goodness-of-fit of the measurement are possible using the factor reliability (FR) and the average explained variance (AEV). These two local goodness-of-fit measures can evaluate how well a factor is measured by the totality of indicator variables. Both measures can have values between zero and one with high values showing a high goodness-of-fit of the model. The factor reliability is calculated as follows:

$$\mathrm{FR}(\xi_j)=\frac{\left(\sum_{i=1}^{q}\lambda_{ij}\right)^2\phi_{jj}}{\left(\sum_{i=1}^{q}\lambda_{ij}\right)^2\phi_{jj}+\sum_{i=1}^{q}\theta_{ii}}$$

As a minimum value for an acceptable goodness-of-fit a value of .60 is demanded.[58] The average explained variance shows the shared variance explained by the factor and results form the following calculation:

$$\mathrm{AEV}(\xi_j)=\frac{\sum_{i=1}^{q}\lambda_{ij}^2\phi_{jj}}{\sum_{i=1}^{q}\lambda_{ij}^2\phi_{jj}+\sum_{i=1}^{q}\theta_{ii}}$$

For this value a threshold value of .50 is demanded.[59]

56 Homburg/Baumgartner (1995), p. 170.
57 Homburg/Giering (1996).
58 Homburg/Baumgartner (1995), p. 170.
59 Homburg/Baumgartner (1995), p. 170.

IV Summary

The goodness-of-fit criteria used for evaluating the scales and the corresponding aspiration levels are summarized in the table below.

Criteria	Aspiration level
a) 1st generation criteria	
Item to total correlations	If Cronbach's alpha < .70, elimination of indicator with lowest item-to-total correlation
Cronbach's alpha	$\geq$ .70
Explained variance of exploratory factor analysis	$\geq$ .50
b) 2nd generation criteria	
χ^2/df	$\leq$ 3.00
RMSEA	$\leq$ .08
GFI	$\geq$ .90
AGFI	$\geq$ .85
CFI	$\geq$ .95
Indicator reliability	$\geq$ .40
t statistic of factor loading	$\geq$ 1.645
Factor reliability	$\geq$ .60
Average explained variance (AEV)	$\geq$ .50
χ^2 difference test	Difference $\geq$ 3.841

V References

Anderson, J. C./Gerbing, D. W. (1984): The effect of sampling error on convergence, improper solutions, and goodness-of-fit indices for maximum likelihood confirmatory factor analysis, in: Psychometrika, 49, pp. 155-173.

Anderson, J. C./Gerbing, D. W. (1988): Structural Equation Modeling in Practice: A Review and Recommended Two-Step Approach, in: Psychological Bulletin, Vol. 103, pp. 411-423.

Backhaus, K./Erichson, B./Plinke, W./Weiber, R. (2003): Multivariate Analysemethoden: Eine anwendungsorientierte Einführung, 10th edition, Berlin et al. 2003.

Bagozzi, R. P./Baumgartner, H. (1994): The Evaluation of Structural Equation Models and Hypothesis Testing, in: Bagozzi, R. P. (Ed.): Principles of Marketing Research, Cambridge 1994, pp. 386-422.

Bagozzi, R. P./Phillips, L. W. (1982): Representing and Testing Organizational Theories: A Holistic Construal, in: Administrative Science Quarterly, Vol. 27, pp. 459-489.

Bagozzi, R. P./Yi, Y./Phillips, L. W. (1991): Assessing Construct Validity in Organizational Research, in: Administrative Science Quarterly, Vol. 36, pp. 421-458.

Bollen, K. A./Long, J.S.(1993): Testing Structural Equation Models, Newbury Park 1993.

Carmines, E. G./Zeller, R. A. (1979): Reliability and Validity Assessment, Beverly Hills et al. 1979.

Churchill Jr., G. A. (1979): A Paradigm for Developing Better Measures of Marketing Constructs, in: Journal of Marketing Research, Vol. 16, pp. 64-73.

Churchill Jr., G. A. (1991): Marketing Research: Methodological Foundations, 5. ed., Chicago et al. 1991.

Cronbach, L. J. (1951). Coefficient alpha and the internal structure of tests, in: Psychometrika, Vol. 16, pp. 297-334.

Cudeck, R./Browne, M. W. (1983): Cross-Validation of Covariance Structures, in: Multivariate Behavioral Research, Vol. 18, pp. 147-167.

Fornell, C. (1982): A Second Generation of Multivariate Analysis, New York 1982.

Hartung, J./Elpelt, B. (1992): Multivariate Statistik: Lehr- und Handbuch der Angewandten Statistik, München et al. 1992.

Homburg, C. (2000): Kundennähe von Industriegüterunternehmen: Konzeption - Erfolgswirkungen - Determinanten, 3rd edition, Wiesbaden 2000.

Homburg, C./Baumgartner, H. (1995): Beurteilung von Kausalmodellen - Bestandsaufnahme und Anwendungsempfehlungen, in: Marketing - Zeitschrift für Forschung und Praxis, Vol. 17, pp. 162-176.

Homburg, C./Giering, A. (1996): Konzeptualisierung und Operationalisierung komplexer Konstrukte: Ein Leitfaden für die Marketingforschung, in: Marketing - Zeitschrift für Forschung und Praxis, Vol. 18, pp. 5-24.

Hu, L./Bentler, P. M. (1998): Fit indices in covariance structure analysis: Sensitivity to underparameterized model misspecification, in: Psychological Methods, Vol. 3, pp. 424-453.

Hu, L./Bentler, P. M./Kano, Y. (1992): Can test statistics in covariance structure analysis be trusted?, in: Psychological Bulletin, Vol. 112, pp. 351-362.

Jöreskog, K. G./Sörbom, D. (2001): LISREL 8: User's Reference Guide, Lincolnwood 2001.

Kaiser, H. F. (1974): An Index of Factor Simplicity, in: Psychometrika, Vol. 39, pp. 31-36.

Long, J. S. (1983): Covariance Structure Models: An Introduction to LISREL, Beverly Hills 1983.

Lord, F. M./Novick, M. R. (1968): Statistical theories of mental test scores, Reading 1968.

Malhotra, N. K./Birks, D. F. (2003): Marketing Research: An Applied Orientation, 3rd ed., London et al. 2003.

Marsh, H. W./Grayson, D. (1995): Latent variable models of multitrait-multimethod data, in: R. Hoyle (Ed.): Structural equation modeling: Concepts, issues and applications, Thousand Oaks 1995, pp. 177-198.

Moosbrugger, H. (in press): Klassische Testtheorie, in: Moosbrugger, H./Kelava, A. (Eds.): Testtheorie und Fragebogenkonstruktion, Berlin in press.

Moosbrugger, H./Schermelleh-Engel, K. (in press): Exploratorische (EFA) und Konfirmatorische Faktorenanalyse (CFA), in: Moosbrugger, H./Kelava, A. (Eds.): Testtheorie und Fragebogenkonstruktion, Berlin in press.

Norušis, M. J. (1993): SPSS for Windows: Professional Statistics, Release 6.0, Chicago 1993.

Nunnally, J. C./Bernstein, I. H. (1994): Psychometric Theory, 3rd ed., New York et al. 1994.

Peter, J. P. (1979): Reliability: A Review of Psychometric Basics and Recent Marketing Practices, in: Journal of Marketing Research, Vol. 16, pp. 6-17.

Peterson, R. A. (1994): A Meta-Analysis of Cronbach's Coefficient Alpha, in: Journal of Consumer Research, Vol. 21, pp. 381-391.

Schermelleh-Engel, K., Moosbrugger, H./Müller, H. (2003): Evaluating the fit of structural equation models: Tests of significance and descriptive goodness-of-fit measures, in: Methods of Psychological Research-Online, Vol. 8, pp. 23–74.

Schermelleh-Engel, K./Werner, C.S. (in press): Methoden der Reliabilitätsbestimmung, in: Moosbrugger, H./Kelava, A. (Eds.): Testtheorie und Fragebogenkonstruktion, Berlin in press.

Sharma, S. (1996): Applied Multivariate Techniques, New York et al. 1996.

Van der Linden, W. J./Hambleton, R. K. (1997): Handbook of modern item response theory, New York 1997.

Westen, D./Rosenthal, R. (2003): Quantifying construct validity: Two simple measures, in: Journal of Personality & Social Psychology, Vol. 84, pp. 608-618.

1. Accounting Control (in R&D Organizations)

Scale Description

The scale describes the extent to which accounting is used as a form of control. Respondents were asked to indicate the extent to which each of three items represented the use of accounting control in their unit.

Origin

Based on early work of Hopwood (1972) and others.

Samples

Survey data were collected by both questionnaire and interview, administered to 150 senior research officers in the research and development (R&D) divisions of a large Australian industrial company and a major US scientific organization. A total of 138 questionnaires (92%) was returned, eleven of which were incomplete, resulting in a useable sample set of 127. On average, the respondents were 40 years of age, had worked for their present employer for 10 years, and had been in their current position for three years. The respondents all held first-line supervisory positions and were responsible for managing separate, identifiable work groups.

Comments

The highest inter-item correlation obtained from the use of this measure was only 0.20, suggesting reliability problems and the need to exercise caution in interpreting the results. Abernethy and Brownell (1997) reported a mean of 10.40 and standard deviation of 3.23 on a theoretical range of 3-21.

Scale Indicators and Reliability / Validity Parameters

Scale: from 1 (definitely false) to 7 (definitely true)

Information on individual indicators regarding "Accounting control (in R&D Organizations)"
Description of indicators
1. No accounting numbers of any sort figure prominently when my performance is judged. (R)
2. Control over the activities of research departments is achieved principally with periodic reporting of accounting information.
3. My ability to meet financial targets is a preoccupation of my superior.

Information on scale "Accounting Control (in R&D Organizations)"			
Descriptive Statistics		*Result of Exploratory Factor Analysis*	
Cronbach's alpha:	–*	Total variance explained:	–*

*Not available

References

Abernethy, M. A./Brownell, P. **(1997): Management Control Systems in Research and Development Organizations: The Role of Accounting, Behavior, and Personnel Controls, in: Accounting, Organizations and Society, Vol. 22, pp. 233-248.**

Hopwood, A. G. (1972): An Empirical Study of the Role of Accounting Data in Performance Evaluation, in: Journal of Accounting Research, Vol. 10, pp. 156-182.

2. Adaptation of Metrics [Anpassung der Kennzahlen]

Scale Description

The scale measures manager's assessment of regular revision of the Metrics used to monitor their business unit.

Origin

The scale was newly developed by Sandt (2004).

Samples

The questionnaire was sent to 2,386 German upper level managers. 254 responses could be integrated into the analysis, yielding a response rate of 11.1%.

Scale Indicators and Reliability / Validity Parameters

Scale: from 1 (definitely false) to 5 (definitely true)

Information on individual indicators regarding "Adaptation of metrics [Anpassung der Kennzahlen]"			
Description of indicators	*Item to Total-Correlation*	*Indicator-Reliability*	*t statistic*
1. Die Kennzahlen werden von Zeit zu Zeit an neue Anforderungen angepasst.	0.69	0.61	16.47
2. Die Kennzahlen wurden einmal entwickelt und sind seitdem nicht verändert worden. (R)	0.63	0.50	15.57
3. Bei organisationalen Änderungen, z.B. neue Strategie, Organisationsstruktur, neue Technologien, werden die Kennzahlen angepasst.	0.65	0.57	16.18
4. Bei wesentlichen Änderungen des Marktumfeldes werden die Kennzahlen hinsichtlich ihrer Zweckmäßigkeit überprüft.	0.64	0.54	15.93
5. In der Vergangenheit wurden neue Kennzahlen aufgenommen.	0.60	0.51	15,77

Information on scale "Adaptation of Metrics [Anpassung der Kennzahlen]"			
Descriptive Statistics		*Result of Exploratory Factor Analysis*	
Cronbach's alpha:	0.84	Total variance explained:	0.61
Results of Confirmatory Factor Analysis			
χ^2-Value (Degrees of Freedom):	9.62 (5)	χ^2-Value/Degrees of Freedom:	1.92
p Value:	0.09	RMSEA:	0.06
SRMR:	–*	CFI:	0.99
GFI:	0.99	AGFI:	0.98
Factor reliability:	0.86	Average variance explained:	0.55

*Not available

References

***Sandt, J.* (2004): Management mit Kennzahlen und Kennzahlensystemen. Bestandsaufnahme, Determinanten und Erfolgswirkungen, Wiesbaden 2004, pp. 139-140.**

3. Adaptiveness [Anpassungsfähigkeit]

Scale Description

The scale measures manager's assessment of the company's ability to adapt to change in the company's environment, e.g. changes in the customer's needs.

Origin

The scale was newly developed by Spillecke (2006). He based the items on research of Krohmer (1999) and Dehler (2001). Willauer (2005) used a similar approach.

Samples

Survey data were collected by a questionnaire, administered via e-mail to 3,312 German managers of companies with at least 200 employees from different industrial sectors. A total of 415 usable questionnaires (12.5%) were returned.

Scale Indicators and Reliability / Validity Parameters

Scale: from 1 (very bad) to 5 (very good)

Information on individual indicators regarding "Adaptiveness [Anpassungsfähigkeit]"			
Description of indicators	*Item to Total-Correlation*	*Indicator-Reliability*	*t statistic*
1. Schnelle Anpassung der Produkte an neue Kundenbedürfnisse	0.72	0.61	–
2. Schnelle Reaktion auf neue Entwicklungen am Markt	0.84	0.98	17.59
3. Schnelle Nutzung neuer Marktchancen	0.66	0.49	15.60

Information on scale "Adaptiveness [Anpassungsfähigkeit]"			
Descriptive Statistics		*Result of Exploratory Factor Analysis*	
Cronbach's alpha:	0.86	Total variance explained:	0.69
Results of Confirmatory Factor Analysis			
Factor reliability:	0.87	Average variance explained:	0.70

*Not feasible

References

***Spillecke, D.* (2006): Interne Kundenorientierung des Controllerbereichs. Messung – Erfolgsauswirkungen – Determinanten, Wiesbaden 2006, pp. 166-167.**

Dehler, M. (2001): Entwicklungsstand der Logistik. Messung – Determinanten – Erfolgswirkungen, Wiesbaden 2001.

Krohmer, H. (1999): Marktorientierte Unternehmenskultur als Erfolgsfaktor der Strategieimplementierung, Wiesbaden 1999.

Willauer, B. (2005): Consensus as a Key Success Factor in Strategy-Making, Wiesbaden 2005.

4. Affective Conflicts [Affektive Konflikte]

Scale Description

The scale measures the extent to which opinions are discussed in management teams on a personal or emotional level, potentially leading to conflicts.

Origin

The scale was newly developed by Spieker (2004).

Samples

Survey data were collected by questionnaire, administered via internet to 353 managers of German start-up companies. A total of 145 usable questionnaires (41.1%) were returned.

Scale Indicators and Reliability / Validity Parameters

Scale: from 1 (definitely false) to 7 (definitely true)

Information on individual indicators regarding "Affective Conflicts [Affektive Konflikte]"			
Description of indicators	*Item to Total-Correlation*	*Indicator-Reliability*	*t statistic*
1. Es entstehen häufig Konflikte, die aus persönlichen Unverträglichkeiten resultieren.	0.86	0.83	14.37
2. Sachliche Diskussionen über wichtige Entscheidungen gleiten in emotionale, persönlich gefärbte Konflikte ab.	0.88	0.89	14.58
3. Wir schreien und in Diskussionen an.	0.61	0.47	12.65
4. Nach Diskussionen ist das emotionale Klima im Team sehr angespannt.	0.91	0.95	14.74

Information on scale "Affective Conflicts [Affektive Konflikte]"			
Descriptive Statistics		*Result of Exploratory Factor Analysis*	
Cronbach's alpha:	0.91	Total variance explained:	0.80
Results of Confirmatory Factor Analysis			
χ^2-Value (Degrees of Freedom):	2.57 (2)	χ^2-Value/Degrees of Freedom:	1.28
p Value:	0.00	RMSEA:	0.04
SRMR:	–*	CFI:	1.00
GFI:	0.99	AGFI:	0.98
Factor reliability:	0.94	Average variance explained:	0.79

*Not available

References

Spieker, M. (2004): Entscheidungen in Gründerteams. Determinanten – Parameter – Erfolgsauswirkungen, Wiesbaden 2004, pp. 235-236.

5. Allocation (in the Context of Business Networks) [Allokation im Kontext von Unternehmensnetzwerken]

Scale Description

The scale measures the degree of formalization in allocating resources to the participants of business networks.

Origin

The scale was first used by Möller (2006).

Samples

Survey data were collected by questionnaire, administered to business unit leaders or responsible controllers of 5,717 German companies. A total of 102 usable questionnaires (1.9%) were returned.

Scale Indicators and Reliability / Validity Parameters

Scale: from 1 (definitely false) to 5 (definitely true)

Information on individual indicators regarding "Allocation (in the Context of Business Networks) [Allokation im Kontext von Unternehmensnetzwerken]"			
Description of indicators	*Item to Total-Correlation*	*Indicator-Reliability*	*t statistic*
1. Wie hoch ist der Standardisierungsgrad hinsichtlich der eingebrachten Ressourcen?	0.53	0.40	–*
2. Wie hoch ist der Standardisierungsgrad hinsichtlich der Verantwortlichkeiten?	0.65	0.63	5.70
3. Wie hoch ist der Standardisierungsgrad hinsichtlich der laufenden Investitionen?	0.55	0.38	4.61
4. Wie hoch ist der Standardisierungsgrad hinsichtlich der Marktverantwortung?	0.58	0.46	4.81

Information on scale "Allocation (in the Context of Business Networks) [Allokation im Kontext von Unternehmensnetzwerken]"			
Descriptive Statistics		*Result of Exploratory Factor Analysis*	
Cronbach's alpha:	0.77	Total variance explained:	0.60
Results of Confirmatory Factor Analysis			
Factor reliability:	0.77	Average variance explained:	0.46

*Not feasible

References

Möller, K. (2006): Unternehmensnetzwerke und Erfolg – eine empirische Analyse von Einfluss- und Gestaltungsfaktoren, in: Zeitschrift für betriebswirtschaftliche Forschung (zfbf), Vol. 58, pp. 1051-1076.

6. Analysis and Creativity in Planning Behavior [Analyse und Kreativität im Planungsverhalten]

Scale Description

The scale measures the extent to which the strategic planning process is characterized by an in-depth questioning of the underlying premises.

Origin

The scale was newly developed by Willauer as part of a doctoral research project. Results were published in Weber/Schäffer/Willauer (2003).

Samples

Survey data were collected by questionnaire, administered to managers of planning departments of 4,186 German companies from the industrial sector. A total of 298 usable questionnaires (7.1%) were returned.

Scale Indicators and Reliability / Validity Parameters

Scale: from 1 (definitely false) to 7 (definitely true)

Information on individual indicators regarding "Analysis and Creativity in Planning Planning Behavior [Analyse und Kreativität im Planungverhalten]"			
Description of indicators	*Item to Total-Correlation*	*Indicator-Reliability*	*t statistic*
1. In der Regel versuchen wir im Rahmen der strategischen/ langfristigen Planung, von Grund auf neu die relevanten Märkte zu beleuchten.	0.44	0.29	8.98
2. Wir bemühen uns im Rahmen der strategischen/langfristigen Planung, den zugrunde liegenden Leistungsprozess analytisch zu durchdringen.	0.56	0.75	8.98
3. Im Rahmen der strategischen/langfristigen Planung stellen wir systematisch die zugrunde liegenden Prämissen in Frage.	0.58	0.79	8.98

Information on scale "Analysis and Creativity in Planning Behavior [Analyse und Kreativität im Planungverhalten]"			
Descriptive Statistics		*Result of Exploratory Factor Analysis*	
Cronbach's alpha:	0.71	Total variance explained:	0.63
Results of Confirmatory Factor Analysis			
Factor reliability:	0.82	Average variance explained:	0.61

References

Weber, J /Schäffer, U./Willauer, B. (2003): Skalenübersicht, in: Weber, J./Kunz, J. (Ed.): Empirische Controllingforschung: Begründung, Beispiele, Ergebnisse, Wiesbaden 2003, pp. 385-467.

7. Anticipation of Decision Enforcement [Antizipation der Willensdurchsetzung]

Scale Description

The scale measures the extent to which management teams use formal processes, e.g. plans, to communicate business decisions to subordinates.

Origin

The scale was newly developed by Spieker (2004).

Samples

Survey data were collected by questionnaire, administered via internet to 353 managers of German start-up companies. A total of 145 usable questionnaires (41.1%) were returned.

Scale Indicators and Reliability / Validity Parameters

Scale: from 1 (definitely false) to 7 (definitely true)

Information on individual indicators regarding "Anticipation of Decision Enforcement [Antizipation der Willensdurchsetzung]"			
Description of indicators	*Item to Total-Correlation*	*Indicator-Reliability*	*t statistic*
1. Die Kommunikation wichtiger Entscheidungen an die Mitarbeiter erfolgt formalisiert.	0.73	0.60	14.37
2. Für die Umsetzung wichtiger Entscheidungen durch unsere Mitarbeiter erarbeiten wir schriftliche Pläne, aus denen sich ihre Aufgaben ergeben.	0.78	0.70	14.72
3. Wir erarbeiten Vorgaben für unsere Mitarbeiter, an denen sie sich später messen müssen.	0.72	0.61	14.17
4. Die Kommunikation wichtiger Teamentscheidungen an die Mitarbeiter erfolgt geplant und einheitlich.	0.77	0.66	14.69
5. Wichtige Entscheidungen werden meistens uneinheitlich durch direkte persönliche Ansprache der Mitarbeiter kommuniziert. (R)	0.76	0.65	14.68

Information on scale "Anticipation of Decision Enforcement [Antizipation der Willens-durchsetzung]"			
Descriptive Statistics		*Result of Exploratory Factor Analysis*	
Cronbach's alpha:	0.91	Total variance explained:	0.80
Results of Confirmatory Factor Analysis			
χ^2-Value (Degrees of Freedom):	6.84 (5)	χ^2-Value/Degrees of Freedom:	1.37
p Value:	0.02	RMSEA:	0.05
SRMR:	–*	CFI:	0.99
GFI:	0.99	AGFI:	0.98
Factor reliability:	0.91	Average variance explained:	0.66

*Not available

References

Spieker, M. **(2004): Entscheidungen in Gründerteams. Determinanten – Parameter – Erfolgsauswirkungen, Wiesbaden 2004, pp. 240-241.**

8. Balance of Metrics [Ausgewogenheit der Kennzahlen]

Scale Description

The scale measures manager´s assessment of balance between financial and non-financial metrics used to monitor their business unit.

Origin

The scale was newly developed by Sandt (2004).

Samples

The questionnaire was sent to 2,386 German upper level managers. 254 responses could be integrated into the analysis, yielding a response rate of 11.1%.

Scale Indicators and Reliability / Validity Parameters

Scale: from 1 (definitely false) to 5 (definitely true)

Information on individual indicators regarding "Balance of Metrics [Ausgewogenheit der Kennzahlen]"			
Description of indicators	*Item to Total-Correlation*	*Indicator-Reliability*	*t statistic*
1. Die Kennzahlen decken umfassend sowohl die „harten" Aspekte der Geschäftseinheit ab als auch die „weichen".	0.72	0.70	12.12
2. Ich muß nicht lange über die Bedeutung nachdenken.	0.74	0.77	12.12
3. Die Kennzahlen berücksichtigen neben quantitativen auch qualitative Perspektiven der Geschäftseinheit.	0.65	0.54	12.12

Information on scale „Balance of Metrics (Ausgewogenheit der Kennzahlen)"			
Descriptive Statistics		*Result of Exploratory Factor Analysis*	
Cronbach's alpha:	0.84	Total variance explained:	0.76
Results of Confirmatory Factor Analysis			
Factor reliability:	0.86	Average variance explained:	0.67

References

***Sandt, J.* (2004): Management mit Kennzahlen und Kennzahlensystemen. Bestandsaufnahme, Determinanten und Erfolgswirkungen, Wiesbaden 2004, pp. 136-137.**

9. Behavior Control (in R&D Organizations)

Scale Description

The scale measures the extent to which reliance is placed on behavior control. The scale comprises four dimensions: hierarchy of authority, job codification, rule observation and formalization.

Origin

Abernethy and Brownell (1997) used the 21-item scale from Hage and Aiken (1967) in a modified form to measure behavior control. The instrument was developed by Hage and Aiken to measure the degree of centralization and was initially conceived as having five dimensions: participation in decision making, hierarchy of authority, job codification, rule observation and formalization. Behavior controls have often been described in terms of the last four dimensions of this instrument (Ouchi (1979); Merchant (1985)), so the items relating to these four dimensions were summed to measure the extent to which reliance is placed on behavior control.

Samples

Survey data were collected by both questionnaire and interview, administered to 150 senior research officers in the research and development (R&D) divisions of a large Australian industrial company and a major US scientific organization.
A total of 138 questionnaires (92%) was returned, eleven of which were incomplete, resulting in a useable sample set of 127. On average, the respondents were 40 years of age, had worked for their present employer for 10 years, and had been in their current position for three years. The respondents all held first-line supervisory positions and were responsible for managing separate, identifiable work groups.

Comments

While the Hage and Aiken (1967) instrument has been in the literature for many years, its recent use by other researchers (e.g. Banker et al. (1993)), who have found excellent reliability coefficients, supports its continuing suitability for operationalizing this construct.
The highest inter-item correlation obtained from the use of this measure was only 0.20, suggesting reliability problems and the need to exercise caution in interpreting the results. Abernethy/Brownell reported a mean of 50.64 and standard deviation of 13.06 on a theoretical range of 17-119.

Scale Indicators and Reliability / Validity Parameters

Scale: from 1 (definitely false) to 4 (definitely true)

Information on individual indicators regarding "Behavior Control (in R&D Organizations)"
Description of indicators
1. There can be little action taken here until a supervisor approves a decision.
2. A person who wants to make his own decisions would be quickly discouraged here.

3. Even small matters have to be referred to someone higher up for a final answer.			
4. I have to ask my boss before I do almost anything.			
5. Any decision I make has to have my boss's approval.			
6. I feel that I am my own boss in most matters. (R)			
7. A person can make his own decisions without checking with anybody else. (R)			
8. How things are done here is left up to the person doing the work. (R)			
9. People here are allowed to do almost as they please. (R)			
10. Most people here make their own rules on the job. (R)			
11. The employees are constantly being checked on for rule violations.			
12. People here feel as though they are constantly being watched to see that they obey all the rules.			
Information on scale "Behavior Control (in R&D Organizations)"			
Cronbach's alpha:	0.82	Total variance explained:	–*

*Not available

References

***Abernethy, M. A./Brownell, P.* (1997): Management Control Systems in Research and Development Organizations: The Role of Accounting, Behavior, and Personnel Controls, in: Accounting, Organizations and Society, Vol. 22, pp. 233-248.**

Banker, R. D./Potter, G./Schroeder, R. G. (1993): Reporting Manufacturing Performance Measures to Workers: An Empirical Study, in: Journal of Management Accounting Research, Vol. 5, pp. 33-55.

Hage, J./Aiken, M. (1967): Relationship of Centralization to Other Structural Properties, in: Administrative Science Quarterly, Vol. 12, pp. 72-92.

Merchant, K. A. (1985): Control in Business Organizations, Boston 1985.

Ouchi, W. G. (1979): A Conceptual Framework for the Design of Organizational Control Mechanisms, in: Management Science, Vol. 25, pp. 833-838.

10. Benchmarking

Scale Description

The scale measures the extent to which external benchmarking of production, marketing, sales, and logistics operations is used to monitor the organization's strategic position.

Origin

A major international management consulting firm developed the construct in 1991.

Samples

Ittner and Larcker (1997) examined the use and performance consequences of strategic control systems using survey data collected by a major international management consulting firm during 1991. The survey covered the automobile and computer industries in Canada, Germany, Japan, and the United States. All automobile assemblers and a random sample of their suppliers were invited to participate. A total of 249 organizations agreed to participate, representing an 85% response rate.

Comments

The scale emerged from a principal component analysis used to reduce the dimensionality of 36 questions from a survey assessing the extent to which organizations employ strategic control practices discussed in the quality literature.

Scale Indicators and Reliability / Validity Parameters

Scale: from 1 (never) to 4 (regularly)

Information on individual indicators regarding "Benchmarking"			
Description of indicators			
How often is benchmarking used to monitor the position of your operation in the following areas?			
1. Marketing systems			
2. Sales systems			
3. Delivery and distribution systems			
4. Service-after-delivery systems			
5. Process or operation methods			
6. Products/services			
Information on scale "Benchmarking"			
Cronbach's alpha:	0.84	Total variance explained:	–*

*Not available

References

Ittner, C. D./Larcker, D. F. **(1997): Quality Strategy, Strategic Control Systems, and Organizational Performance, in: Accounting, Organizations and Society, Vol. 22, pp. 293-314.**

11. Board Director Review

Scale Description

The scale measures the frequency of board of director reviews of quality plans, problems, and achievements.

Origin

Developed by a major international management consulting firm in 1991.

Samples

Ittner and Larcker (1997) examined the use and performance consequences of strategic control systems using survey data collected by a major international management consulting firm during 1991. The survey covered the automobile and computer industries in Canada, Germany, Japan, and the United States. All automobile assemblers and a random sample of their suppliers were invited to participate. A total of 249 organizations agreed to participate, representing an 85% response rate.

Comments

The scale emerged from a principal component analysis used to reduce the dimensionality of 36 questions from a survey assessing the extent to which organizations employ strategic control practices discussed in the quality literature.

Scale Indicators and Reliability / Validity Parameters

Scale: 1 (never), 2 (seldom), 3 (occasionally), 4 (usually), 5 (always or almost always)

Information on individual indicators regarding "Board Director Review"			
Description of indicators			
1. How frequently does the board of directors report on quality plans compared to prior achievements?			
2. How frequently does the board of directors report on quality plans compared to competitors' achievements?			
3. How frequently does the board of directors report on quality problems compared to prior achievements?			
4. How frequently does the board of directors report on quality problems compared to competitors' achievements?			
5. How frequently does the board of directors report on quality achieved compared to prior achievements?			
6. How frequently does the board of directors report on quality achieved compared to competitors' achievements?			
Information on scale "Board Director Review"			
Cronbach's alpha:	0.94	Total variance explained:	–*

*Not available

References

Ittner, C. D./Larcker, D. F. **(1997): Quality Strategy, Strategic Control Systems, and Organizational Performance, in: Accounting, Organizations and Society, Vol. 22, pp. 293-314.**

12. Breadth of ABC Use

Scale Description

The scale measures the use of ABC by organizational functions (e.g. manufacturing, engineering, top management).

Origin

Adapted from Swenson (1995).

Samples

A questionnaire was distributed to 1,058 internal auditing professionals. 204 completed usable responses were received. 134 are from the first and 67 from the second mailings, yielding a response rate of 21.2%. 65 responses (31.8%) indicate some use of ABC. The remaining 139 responses serve as a non-using control group.

Scale Indicators and Reliability / Validity Parameters

Scale: from 1 (strongly disagree) to 5 (strongly agree)

Information on individual indicators regarding "Breadth of ABC Use"			
Description of indicators			
The following functions routinely use the ABC information for decision-making			
1. Design engineering			
2. Manufacturing engineering			
3. Production management			
4. Plant manager			
5. Top management			
6. Marketing			
7. Corporate finance			
Information on scale "Breadth of ABC Use"			
Descriptive Statistics		*Result of Exploratory Factor Analysis*	
Cronbach's alpha:	0.90	Total variance explained:	–*
Results of Confirmatory Factor Analysis			
χ^2-Value (Degrees of Freedom):	2.96 (7)	χ^2-Value/Degrees of Freedom:	0.42
p Value:	0.89	RMSEA:	0.026
NFI:	0.99	NNFI:	–*
GFI:	0.99	AGFI:	0.95
Factor reliability:	–*	Average variance explained:	–*

*Not available

References

***Cagwin, D./Bouwman, M. J.* (2002): The Association between Activity-Based Costing and Improvement in Financial Performance, in: Management Accounting Research, Vol. 13, pp. 1-39.**

Swenson, D. (1995): The Benefits of Activity-Based Cost Management to the Manufacturing Industry, in: Journal of Management Accounting Research, Vol. 7, pp. 167-180.

13. Budget Adequacy

Scale Description

The scale determines whether individuals perceive their budgeted resources as adequate for the performance of job duties.

Origin

Developed by Nouri and Parker (1998).

Samples

Data was collected using a survey questionnaire sent to a large multi-national corporation engaged primarily in chemical production. Questionnaires were sent to 203 American managers and supervisors whom top management has identifies as having budget responsibilities. Of the 203 questionnaires distributed, respondents returned 139, a response rate of 68.5%. Since four respondents failed to complete the entire questionnaire, 135 responses (66.5%) were used in the data analysis.

Comments

Nouri and Parker (1998) reported a scale mean of 15.81 and a standard deviation of 3.22 on an observed range of 6-21.

Scale Indicators and Reliability / Validity Parameters

Scale: from 1 (strongly disagree) to 7 (strongly agree)

Information on individual indicators regarding "Budget Adequacy"			
Description of indicators			
1. By budget does not allow me to perform what is expected of me. (R)			
2. What is expected of me is achievable under my budget.			
3. I am pretty much confident that I can achieve what is expected of me under my budget.			
Information on scale "Budget Adequacy"			
Cronbach's alpha:	0.89	Total variance explained:	–*

*Not available

References

***Nouri, H./Parker, P. J.* (1998): The Relationship between Budget Participation and Job Performance: The Roles of Budget Adequacy and Organizational Commitment, in: Accounting, Organizations and Society, Vol. 23, pp. 467-483.**

14. Budget Goal Commitment

Scale Description

The measure reflects the view of commitment as being an attitude about a goal (i.e. cognitive, affective, and behavioral) and the maintenance of that determination (Wright et al. (1994)). This measure derives commitment levels by asking directly about the goal.

Origin

Developed by Hollenback et al. (1989).

Samples

Chong and Chong (2002) drew a total of 80 manufacturing companies randomly from the Kompass Australia (1996/1997) business directory. From the 80 companies, the names of 120 middle-level managers were included in the sample. 84 questionnaires were returned, which yielded a response rate of 70 percent. A wide range of manufacturing was represented in their final sample. These industries included electrical and electronics products, consumer durable products, furniture, printing and publishing, steel and metal products, wire and cable, plastic, rubber and tire, medical and health products, food products and textile, clothing and footwear.

Comments

Chong and Chong (2002) reported a scale mean of 6.205 and a standard deviation of 0.812 on an actual (theoretical) range of 4.25-7.00 (1.00-7.00).

Scale Indicators and Reliability / Validity Parameters

Scale: from 1 (strongly disagree) to 7 (strongly agree)

<table>
<tr><th colspan="5">Information on individual indicators regarding "Budget Goal Commitment"</th></tr>
<tr><td colspan="2">Description of indicators</td><td>Item to Total-Correlation</td><td>Indicator-Reliability</td><td>t statistic</td></tr>
<tr><td colspan="2">1. Quite frankly, I don't care if I achieve the budget objectives or not.</td><td>_*</td><td>0.33</td><td>_*</td></tr>
<tr><td colspan="2">2. It wouldn't take much for me to abandon the budget objectives.</td><td>_*</td><td>0.30</td><td>_*</td></tr>
<tr><td colspan="2">3. It is unrealistic for me to expect to reach the budget objectives.</td><td>_*</td><td>0.54</td><td>_*</td></tr>
<tr><td colspan="2">4. Since it is not always possible to tell how tough meeting the budget is until you have worked on it for a while, it is hard to take the budget objectives seriously.</td><td>_*</td><td>0.32</td><td>_*</td></tr>
<tr><th colspan="5">Information on scale "Budget Goal Commitment"</th></tr>
<tr><td colspan="2">Descriptive Statistics</td><td colspan="3">Result of Exploratory Factor Analysis</td></tr>
<tr><td>Cronbach's alpha:</td><td>_*</td><td colspan="2">Total variance explained:</td><td>_*</td></tr>
<tr><td colspan="5">Results of Confirmatory Factor Analysis</td></tr>
<tr><td>Factor reliability:</td><td>0.70</td><td colspan="2">Average variance explained:</td><td>0.37</td></tr>
</table>

*Not available

References

***Chong, V. K./Chong, K. M.* (2002): Budget Goal Commitment and Informational Effects of Budget Participation on Performance: A Structural Equation Modeling Approach, in: Behavioral Research in Accounting, Vol. 14, pp. 65-86.**

Hollenback, J. R./Williams, C. R./Klein, H. J. (1989): An Empirical Examination of the Antecedents of Commitment to Difficult Goals, in: Journal of Applied Psychology, Vol. 74, pp. 18-23.

Wright, P. M./O'Leary-Kelly, A. M./Cortina, J. M./Klein, H. J./Hollenbeck, J. R. (1994): On the Meaning and Measurement of Goal Commitment, in: Journal of Applied Psychology, Vol. 79, pp. 795-803.

15. Budget Participation

Scale Description
The six-item, seven-point Likert-type was used to measure budget participation.

Origin
Developed by Milani (1975).

Samples
Chong and Chong (2002) drew a total of 80 manufacturing companies randomly from the Kompass Australia (1996/1997) business directory. From the 80 companies, the names of 120 middle-level managers were included in the sample. 84 questionnaires were returned, which yielded a response rate of 70 percent. A wide range of manufacturing was represented in their final sample. These industries included electrical and electronics products, consumer durable products, furniture, printing and publishing, steel and metal products, wire and cable, plastic, rubber and tire, medical and health products, food products and textile, clothing and footwear.

Comments
Chong and Chong (2002) reported a scale mean of 5,135 and a standard deviation of 1,505 on an actual (theoretical) range of 1-7 (1-7). The scale has been used and validated extensively in accounting studies of budget participation (e.g. Brownell and McInnes (1986); Chenhall and Brownell (1988); Mia (1989); Dunk (1993); Lau et al. (1995); Lau et al. (1997); Nouri and Parker (1998); Chong and Bateman (2000)).

Scale Indicators and Reliability / Validity Parameters
Scale: from 1 (strongly disagree) to 7 (strongly agree)

Information on individual indicators regarding "Budget Participation"			
Description of indicators	*Item to Total-Correlation*	*Indicator-Reliability*	*t statistic*
1. The extent of involvement in setting budget.	–*	0.79	–*
2. Reasoning of budget revisions.	–*	0.40	–*
3. Frequencies of requests, opinions, and/or suggestions about budget.	–*	0.79	–*
4. Influence on the final budget.	–*	0.88	–*
5. Importance of contribution to the budget.	–*	0.72	–*
6. Frequency of requests, opinions, and/or suggestions sought by your superior.	–*	0.91	–*

Information on scale "Budget Participation"			
Descriptive Statistics		*Result of Exploratory Factor Analysis*	
Cronbach's alpha:	–*	Total variance explained:	–*
Results of Confirmatory Factor Analysis			
Factor reliability:	0.94	Average variance explained:	0.74

*Not available

References

***Chong, V. K./Chong, K. M.* (2002): Budget Goal Commitment and Informational Effects of Budget Participation on Performance: A Structural Equation Modeling Approach, in: Behavioral Research in Accounting, Vol. 14, pp. 65-86.**

Brownell, P./McInnes, M. (1986): Budgetary Participation, Motivation, and Managerial Performance, in: The Accounting Review, Vol. 61, pp. 587-600.

Chenhall, R. H./Brownell, P. (1988): The Effect of Participative Budgeting on Job Satisfaction and Performance: Role Ambiguity as an Intervening Variable, in: Accounting, Organizations and Society, Vol. 13, pp. 225-233.

Chong, V. K./Bateman, D. (2000): The Effects of Role Stress on Budgetary Participation and Job Satisfaction-Performance Linkages: A Test of Two Different Models, in: Advances in Accounting Behavioral Research, Vol. 3, pp. 91-118.

Dunk, A. S. (1993): The Effects of Job-Related Tension on Managerial Performance in Participative Budgetary Settings, in: Accounting, Organizations and Society, Vol. 18, pp. 575-585.

Lau, C. M./Low, L. C./Eggleton, I. R. C. (1995): The Impact of Reliance on Accounting Performance Measures on Job-Related Tension and Managerial Performance: Additional Evidence, in: Accounting, Organizations and Society, Vol. 20, pp. 359-381.

Lau, C. M./Low, L. C./Eggleton, I. R. C. (1997): The Interactive Effect of Budget Emphasis, Participation and Task Difficulty on Managerial Performance: A Cross-Cultural Study, in: Accounting, Auditing & Accountability Journal, Vol. 10, pp. 175-197.

Mia, L. (1989): The Impact of Participation in Budgeting and Job Difficulty on Managerial Performance and Work Motivation: A Research Note, in: Accounting, Organizations and Society, Vol. 14, pp. 347-357.

Milani, K. (1975): The Relationship of Participation in Budget-Setting to Industrial Supervisor Performance and Attitudes - a Field Study, in: The Accounting Review, Vol. 50, pp. 274-284.

Nouri, H./Parker, P. J. (1998): The Relationship between Budget Participation and Job Performance: The Roles of Budget Adequacy and Organizational Commitment, in: Accounting, Organizations and Society, Vol. 23, pp. 467-483.

16. Centralisation [Zentralisierung]

Scale Description

The scale measures the extent to which the power for decision-making within a firm is concentrated on upper echelon managers.

Origin

Based on a scale developed by Menon et al. (1999).

Samples

Survey data were collected by questionnaire, administered to business unit leaders of 3,500 German companies with 100 to 2,000 employees from the industrial sector. A total of 449 usable questionnaires (12.8%) were returned.

Scale Indicators and Reliability / Validity Parameters

Scale: from 1 (definitely false) to 5 (definitely true)

Information on individual indicators regarding "Centralisation [Zentralisierung]"			
Description of indicators	*Item to Total-Correlation*	*Indicator-Reliability*	*t statistic*
1. Mitarbeiter in diesem Unternehmen können in der Regel Entscheidungen treffen, ohne die Zustimmung eines Vorgesetzten einholen zu müssen. (R)	0.65	0.54	16.34
2. Die einzelnen Entscheidungsträger haben große Freiheiten bei der Wahl der Mittel zur Zielerreichung. (R)	0.73	0.78	20.08
3. Wie sie ihre Arbeit erledigen, bleibt den Mitarbeitern dieses Unternehmens weitgehend selbst überlassen. (R)	0.63	0.51	15.78

Information on scale „Centralisation [Zentralisierung]"			
Descriptive Statistics		*Result of Exploratory Factor Analysis*	
Cronbach's alpha:	0.82	Total variance explained:	0.74
Results of Confirmatory Factor Analysis			
Factor reliability:	0.82	Average variance explained:	0.61

References

***Schäffer, U./Steiners, D.* (2004): Zur Nutzung von Controllinginformationen, in: Zeitschrift für Planung und Unternehmenssteuerung, Vol. 15, pp. 377-404.**

Menon, A./Bharadwaj, S./Adidam, P. T./Edison, S. W. (1999): Antecedents and Consequences of Marketing Strategy Making: A Model and a Test, in: Journal of Marketing, Vol. 63, pp. 18-40.

17. Championing in Strategy Implementation

Scale Description

The scale measures the extent to which it is perceived that a strategy is being led through the implementation process by a specific individual.

Origin

Developed by Noble and Mokwa (1999).

Samples

The survey-based study conducted by Noble and Mokwa (1999) involved sampling from two firms: One firm was a large, multi state, financial services organization. Subjects were managers with extensive responsibilities for the implementation of marketing strategies. The other firm was a market share leader in the packaged goods industry. In this company, participants were regional sales managers with full responsibility for a geographic area, including discretionary budgets for promotions and responsibility for implementing corporate promotional strategies. The sample consisted of 254 managers in the financial services company and 534 managers in the packaged goods industry. Usable responses were 161 from the financial service company (63% response rate) and 325 from the other company (61% response rate). The total of 486 usable responses represents an overall 62% response rate.

Scale Indicators and Reliability / Validity Parameters

Scale: from 1 (strongly agree) to 5 (strongly disagree)

Information on individual indicators regarding "Championing in Strategy Implementation"			
Description of indicators	*Item to Total-Correlation*	*Indicator-Reliability*	*t statistic*
1. I felt that this strategy lacked a true leader in the company. (R)	–*	0.615	5.65
2. One person in the organization definitely took charge of making this strategy happen.	–*	0.428	4.51
3. The strategy had a champion to guide it through the implementation process.	–*	0.785	6.35

Information on scale "Championing in Strategy Implementation"			
Descriptive Statistics		*Result of Exploratory Factor Analysis*	
Cronbach's alpha:	0.62	Total variance explained:	–*

*Not available

References

Noble, C. H./Mokwa, M. P. **(1999): Implementing Marketing Strategies: Developing and Testing a Managerial Theory, in: Journal of Marketing, Vol. 63, pp. 57-73.**

18. Cognitive Conflicts [Kognitive Konflikte]

Scale Description

The scale measures the extent to which opposing opinions are discussed in teams.

Origin

The scale was newly developed by Spieker (2004) adapting items from Amason (1996) and Jehn (1997).

Samples

Survey data were collected by questionnaire, administered via internet to 353 managers of German start-up companies. A total of 145 usable questionnaires (41.1%) were returned.

Scale Indicators and Reliability / Validity Parameters

Scale: from 1 (definitely false) to 7 (definitely true)

Information on individual indicators regarding "Cognitive Conflicts [Kognitive Konflikte]"			
Description of indicators	*Item to Total-Correlation*	*Indicator-Reliability*	*t statistic*
1. In Diskussionen vertreten wir häufig kontroverse Meinungen.	0.77	0.76	12.08
2. Im Verlauf von Diskussionen geben wir uns häufig „contra".	0.80	0.80	12.20
3. Wir sind uns häufig uneinig über die Bedeutung und Bewertung einzelner Argumente.	0.53	0.43	10.60
4. Eigentlich vertreten wir selten kontroverse Standpunkte. (R)	0.70	0.58	11.51

Information on scale "Cognitive Conflicts [Kognitive Konflikte]"			
Descriptive Statistics		*Result of Exploratory Factor Analysis*	
Cronbach's alpha:	0.86	Total variance explained:	0.71
Results of Confirmatory Factor Analysis			
χ^2-Value (Degrees of Freedom):	0.67 (2)	χ^2-Value/Degrees of Freedom:	0.34
p Value:	0.00	RMSEA:	0.00
SRMR:	–*	CFI:	1.00
GFI:	1.00	AGFI:	0.99
Factor reliability:	0.88	Average variance explained:	0.64

*Not available

References

Spieker, M. (2004): Entscheidungen in Gründerteams. Determinanten – Parameter – Erfolgsauswirkungen, Wiesbaden 2004, pp. 234-235.

Amason, A. C. (1996): Distinguishing the effects of functional and dysfunctional conflict on strategic decision making: Resolving a paradox for top management teams, in: Academy of Management Journal, Vol. 39, pp. 123-148.

Jehn, K. A. (1997): A Qualitative Analysis of Conflict Types and Dimensions in Organizational Groups, Administrative Science Quarterly, Vol. 52, pp. 530-557.

19. Coherence of Metrics [Zusammenhang der Kennzahlen]

Scale Description

The scale measures manager´s assessment of coherence in the metrics used to monitor their business unit.

Origin

The scale was newly developed by Sandt (2004).

Samples

The questionnaire was sent to 2,386 German upper level managers. 254 responses could be integrated into the analysis, yielding a response rate of 11.1%.

Scale Indicators and Reliability / Validity Parameters

Scale: from 1 (definitely false) to 5 (definitely true)

Information on individual indicators regarding „Coherence of Metrics [Zusammenhang der Kennzahlen]"			
Description of indicators	*Item to Total-Correlation*	*Indicator-Reliability*	*t statistic*
1. Die mir zur Verfügung stehenden Kennzahlen aus den verschiedenen Gruppen stehen in einem sehr gut nachvollziehbaren Zusammenhang zueinander.	0.63	0.52	9.75
2. Die verschiedenen Kennzahlen bauen sehr stark aufeinander auf.	0.64	0.59	9.75
3. Die verschiedenen Kennzahlen ergänzen sich zu einem Kennzahlensystem.	0.70	0.76	9.75

Information on scale „Coherence of Metrics [Zusammenhang der Kennzahlen]"			
Descriptive Statistics		*Result of Exploratory Factor Analysis*	
Cronbach's alpha:	0.80	Total variance explained:	0.72
Results of Confirmatory Factor Analysis			
Factor reliability:	0.83	Average variance explained:	0.62

References

***Sandt, J.* (2004): Management mit Kennzahlen und Kennzahlensystemen. Bestandsaufnahme, Determinanten und Erfolgswirkungen, Wiesbaden 2004, pp. 137-138.**

20. Collaboration

Scale Description

The scale measures the degree of collaboration measured by asking respondents to evaluate the degree to which their departments and other departments achieved collective goals, had mutual understanding, informally worked together, shared the same vision for the company, and shared ideas, information, and/or resources.

Origin

Developed by Kahn and McDonough III (1997).

Samples

The survey sample of Kahn and McDonough III (1997) was comprised of department managers whose companies were members of the Electronic Industries Association (EIA). After qualifying survey participants, a sample of 860 „valid“ companies were identified from the EIA membership directory - a valid company was a manufacturer with marketing, manufacturing, and R&D departments. Questionnaires were then mailed to the manager in each of these three departments. The response rate was 514 managers or 20%. Of these 514 managers, 177 were marketing managers, 157 manufacturing managers, and 180 R&D managers.

Scale Indicators and Reliability / Validity Parameters

Scale: from 1 (never) to 5 (quite frequently)

Information on individual indicators regarding "Collaboration"			
Description of indicators			
During the last 3 months, to what degree did your department pursue the following activities with the other two departments?			
1. Achieve goals collectively			
2. Have a mutual understanding			
3. Informally work together			
4. Share ideas, information, and/or resources			
5. Share the same vision for the company			
6. Work together as a team			
Information on scale "Collaboration"			
Descriptive Statistics		*Result of Exploratory Factor Analysis*	
Cronbach's alpha:	0.92	Total variance explained:	0.72

References

***Kahn, K. B./McDonough III, E. F.* (1997): An Empirical Study of the Relationships among Co-Location, Integration, Performance, and Satisfaction, in: Journal of Product Innovation Management, Vol. 14, pp. 161-176.**

21. Collateral Learning [Mittelbares Lernen]

Scale Description

The scale measures the extent to which managers use MAS information for indirect learning (learning that is not directed towards a specific present goal).

Origin

The scale was newly developed by Schäffer/Steiners (2004).

Samples

Survey data were collected by questionnaire, administered to business unit leaders of 3,500 German companies with 100 to 2,000 employees from the industrial sector. A total of 449 usable questionnaires (12.8%) were returned.

Scale Indicators and Reliability / Validity Parameters

Scale: from 1 (definitely false) to 5 (definitely true)

Information on individual indicators regarding "Collateral Learning [Mittelbares Lernen]"			
Description of indicators	*Item to Total-Correlation*	*Indicator-Reliability*	*t statistic*
1. Ich nutze unser Controllingsystem auch ohne eine konkrete Entscheidung treffen zu müssen oder ein spezifisches Problem lösen zu wollen.	0.41	0.27	9.71
2. Ich nutze die Informationen, um mein allgemeines Verständnis der Unternehmenssituation zu verbessern.	0.52	0.93	14.16
3. Ich blättere häufig durch die Berichte mit Informationen aus unserem Controllingsystem, auch ohne ein konkretes Ziel zu verfolgen.	0.32	0.27	7.47
4. Ich nutze die Informationen, um Zusammenhänge in meinem Unternehmen zu erkennen.	0.44	0.30	10.17

Information on scale "Collateral Learning [Mittelbares Lernen]"			
Descriptive Statistics		*Result of Exploratory Factor Analysis*	
Cronbach's alpha:	0.63	Total variance explained:	0.50
Results of Confirmatory Factor Analysis			
χ^2-Value (Degrees of Freedom):	0.21 (1)	χ^2-Value/Degrees of Freedom:	0.21
p Value:	0.65	RMSEA:	0.0
NFI:	1.0	NNFI:	1.0
SRMR:	0.01	CFI:	1.0
GFI:	1.0	AGFI:	1.0
Factor reliability:	0.74	Average variance explained:	0.44

References

***Schäffer, U./Steiners, D.* (2004): Zur Nutzung von Controllinginformationen, in: Zeitschrift für Planung und Unternehmenssteuerung, Vol. 15, pp. 377-404.**

22. Company Training

Scale Description

The scale measures the degree of training being offered by the firm.

Origin

Anderson and Robertson (1995) used the scale from Churchill Jr. et al. (1985).

Samples

Anderson and Robertson (1995) model dependence and exit barriers using perceptual data gathered directly from 208 salespeople of several cooperating firms that supplied names and addresses of a cross section of their salespeople. Surveys were sent by the researchers to home addresses and solicited cooperation in exchange for an executive summary of results. These 208 responses represent 49.5% of the 420 brokers sampled and are the basis for measure development and for modeling dependence and perceptions of the hazards of selling house brands.

Comments

Anderson and Robertson (1995) reported a mean of 0.00 and a standard deviation of 0.78.

Scale Indicators and Reliability / Validity Parameters

Scale: from 1 (strongly disagree) to 7 (strongly agree)

Information on individual indicators regarding "Company Training"			
Description of indicators			
1. I go in for a lot of refresher training courses.			
2. I've spent significant time in my firm's classes and seminars this year.			
3. Over the years I've had a lot of training from my present firm.			
4. How much time have you spent in company-sponsored training programs in the last 18 months? ____ days.			
5. Our training program is a joke. (R)			
Information on scale "Company Training"			
Descriptive Statistics		*Result of Exploratory Factor Analysis*	
Cronbach's alpha:	0.82	Total variance explained:	–*

*Not available

References

***Anderson, E./Robertson, T. S.* (1995): Inducing Multiline Salespeople to Adopt House Brands, in: Journal of Marketing, Vol. 59, pp. 16-31.**

Churchill Jr., G. A./Ford, N. M./Hartley, S. W./Walker Jr., O. C. (1985): The Determinants of Salesperson Performance: A Meta-Analysis, in: Journal of Marketing Research, Vol. 22, pp. 103-118.

23. Competitive Intensity [Wettbewerbsintensität]

Scale Description

The scale measures manager's assessment of the competitive intensity of the company's branch, e.g. regular price competitions.

Origin

The scale is based on items by Farrell (2000).

Samples

Survey data were collected by questionnaire, administered to business unit leaders of 3,500 German companies with 100 to 2,000 employees from the industrial sector. A total of 449 usable questionnaires (12.8%) were returned.

Comment

The scale initially consisted of 5 items. 2 items had to be eliminated due to a lack of Item-to-Total Correlation.

Scale Indicators and Reliability / Validity Parameters

Scale: from 1 (definitely false) to 5 (definitely true)

Information on individual indicators regarding "Competitive Intensity [Wettbewerbsintensität]"			
Description of indicators	*Item to Total-Correlation*	*Indicator-Reliability*	*t statistic*
1. Der Wettbewerb in unserer Branche ist sehr stark.	0.64	0.75	15.47
2. Bei allem, was wir anbieten, können die Wettbewerber mithalten.	0.44	0.25	9.99
3. Unsere Branche ist durch einen starken Preiswettbewerb gekennzeichnet.	0.57	0.51	13.46
Information on scale "Competitive Intensity [Wettbewerbsintensität]"			
Descriptive Statistics		*Result of Exploratory Factor Analysis*	
Cronbach's alpha:	0.72	Total variance explained:	0.65
Results of Confirmatory Factor Analysis			
Factor reliability:	0.74	Average variance explained:	0.50

References

Schäffer, U./Steiners, D. **(2004): Zur Nutzung von Controllinginformationen, in: Zeitschrift für Planung und Unternehmenssteuerung, Vol. 15, pp. 377-404.**

Farrell, M. A. (2000): Developing a Market-Oriented Learning Organisation, in: Australian Journal of Management, Vol. 25, pp. 201-223.

24. Conceptual Use of Controlling Information [Konzeptionelle Nutzung von Controlling-Informationen]

Scale Description

The scale measures the extent to which managers use controlling information for gaining insights into specific business problems. Here controlling information is not used as a means to finding immediate conclusions, but rather to broaden one's knowledge.

Origin

The scale was newly developed by Bauer (2002), adapting items from Karlshaus (2000).

Samples

Survey data were collected by questionnaire, administered via mail to 2,527 German companies. A total of 347 companies sent usable answers, yielding a 14.8% return rate.

Comments

The study used a dyadic design approach, where a manager and a controller of the same company were questioned. The data for this scale sole stem from the answers of the managers.

Scale Indicators and Reliability / Validity Parameters

Scale: from 1 (definitely false) to 7 (definitely true)

Information on individual indicators regarding "Conceptual Use of Controlling Information [Konzeptionelle Nutzung von Controlling-Informationen]"			
Description of indicators	*Item to Total-Correlation*	*Indicator-Reliability*	*t statistic*
1. Durch das Controlling erhalte ich einen Überblick über die Zusammenhänge in meinem Geschäftsbereich.	0.69	0.63	17.8
2. Die Informationen aus dem Controlling tragen sehr zum allgemeinen Verständnis der aktuellen Situation meiner Geschäftseinheit bei.	0.83	0.88	18.6
3. Meine Kenntnisse der Wirkung meiner Geschäftsführung werden durch Informationen des Controlling wesentlich erweitert.	0.76	0.72	18.3
4. Das Abschätzen der zukünftigen Verhältnisse in meinem Geschäftsbereich wird durch die Leistungen und die Informationen des Controlling wesentlich unterstützt.	0.63	0.53	16.9

Information on scale "Conceptual Use of Controlling Information [Konzeptionelle Nutzung von Controlling-Informationen]"			
Descriptive Statistics		*Result of Exploratory Factor Analysis*	
Cronbach's alpha:	0.87	Total variance explained:	0.72
Results of Confirmatory Factor Analysis			
χ^2-Value (Degrees of Freedom):	3.13 (2)	χ^2-Value/Degrees of Freedom:	1.57
p Value:	0.21	RMSEA:	0.04
NFI:	1.00	NNFI:	–*
GFI:	1.00	AGFI:	0.99
Factor reliability:	0.88	Average variance explained:	0.71

*Not available

References

***Bauer, M.* (2002): Controllership in Deutschland. Zur erfolgreichen Zusammenarbeit von Controllern und Managern, Wiesbaden 2002, pp. 206-207.**

Karlshaus, J. T. (2000): Die Nutzung von Kostenrechnungsinformationen im Marketing, Wiesbaden 2000.

25. Conceptual Use of Metrics [Konzeptionelle Nutzung von Kennzahlen]

Scale Description

The scale measures the extent to which managers use metrics in the decision-making process for gaining insights into a specific business problem. Here metrics are not used as a means to finding conclusions, but rather to broaden one's knowledge.

Origin

The scale was adopted by Sandt (2004) from Karlshaus (2000). A similar approach concerning accounting data was used by Hunold (2003).

Samples

The questionnaire was sent to 2,386 German upper level managers. 254 responses could be integrated into the analysis, yielding a response rate of 11.1%.

Scale Indicators and Reliability / Validity Parameters

Scale: from 1 (definitely false) to 5 (definitely true)

Information on individual indicators regarding "Conceptual Use of Metrics [Konzeptionelle Nutzung von Kennzahlen]"			
Description of indicators	*Item to Total-Correlation*	*Indicator-Reliability*	*t statistic*
1. Durch die Kennzahlen erhalte ich einen Überblick über die Zusammenhänge in meiner Geschäftseinheit.	0.75	0.76	13.08
2. Die Kennzahlen tragen sehr zum allgemeinen Verständnis der aktuellen Situation meiner Geschäftseinheit bei.	0.81	0.89	13.08
3. Meine Kenntnisse über die Wirkung meiner Geschäftseinheit werden durch die Kennzahlen wesentlich erweitert.	0.68	0.55	13.08

Information on individual indicators on "Conceptual Use of Metrics [Konzeptionelle Nutzung von Kennzahlen]"			
Descriptive Statistics		*Result of Exploratory Factor Analysis*	
Cronbach's alpha:	0.86	Total variance explained:	0.79
Results of Confirmatory Factor Analysis			
Factor reliability:	0.89	Average variance explained:	0.73

References

Sandt, J. (2004): Management mit Kennzahlen und Kennzahlensystemen. Bestandsaufnahme, Determinanten und Erfolgswirkungen, Wiesbaden 2004, pp. 162-163.

Hunold, C. (2003): Kommunale Kostenrechnung. Gestaltung, Nutzung und Erfolgsfaktoren, Wiesbaden 2003.

Karlshaus, J. T. (2000): Die Nutzung von Kostenrechnungsinformationen im Marketing, Wiesbaden 2000.

26. Conflict Intensity [Konfliktausmaß]

Scale Description

The scale measures manager's assessment of the regularity disagreements with the accounting staff.

Origin

The scale was newly developed by Aust (1999).

Samples

The scale stems from a questionnaire sent to 1,163 German industrial companies, of which 143 participated, yielding a return rate of 12.3%. The study used a triadic design approach, where the general manager, the marketing or sales director and an accountant of the same company were questioned. Altogether, 105 usable triads were returned.

Scale Indicators and Reliability / Validity Parameters

Scale: from 1 (definitely false) to 5 (definitely true)

Information on individual indicators regarding "Conflict Intensity [Konfliktausmaß]"			
Description of indicators	*Item to Total-Correlation*	*Indicator-Reliability*	*t statistic*
1. Bei der Zusammenarbeit mit den Kostenrechnern kommt es häufig zu Spannungen.	0.65	0.69	17.68
2. Es gibt häufig Meinungsverschiedenheiten über die Art die Bereitstellung von Informationen durch die Kostenrechnung.	0.67	0.68	17.53
3. Es gibt keine oder nur sehr wenige Konflikte mit den Kostenrechnern. (R)	0.50	0.42	12.86
4. Es gibt häufig Unstimmigkeiten über die Art der Zusammenarbeit zwischen mir und den Kostenrechnern.	0.50	0.49	14.04

Information on scale "Conflict Intensity [Konfliktausmaß]"			
Descriptive Statistics		*Result of Exploratory Factor Analysis*	
Cronbach's alpha:	0.77	Total variance explained:	0.60
Results of Confirmatory Factor Analysis			
Factor reliability:	0.84	Average variance explained:	0.57

References

***Aust, R.* (1999): Kostenrechnung als unternehmensinterne Dienstleistung, Wiesbaden 1999, pp. 162-163.**

27. Conflict Resolution

Scale Description

The scale measures the degree to which ABC team members are friendly toward each other (Goodman et al. (1987)).

Origin

Developed by Anderson et al. (2002).

Samples

Data from 18 ABC projects in two automobile manufacturing firms and survey data from 89 individual ABC team members were collected.

Comments

Anderson et al. (2002) reported an item mean of 4.0 and a standard deviation of 0.59.

Scale Indicators and Reliability / Validity Parameters

Scale: from 1 (strongly disagree) to 5 (strongly agree)

Information on individual indicators regarding "Conflict Resolution"			
Description of indicators			
1. On the ABC team, everyone's opinions were heard.			
2. When a decision was required, every member of the ABC team was involved.			
3. If a disagreement arose between ABC team members, the issue was dealt with in an open fashion.			
4. When a disagreement arose between ABC team members everyone tried to find a workable solution.			
Information on scale "Conflict Resolution"			
Descriptive Statistics		*Result of Exploratory Factor Analysis*	
Cronbach's alpha:	0.76	Total variance explained:	–*

*Not available

References

***Anderson, S./Hesford, J./Young, S. M.* (2002): Factors Influencing the Performance of Activity Based Costing Teams: A Field Study of ABC Model Development Time in the Automobile Industry, in: Accounting, Organizations and Society, Vol. 27, pp. 195-211.**

Goodman, P. S./Ravlin, E./Schminke, M. (1987): Understanding Teams in Organizations, in: Cummings, L./Staw, B. (Ed.): Research in Organizational Behavior, Greenwich, Conn. 1987, pp. 121-183.

28. Connection of Strategic and Operative Planning [Verknüpfung der strategischen mit der operativen Planung]

Scale Description

The scale measures the extent to which the process of strategic planning within a firm is connected to the process of operative planning.

Origin

The scale was newly developed by Willauer as part of a doctoral research project. Results were published in Weber/Schäffer/Willauer (2003).

Samples

Survey data were collected by questionnaire, administered to managers of planning departments of 4,186 German companies from the industrial sector. A total of 298 usable questionnaires (7.1%) were returned.

Scale Indicators and Reliability / Validity Parameters

Scale: from 1 (definitely false) to 7 (definitely true)

Information on individual indicators regarding "Connection of Strategic and Operative Planning [Verknüpfung der strategischen mit der operativen Planung]"			
Description of indicators	*Item to Total-Correlation*	*Indicator-Reliability*	*t statistic*
1. Die strategische/langfristige Planung ist mit der operativen eng verknüpft.	0.65	0.47	16.76
2. Ziele und Maßnahmen in der operativen Planung sind auf die Ziele und Maßnahmen der strategischen/langfristigen Planung ausgerichtet.	0.84	0.93	19.26
3. Ziele und Maßnahmen in der operativen Planung sind mit der strategischen/langfristigen Planung im Sinne von Ursache-Wirkungs-Zusammenhängen verknüpft.	0.75	0.74	18.66
4. Die strategische/langfristige Planung setzt bei uns die Eckpunkte für die operative Planung.	0.72	0.65	18.18

Information on scale "Connection of Strategic and Operative Planning [Verknüpfung der strategischen mit der operativen Planung]"			
Descriptive Statistics		*Result of Exploratory Factor Analysis*	
Cronbach's alpha:	0.88	Total variance explained:	0.74
Results of Confirmatory Factor Analysis			
χ^2-Value (Degrees of Freedom):	0.03 (2)	χ^2-Value/Degrees of Freedom:	0.01
p Value:	0.99	RMSEA:	0.00
SRMR:	–*	CFI:	1.00
GFI:	1.00	AGFI:	0.95
Factor reliability:	0.90	Average variance explained:	0.70

*Not available

References

Weber, J /Schäffer, U./Willauer, B. **(2003): Skalenübersicht, in: Weber, J./Kunz, J. (Ed.): Empirische Controllingforschung: Begründung, Beispiele, Ergebnisse, Wiesbaden 2003, pp. 385-467.**

29. Connection of Strategy Development and Strategic Planning [Verknüpfung der Strategieentwicklung mit der strategischen Planung]

Scale Description

The scale measures the extent to which the goals of a strategy are represented in the strategic planning process.

Origin

The scale was newly developed by Willauer as part of a doctoral research project. Results were published in Weber/Schäffer/Willauer (2003).

Samples

Survey data were collected by questionnaire, administered to managers of planning departments of 4,186 German companies from the industrial sector. A total of 298 usable questionnaires (7.1%) were returned.

Scale Indicators and Reliability / Validity Parameters

Scale: from 1 (definitely false) to 7 (definitely true)

Information on individual indicators regarding "Connection of Strategy Development and Strategic Planning [Verknüpfung der Strategieentwicklung mit der strategischen Planung]"			
Description of indicators	*Item to Total-Correlation*	*Indicator-Reliability*	*t statistic*
1. Die Strategieentwicklung im Top-Management setzt bei uns die Eckpunkte für die Strategische Planung.	0.48	0.36	10.75
2. Die Ziele und Maßnahmen in der strategischen/lang-fristigen Planung sind auf die Ziele und Maßnahmen der Strategie ausgerichtet.	0.68	0.84	10.75
3. Ziele und Maßnahmen in der strategischen/ langfristigen Planung sind mit der Strategie im Sinne von Ursache-Wirkungs-Zusammenhängen verbunden.	0.60	0.57	10.75

Information on scale "Connection of Strategy Development and Strategic Planning [Verknüpfung der Strategieentwicklung mit der strategischen Planung]"			
Descriptive Statistics		*Result of Exploratory Factor Analysis*	
Cronbach's alpha:	0.76	Total variance explained:	0.68
Results of Confirmatory Factor Analysis			
Factor reliability:	0.81	Average variance explained:	0.59

References

***Weber, J./Schäffer, U./Willauer, B.* (2003): Skalenübersicht, in: Weber, J./Kunz, J. (Ed.): Empirische Controllingforschung: Begründung, Beispiele, Ergebnisse, Wiesbaden 2003, pp. 385-467.**

30. Consensus

Scale Description

The scale measures the extent to which managers believe that consensus exists among a business unit's managers concerning relevant business topics, e.g. market and competitors or technology development.

Origin

The scale was developed by Willauer (2005) based on Iaquinto/Fredrickson (1997).

Samples

Survey data were collected by questionnaire, administered to managers of planning departments of 4,186 German companies from the industrial sector. A total of 298 usable questionnaires (7.1%) were returned.

Scale Indicators and Reliability / Validity Parameters

Scale: from 1 (definitely false) to 7 (definitely true)

Information on individual indicators regarding "Consensus"			
Description of indicators	*Item to Total-Correlation*	*Indicator-Reliability*	*t statistic*
1. There is consensus among functional managers concerning the assessment of the market and competitors.	0.66	0.51	25.61
2. There is consensus among functional managers concerning technologies and their development.	0.68	0.56	27.20
3. There is consensus among functional managers concerning the assessment of customers and their needs.	0.68	0.54	26.32
4. There is consensus among functional managers concerning the assessment of strengths and weaknesses of the SBU.	0.58	0.40	23.59
5. There is consensus among functional managers concerning the strategies set by the SBU.	0.69	0.55	26.82
6. There is consensus among functional managers on how goals are to be reached.	0.71	0.61	28.14
7. There is consensus among functional managers concerning the resources needed in order to reach the goals.	0.69	0.57	27.32
8. There is consensus among functional managers concerning the means needed to reach the goals.	0.71	0.61	28.00
9. Functional managers are committed to realize the goals.	0.64	0.50	25.84
10. There is consensus among functional managers on the priorities put on the achievement of the goals.	0.71	0.60	27.99

Information on scale "Consensus"			
Descriptive Statistics		*Result of Exploratory Factor Analysis*	
Cronbach's alpha:	0.91	Total variance explained:	0.56
Results of Confirmatory Factor Analysis			
χ^2-Value (Degrees of Freedom):	120.56 (35)	χ^2-Value/Degrees of Freedom:	3.44
p Value:	0.00	RMSEA:	0.09
SRMR:	–*	CFI:	0.98
GFI:	0.98	AGFI:	0.97
Factor reliability:	0.92	Average variance explained:	0.55

*Not available

References

Willauer, B. **(2005): Consensus as a Key Success Factor in Strategy-Making, Wiesbaden 2003, pp. 204-206.**

Iaquinto, A. L./Fredrickson, J. W. (1997): Top Management Team Agreement about The Strategic Decision Process: A Test of Some of Its Determinants and Consequences, in: Strategic Management Journal, Vol. 18, pp. 63-75.

31. Consensus Orientation [Konsensorientierung]

Scale Description

The scale measures the extent to which the process of interaction between team members is headed towards reaching unanimous decisions.

Origin

The scale was adapted by Spieker (2004) following an approach of Reitmeyer (2000).

Samples

Survey data were collected by questionnaire, administered via internet to 353 managers of German start-up companies. A total of 145 usable questionnaires (41.1%) were returned.

Scale Indicators and Reliability / Validity Parameters

Scale: from 1 (definitely false) to 7 (definitely true)

Information on individual indicators regarding "Consensus Orientation [Konsensorientierung]"			
Description of indicators	*Item to Total-Correlation*	*Indicator-Reliability*	*t statistic*
1. Wichtige Entscheidungen werden nur gemeinsam im Team getroffen.	0.90	0.91	15.98
2. Bei wichtigen Entscheidungen legen wir sehr viel Wert darauf, dass sich alle einig sind.	0.94	0.97	16.12
3. Es ist wichtig, dass alle Mitglieder des Management-Teams wirklich von einer Entscheidung überzeugt sind.	0.94	0.95	16.07
4. Wir machen uns viele Gedanken über die Art der Interaktion in unserem Team.	0.80	0.61	14.55

Information on scale "Consensus Orientation [Konsensorientierung]"			
Descriptive Statistics		*Result of Exploratory Factor Analysis*	
Cronbach's alpha:	0.96	Total variance explained:	0.89
Results of Confirmatory Factor Analysis			
χ^2-Value (Degrees of Freedom):	0.15 (2)	χ^2-Value/Degrees of Freedom:	0.08
p Value:	0.00	RMSEA:	0.00
SRMR:	–*	CFI:	1.00
GFI:	1.00	AGFI:	1.00
Factor reliability:	0.96	Average variance explained:	0.86

*Not available

References

***Spieker, M.* (2004): Entscheidungen in Gründerteams. Determinanten – Parameter – Erfolgsauswirkungen, Wiesbaden 2004, pp. 236-237.**

Reitmeyer, T. (2000): Qualität von Entscheidungsprozessen der Geschäftsleitung: Eine empirische Untersuchung mittelständischer Unternehmen 2000, Wiesbaden.

32. Constructive Transparency [Konstruktive Transparenz]

Scale Description
The scale measures the extent to which deviations from planned budgets are communicated openly and these data are used for organizational learning.

Origin
The scale was newly developed by Bauer (2002).

Samples
Survey data were collected by questionnaire, administered via mail to 2,527 German companies. A total of 347 companies sent usable answers, yielding a 14.8% return rate.

Comments
The study used a dyadic design approach, where a manager and a controller of the same company were questioned. The data for this scale solely stem from the answers of the managers.

Scale Indicators and Reliability / Validity Parameters
Scale: from 1 (definitely false) to 7 (definitely true)

Information on individual indicators regarding "Constructive Transparency [Konstruktive Transparenz]"			
Description of indicators	*Item to Total-Correlation*	*Indicator-Reliability*	*t statistic*
1. Planabweichungen werden bei uns offen kommuniziert und analysiert.	0.60	0.60	15.06
2. Bei größeren Problemen führen wir umgehend alle Betroffenen zu einer gemeinsamen Lösungsfindung zusammen.	0.61	0.66	15.06
3. Kontrolle ist v.a. wichtig, um aus Fehlern lernen zu können.	0.55	0.42	15.06

Information on scale "Constructive Transparency [Konstruktive Transparenz]"			
Descriptive Statistics		*Result of Exploratory Factor Analysis*	
Cronbach's alpha:	0.76	Total variance explained:	0.67
Results of Confirmatory Factor Analysis			
Factor reliability:	0.79	Average variance explained:	0.56

References

***Bauer, M.* (2002): Controllership in Deutschland. Zur erfolgreichen Zusammenarbeit von Controllern und Managern, Wiesbaden 2002, pp. 187.**

33. Contact Frequency [Kontakthäufigkeit]

Scale Description

The scale measures manager's assessment of the regularity of having contacts with the accounting staff.

Origin

The scale was newly developed by Aust (1999). Hunold (2003) used a similar approach.

Samples

The scale stems from a questionnaire sent to 1,163 German industrial companies, of which 143 participated, yielding a return rate of 12.3%. The study used a triadic design approach, where the general manager, the marketing or sales director and an accountant of the same company were questioned. Altogether, 105 usable triads were returned.

Scale Indicators and Reliability / Validity Parameters

Scale: from 1 (definitely false) to 5 (definitely true)

Information on individual indicators regarding "Contact Frequency [Kontakthäufigkeit]"			
Description of indicators	*Item to Total-Correlation*	*Indicator-Reliability*	*t statistic*
1. Ich komme mit den Informationen der Kostenrechnung häufig in Berührung.	0.63	–*	–*
2. Mit den Kostenrechnern habe ich einen häufigen Kontakt.	0.63	–*	–*

Information on scale "Contact Frequency [Kontakthäufigkeit]"			
Descriptive Statistics		*Result of Exploratory Factor Analysis*	
Cronbach's alpha:	0.77	Total variance explained:	0.82

*Not feasible

References

***Aust, R.* (1999): Kostenrechnung als unternehmensinterne Dienstleistung, Wiesbaden 1999, pp. 162.**

Hunold, C. (2003): Kommunale Kostenrechnung. Gestaltung, Nutzung und Erfolgsfaktoren, Wiesbaden 2003.

34. Controller Support [Controllerunterstützung]

Scale Description

The scale measures the extent to which controllers support the process of budgeting. The scale comprises four dimensions: timeliness of supplied information, relevance of supplied information, adaptiveness of supplied information as well as explanations and advice from controllers.

Origin

Künkele and Schäffer (2007) developed the scale based on the measure of process quality of Aust (1999). The third indicator of Aust's scale was eliminated; the remaining four indicators were related to budgeting.

Samples

Survey data were collected by questionnaire, administered to business unit leaders and the responsible controllers of these business units of 1,120 German companies from 500 to 5,000 employees. The companies were from services and industrial sectors. A total of 140 usable pairs of questionnaires (12.5%) were returned.

Scale Indicators and Reliability / Validity Parameters

Scale: from 1 (definitely false) to 5 (definitely true)

Information on individual indicators regarding "Controller Support [Controllerunterstützung]"			
Description of indicators	*Item to Total-Correlation*	*Indicator-Reliability*	*t statistic*
1. Die Budgetierung wird von Beratungen bzw. Erläuterungen durch die Controller begleitet.	0.59	_*	_*
2. Die Controller gehen sehr spezifisch auf die individuellen Bedürfnisse der Budgetverantwortlichen ein.	0.59	_*	_*

Information on scale "Controller Support [Controllerunterstützung]"			
Descriptive Statistics		*Result of Exploratory Factor Analysis*	
Cronbach's alpha:	0.74	Total variance explained:	0.79

*Not feasible

References

***Künkele, J./Schäffer, U.* (2007): Zur erfolgreichen Gestaltung der Budgetkontrolle, in: Die Betriebswirtschaft, Vol. 67, pp. 75-92.**

Aust, R. (1999): Kostenrechnung als unternehmensinterne Dienstleistung, Wiesbaden 1999.

35. Coordination through Personal Order [Koordination durch persönliche Weisung]

Scale Description

The scale measures the extent to which managers use personal communication as a means of coordinating the tasks of subordinates.

Origin

The scale was newly developed by Reitmeyer (2000).

Samples

Survey data were collected by questionnaire, administered via mail to 3,000 top managers of German industrial companies. A total of 500 usable questionnaires (16.6%) were returned.

Scale Indicators and Reliability / Validity Parameters

Scale: from 1 (definitely false) to 7 (definitely true)

Information on individual indicators regarding "Coordination through Personal Order [Koordination durch persönliche Weisung]"			
Description of indicators	*Item to Total-Correlation*	*Indicator-Reliability*	*t statistic*
1. Ich möchte auch bei vermeintlich kleineren Entscheidungen eingebunden werden.	0.49	0.24	9.41
2. Die Mitarbeiter fragen häufig bei ihrer täglichen Arbeit um Rat oder Entscheidungen nach.	0.52	0.28	9.88
3. Viele Probleme könnten ohne meine persönliche Anwesenheit nicht oder nur schlechter gelöst werden.	0.53	0.28	9.91
4. Ich mische ich gerne ein und gebe den Mitarbeitern häufig Hinweise, wie sie ihre Arbeit besser erledigen können.	0.54	0.29	12.08

Information on scale "Coordination through Personal Order [Koordination durch persönliche Weisung]"			
Descriptive Statistics		*Result of Exploratory Factor Analysis*	
Cronbach's alpha:	0.73	Total variance explained:	0.55
Results of Confirmatory Factor Analysis			
χ^2-Value (Degrees of Freedom):	2.78 (2)	χ^2-Value/Degrees of Freedom:	1.39
p Value:	–*	RMSEA:	0.06
SRMR:	–*	CFI:	0.99
GFI:	0.99	AGFI:	0.97
Factor reliability:	0.73	Average variance explained:	0.27

*Not available

References

***Reitmeyer, T.* (2000): Qualität von Entscheidungsprozessen der Geschäftsleitung: Eine empirische Untersuchung mittelständischer Unternehmen, Wiesbaden 2000, pp. 77-78.**

36. Coordination through Plans [Koordination durch Pläne]

Scale Description

The scale measures the extent to which managers use planning systems as means of coordinating the tasks of subordinates.

Origin

The scale was newly developed by Reitmeyer (2000).

Samples

Survey data were collected by questionnaire, administered via mail to 3,000 top managers of German industrial companies. A total of 500 usable questionnaires (16.6%) were returned.

Scale Indicators and Reliability / Validity Parameters

Scale: from 1 (definitely false) to 7 (definitely true)

Information on individual indicators regarding "Coordination through Plans [Koordination durch Pläne]"			
Description of indicators	*Item to Total-Correlation*	*Indicator-Reliability*	*t statistic*
1. Wir haben eine jährliche Planung, die wir auch einhalten.	0.69	0.59	7.95
2. Über unsere Planung geben wir die wesentlichen Aufgaben für das Jahr vor.	0.74	0.63	7.94
3. Für unsere Führungskräfte gibt es schriftliche Pläne, aus denen sich unsere Aufgaben ergeben.	0.53	0.33	7.33
4. Bei meinen Entscheidungen hat die ursprüngliche Planung nur eine geringe Bedeutung.	0.34	0.12	8.18

Information on scale "Coordination through Plans [Koordination durch Pläne]"			
Descriptive Statistics		*Result of Exploratory Factor Analysis*	
Cronbach's alpha:	0.77	Total variance explained:	0.60
Results of Confirmatory Factor Analysis			
χ^2-Value (Degrees of Freedom):	0.10 (2)	χ^2-Value/Degrees of Freedom:	0.05
p Value:	–*	RMSEA:	0.00
SRMR:	–*	CFI:	1.00
GFI:	1.00	AGFI:	1.00
Factor reliability:	0.78	Average variance explained:	0.42

*Not available

References

Reitmeyer, T. **(2000): Qualität von Entscheidungsprozessen der Geschäftsleitung: Eine empirische Untersuchung mittelständischer Unternehmen, Wiesbaden, pp. 77-78.**

37. Cost Consciousness

Scale Description

The scale measures cost consciousness of physician managers.

Origin

Abernethy and Vagnoni (2004) used the construct developed by Shields and Young (1994).

Samples

A total of 70 from 135 questionnaires were returned providing an overall response rate of 52%. There were, however, only 56 useable questionnaires. The physician managers in the sample had been in their current position for an average of 10 years and had practiced as a medical practitioner in the hospital for an average of 24 years.

Comments

Abernethy and Vagnoni (2004) reported a mean of 5.22 and a standard deviation of 1.26. Shields and Young (1994) who developed the construct reported a Cronbach's alpha of 0.85.

Scale Indicators and Reliability / Validity Parameters

Scale: from 1 (strongly agree) to 7 (strongly disagree)

Information on individual indicators regarding "Cost Consciousness"			
Description of indicators	*Item to Total-Correlation*	*Indicator-Reliability*	*t statistic*
1. In general, I know how much I have to spend in operating my unit.	–*	–*	–*
2. I have a good knowledge of the way my unit's budget is spent.	–*	–*	–*
3. I make sure those who work in my unit know the spending goals and limits.	–*	–*	–*
4. I am very confident of my ability to manage costs in this unit.	–*	–*	–*
5. I put a lot of effort into reducing costs.	–*	–*	–*
6. When I decide to purchase new supplies or equipment I focus heavily on how much it costs.	–*	–*	–*
7. I am very conscious of how actions in this unit influence overall hospital costs.	–*	–*	–*

Information on scale "Cost Consciousness"			
Descriptive Statistics		*Result of Exploratory Factor Analysis*	
Cronbach's alpha:	–*	Total variance explained:	0.55
Results of Confirmatory Factor Analysis			
χ^2-Value (Degrees of Freedom):	0.157 (1)	χ2-Value/Degrees of Freedom:	0.157
p-Wert:	0.692	RMSEA:	–*
NFI:	0.997	NNFI:	–*
SRMR:	–*	CFI:	–*
GFI:	–*	AGFI:	0.980
Factor reliability:	0.86	Average variance explained:	–*

*Not available

References

***Abernethy, M. A./Vagnoni, E.* (2004): Power, Organization Design and Managerial Behaviour, in: Accounting, Organizations and Society, Vol. 29, pp. 207-225.**

Shields, M. D./Young, S. M. (1994): Managing Innovation Costs: A Study of Cost Conscious Behavior by R&D Professionals, in: Journal of Management Accounting Research, Vol. 6, pp. 175-196.

38. Critical Counterpart [Kritischer Counterpart]

Scale Description

The scale indicates in how far controllers perceive themselves as playing a critical counterpart role, e.g. actively „challenging" the managers.

Origin

The scale was newly developed by Bauer (2002).

Samples

Survey data were collected by questionnaire, administered via mail to 2,527 German companies. A total of 347 companies sent usable answers, yielding a 14.8% return rate.

Comments

The study used a dyadic design approach, where a manager and a controller of the same company were questioned. The data for this scale solely stem from the answers of the controllers.

Scale Indicators and Reliability / Validity Parameters

Scale: from 1 (definitely false) to 7 (definitely true)

Information on individual indicators regarding "Critical Counterpart [Kritischer Counterpart]"			
Description of indicators	*Item to Total-Correlation*	*Indicator-Reliability*	*t statistic*
1. Wir hinterfragen auch inhaltliche Aspekte der Planung generell kritisch.	0.60	0.57	14.9
2. Aussagen zu Ergebniswirkungen von geplanten Maßnahmen prüfen wir.	0.58	0.55	14.8
3. Unsere Rolle bei der Entscheidungsfindung verstehe ich als die eines kritischen und konstruktiven Sparring-Partners.	0.60	0.60	15.2

Information on scale "Critical Counterpart [Kritischer Counterpart]"			
Descriptive Statistics		*Result of Exploratory Factor Analysis*	
Cronbach's alpha:	0.76	Total variance explained:	0.68
Results of Confirmatory Factor Analysis			
Factor reliability:	0.80	Average variance explained:	0.57

References

Bauer, M. (2002): Controllership in Deutschland. Zur erfolgreichen Zusammenarbeit von Controllern und Managern, Wiesbaden 2002, pp. 188-189.

39. Culture of Mutual Trust

Scale Description

The scale measures the extent to which managers believe that trust is an important basis of collaboration.

Origin

The scale was newly developed by Willauer (2005).

Samples

Survey data were collected by questionnaire, administered to managers of planning departments of 4,186 German companies from the industrial sector. A total of 298 usable questionnaires (7.1%) were returned.

Scale Indicators and Reliability / Validity Parameters

Scale: from 1 (definitely false) to 7 (definitely true)

Information on individual indicators regarding "Culture of Mutual Trust"			
Description of indicators	*Item to Total-Correlation*	*Indicator-Reliability*	*t statistic*
1. Trust is a very important topic for us.	0.67	0.58	16.27
2. Caution and mutual distrust are very common in our company. (R)	0.65	0.52	15.70
3. We communicate important connections immediately.	0.68	0.61	16.52
4. Management cooperation is formed by mutual trust.	0.75	0.77	17.00

Information on scale "Culture of Mutual Trust"			
Descriptive Statistics		*Result of Exploratory Factor Analysis*	
Cronbach's alpha:	0.85	Total variance explained:	0.69
Results of Confirmatory Factor Analysis			
χ^2-Value (Degrees of Freedom):	1.38 (2)	χ^2-Value/Degrees of Freedom:	0.69
p Value:	0.50	RMSEA:	0.00
SRMR:	–*	CFI:	1.00
GFI:	1.00	AGFI:	0.99
Factor reliability:	0.87	Average variance explained:	0.62

*Not available

References

***Willauer, B.* (2005): Consensus as a Key Success Factor in Strategy-Making, Wiesbaden 2005, pp. 204-206.**

40. Data Manipulation [Datenmanipulation]

Scale Description

The scale measures the extent to which managers manipulate budgetary data.

Origin

The fist two indicators stem from Merchant's (1990) scale of manipulation of performance measures. The other four indicators are taken from the dysfunctional behavior measure by Jaworski and MacInnis (1989).

Samples

Survey data were collected by questionnaire, administered to business unit leaders and the responsible controllers of these business units of 1,120 German companies from 500 to 5,000 employees. The companies were from services and industrial sectors. A total of 140 usable pairs of questionnaires (12.5%) were returned.

Comments

The dysfunctional behavior measure of Jaworski and MacInnis (1989) has been used by Ramaswami (1996), who found good reliability coefficients (Cronbach's alpha = 0.78). Ramaswami (1996) reported a mean of 2.45 and a standard deviation of 0.75.

Scale Indicators and Reliability / Validity Parameters

Scale: from 1 (definitely false) to 5 (definitely true)

Information on individual indicators regarding "Data Manipulation [Datenmanipulation]"			
Description of indicators	*Item to Total-Correlation*	*Indicator-Reliability*	*t statistic*
1. Auch wenn die Leistung von Managern Inkonsistenzen aufweist, versuchen sie, sie schlüssig zu verkaufen.	0.59	0.47	10.34
2. Bei Berichten an ihre Vorgesetzten versuchen Manager, Daten, die ein positives Licht auf ihre Leistung werfen, in den Vordergrund zu rücken.	0.65	0.79	12.68
3. Bei Berichten an ihre Vorgesetzten versuchen Manager, schlechte Nachrichten zurückzuhalten.	0.48	0.28	8.33

Information on scale "Data Manipulation [Datenmanipulation]"			
Descriptive Statistics		*Result of Exploratory Factor Analysis*	
Cronbach's alpha:	0.74	Total variance explained:	0.66
Results of Confirmatory Factor Analysis			
Factor reliability:	0.75	Average variance explained:	0.51

References

***Künkele, J./Schäffer, U.* (2007): Zur erfolgreichen Gestaltung der Budgetkontrolle, in: Die Betriebswirtschaft, Vol. 67, pp. 75-92.**

Merchant, K. A. (1990): The Effects of Financial Controls on Data Manipulation and Management Myopia, in: Accounting, Organizations and Society, Vol. 15, pp. 297-313.

Ramaswami, S. N. (1996): Marketing Controls and Dysfunctional Employee Behaviors: A Test of Traditional and Contingency Theory Postulates, in: Journal of Marketing, Vol. 60, pp. 105-120.

41. Decision-Making (Learning Ex Ante) [Willensbildung – Lernen ex ante]

Scale Description

The scale measures the extent to which managers use MAS information for the anticipation of specific relations of means and ends in the decision-making process.

Origin

The first three indicators stem from Karlshaus´ (2000) scale of instrumental use of information. The fourth item was newly developed by Schäffer/Steiners (2004).

Samples

Survey data were collected by questionnaire, administered to business unit leaders of 3,500 German companies with 100 to 2,000 employees from the industrial sector. A total of 449 usable questionnaires (12.8%) were returned.

Scale Indicators and Reliability / Validity Parameters

Scale: from 1 (definitely false) to 5 (definitely true)

Information on individual indicators regarding "Decision-Making (Learning Ex Ante) [Willensbildung – Lernen ex ante]"			
Description of indicators	*Item to Total-Correlation*	*Indicator-Reliability*	*t statistic*
1. Ohne die Informationen würden meine Entscheidungen zumeist anders ausfallen.	0.47	0.23	8.31
2. Die Informationen lenken meine Aufmerksamkeit auf Aspekte meiner Entscheidungen, die ich sonst nicht beachten würde.	0.44	0.53	9.02
3. Für meine Entscheidungen benötige ich die Informationen eigentlich kaum. (R)	0.43	0.24	8.35
4. Ich nutze die Informationen unmittelbar zur Entscheidungsfindung bzw. zur Lösung konkreter Probleme.	0.50	0.73	10.41

Information on scale "Decision-Making (Learning Ex Ante) [Willensbildung – Lernen ex ante]"			
Descriptive Statistics		*Result of Exploratory Factor Analysis*	
Cronbach's alpha:	0.67	Total variance explained:	0.66
Results of Confirmatory Factor Analysis			
χ^2-Value (Degrees of Freedom):	5.66 (1)	χ^2-Value/Degrees of Freedom:	5.66
p Value:	0.02	RMSEA:	0.10
NFI:	0.98	NNFI:	0.91
GFI:	0.99	AGFI:	0.94
Factor reliability:	0.74	Average variance explained:	0.43

References

***Schäffer, U./Steiners, D.* (2004): Zur Nutzung von Controllinginformationen, in: Zeitschrift für Planung und Unternehmenssteuerung, Vol. 15, pp. 377-404.**

Karlshaus, J. T. (2000): Die Nutzung von Kostenrechnungsinformationen im Marketing, Wiesbaden 2000.

42. Decision-Making Style [Entscheidungsstil]

Scale Description

The scale measures what type of thinking a person prefers in the process of decision-making (analytic as opposed to intuitive).

Origin

Schäffer/Steiners (2004) based their scale on the Cognitive Style Index (CSI) by Allinson/ Hayes (1996).

Samples

Survey data were collected by questionnaire, administered to business unit leaders of 3,500 German companies with 100 to 2,000 employees from the industrial sector. A total of 449 usable questionnaires (12.8%) were returned.

Comments

The original CSI contains 38 indicators. The items for the scale described here were chosen by expert interviews to specifically fit into the context of decision-making by using MAS information.

Scale Indicators and Reliability / Validity Parameters

Scale: from 1 (definitely false) to 5 (definitely true)

Information on individual indicators regarding "Decision-Making Style [Entscheidungsstil]"			
Description of indicators	*Item to Total-Correlation*	*Indicator-Reliability*	*t statistic*
1. Vor einer Entscheidung nehme ich mir Zeit und berücksichtige sorgfältig alle relevanten Aspekte.	0.55	0.44	13.37
2. Bei wichtigen Entscheidungen erarbeite ich ausführlich mögliche Alternativen.	0.53	0.43	13.18
3. Zur Entscheidungsfindung besorge ich mir alle Informationen, die ich bekommen kann.	0.61	0.57	15.35
4. Wenn ich eine Entscheidung treffen muss, beachte ich deren Einfluss auf künftige Entscheidungen.	0.41	0.24	9.50

Information on scale "Decision-Making Style [Entscheidungsstil]"			
Descriptive Statistics		*Result of Exploratory Factor Analysis*	
Cronbach's alpha:	0.73	Total variance explained:	0.56
Results of Confirmatory Factor Analysis			
χ^2-Value (Degrees of Freedom):	1.59 (2)	χ^2-Value/Degrees of Freedom:	0.80
p Value:	0.45	RMSEA:	0.00
NFI:	1.0	NNFI:	1.0
SRMR:	0.01	CFI:	1.0
GFI:	1.0	AGFI:	0.99
Factor reliability:	0.74	Average variance explained:	0.42

References

Schäffer, U./Steiners, D. **(2004): Zur Nutzung von Controllinginformationen, in: Zeitschrift für Planung und Unternehmenssteuerung, Vol. 15, pp. 377-404.**

Allinson, C. W./Hayes, J. (1996): The Cognitive Style Index: A Measure of Intuition-Analysis for Organizational Research, in: Journal of Management Studies, Vol. 33, pp. 119-153.

43. Decision Quality [Entscheidungsqualität]

Scale Description

The scale measures the extent to which management teams are satisfied with the overall quality of the decision-making process.

Origin

The scale was developed by Spieker (2004) drawing on items from Hauschildt et al. (1983) and Reitmeyer (2000).

Samples

Survey data were collected by questionnaire, administered via internet to 353 managers of German start-up companies. A total of 145 usable questionnaires (41.1%) were returned.

Scale Indicators and Reliability / Validity Parameters

Scale: from 1 (definitely false) to 7 (definitely true)

Information on individual indicators regarding "Decision Quality [Entscheidungsqualität]"			
Description of indicators	*Item to Total-Correlation*	*Indicator-Reliability*	*t statistic*
1. Der Ablauf wichtiger Entscheidungen ist sehr zufriedenstellend.	0.70	0.62	10.25
2. Die Ergebnisse wichtiger Entscheidungen sind sehr zufriedenstellend.	0.83	0.94	10.25
3. Der Umsetzung wichtiger Entscheidungen ist sehr zufriedenstellend.	0.74	0.73	10.25

Information on scale "Decision Quality [Entscheidungsqualität]"			
Descriptive Statistics		*Result of Exploratory Factor Analysis*	
Cronbach's alpha:	0.87	Total variance explained:	0.80
Results of Confirmatory Factor Analysis			
Factor reliability:	0.91	Average variance explained:	0.76

References

Spieker, M. **(2004): Entscheidungen in Gründerteams. Determinanten – Parameter – Erfolgsauswirkungen, Wiesbaden 2004, pp. 247-248.**

Hauschildt, J./Gemünden, H. G./Grotz-Martin, S./Haidle, U. (1983): Entscheidungen in der Geschäftsführung. Typologie, Informationsverhalten, Effizienz, Tübingen 1983.

Reitmeyer, T. (2000): Qualität von Entscheidungsprozessen der Geschäftsleitung: Eine empirische Untersuchung mittelständischer Unternehmen, Wiesbaden 2000.

44. Delegation of Strategic Planning [Delegation der strategischen Planung]

Scale Description

The scale measures the extent to which the strategic planning process within a firm is delegated into functional areas.

Origin

The scale was newly developed by Willauer as part of a doctoral research project. Results were published in Weber/Schäffer/Willauer (2003).

Samples

Survey data were collected by questionnaire, administered to managers of planning departments of 4,186 German companies from the industrial sector. A total of 298 usable questionnaires (7.1%) were returned.

Scale Indicators and Reliability / Validity Parameters

Scale: from 1 (definitely false) to 7 (definitely true)

Information on individual indicators regarding "Delegation of Strategic Planning [Delegation der Strategischen Planung]"			
Description of indicators	*Item to Total-Correlation*	*Indicator-Reliability*	*t statistic*
1. Die strategische/langfristige Planung erfolgt bei uns überwiegend in der Zentrale. (R)	0.64	0.53	16.40
2. Die strategische/langfristige Planung erfolgt bei uns überwiegend in den dezentralen Bereichen.	0.68	0.63	17.07
3. Wir versuchen im Rahmen der strategischen/langfristigen Planung möglichst viel Kompetenz an diejenigen zu delegieren, die später operativ zuständig sind.	0.71	0.68	17.26
4. Die strategische/langfristige Planung wird von denen gemacht, die sie nachher umsetzen.	0.72	0.75	17.63

Information on scale "Delegation of Strategic Planning [Delegation der Strategischen Planung]"			
Descriptive Statistics		*Result of Exploratory Factor Analysis*	
Cronbach's alpha:	0.85	Total variance explained:	0.69
Results of Confirmatory Factor Analysis			
χ^2-Value (Degrees of Freedom):	1.38 (2)	χ^2-Value/Degrees of Freedom:	0.69
p Value:	0.50	RMSEA:	0.00
SRMR:	–*	CFI:	1.00
GFI:	1.00	AGFI:	0.99
Factor reliability:	0.88	Average variance explained:	0.65

*Not available

References

***Weber, J /Schäffer, U./Willauer, B.* (2003): Skalenübersicht, in: Weber, J./Kunz, J. (Ed.): Empirische Controllingforschung: Begründung, Beispiele, Ergebnisse, Wiesbaden 2003, pp. 385-467.**

45. Detail in Reports [Berichtsdetaillierung]

Scale Description

The scale measures the extent to which reports show budget data in a detailed manner and broken down by units, regions, projects, etc.

Origin

The scale was developed based on an overall monitoring measure of Kren (1993). Kren's indicator to measure detail in reports was taken and four additional indicators were added. Kren asked for the detail in controlling reports based on a 7-point-likert scale from 1 (aggregated, summaries only) to 7 (highly detailed, breakdown by unit and tasks).

Samples

Survey data were collected by questionnaire, administered to business unit leaders and the responsible controllers of these business units of 1,120 German companies from 500 to 5,000 employees. The companies were from services and industrial sectors. A total of 140 usable pairs of questionnaires (12.5%) were returned.

Comments

Kren (1993) measured the monitoring ability of companies. Therefore he constructed an overall monitoring measure using the sum of the items of five scales (action control, results control, personnel control, detail of reports and frequency of reporting). He reported a Cronbach's alpha of 0.77 for this overall monitoring measure. Kren (1993) reported a hypothetical range of 10-70, an actual range of 14-68, a mean of 38.1 and a standard deviation of 10.6.

Scale Indicators and Reliability / Validity Parameters

Scale: from 1 (definitely false) to 5 (definitely true)

Information on individual indicators regarding "Detail in Reports [Berichtsdetaillierung]"			
Description of indicators	*Item to Total-Correlation*	*Indicator-Reliability*	*t statistic*
1. Unsere Budgetkontrollberichte weisen einen sehr hohen Detaillierungsgrad auf.	0.57	_*	_*
2. Bei uns gibt es für jeden Verantwortungsbereich (z.B. Funktionen, Regionen, Projekte) separate Budgetkontrollberichte.	0.57	_*	_*
Information on scale "Detail in Reports [Berichtsdetaillierung]"			
Descriptive Statistics		*Result of Exploratory Factor Analysis*	
Cronbach's alpha:	0.72	Total variance explained:	0.78

*Not feasible

References

Künkele, J./Schäffer, U. **(2007): Zur erfolgreichen Gestaltung der Budgetkontrolle, in: Die Betriebswirtschaft, Vol. 67, pp. 75-92.**

Kren, L. (1993): Control System Effects on Budget Slack, in: Advances in Management Accounting, Vol. 2, pp. 109-118.

46. Diagnostic Use of Metrics [Diagnostische Nutzung von Kennzahlen]

Scale Description

The scale measures the extent to which managers use some metrics as means of directing scarce attention towards crucial business aspects. Here, metrics are noticed only if a critical threshold value has been violated.

Origin

The scale was newly developed by Sandt (2004) based on a framework by Simons (1995).

Samples

The questionnaire was sent to 2,386 German upper level managers. 254 responses could be integrated into the analysis, yielding a response rate of 11.1%.

Scale Indicators and Reliability / Validity Parameters

Scale: from 1 (definitely false) to 5 (definitely true)

Information on individual indicators regarding "Diagnostic Use of Metrics [Diagnostische Nutzung von Kennzahlen]"			
Description of indicators	*Item to Total-Correlation*	*Indicator-Reliability*	*t statistic*
1. Die Kennzahlen helfen mir, meine Zeit und Kapazität zu schonen, indem ich lediglich bei bedeutenden Abweichungen eingreife.	0.60	0.49	13.20
2. Die Kennzahlen dienen mir als Ampel, die mir zeigt, wo alles im grünen Bereich ist oder wo etwas aus dem Ruder läuft.	0.62	0.56	13.47
3. Die Kennzahlen sind wie eine Alarmglocke, die ertönt, wenn es nötig ist, ansonsten aber ruhig ist.	0.65	0.49	13.76
4. Mit Hilfe der Kennzahlen verschaffe ich mir einen Überblick über den Stand der Dinge in meiner Geschäftseinheit.	0.61	0.51	13.22

Information on scale "Diagnostic Use of Metrics [Diagnostische Nutzung von Kennzahlen]"			
Descriptive Statistics		*Result of Exploratory Factor Analysis*	
Cronbach's alpha:	0.80	Total variance explained:	0.63
Results of Confirmatory Factor Analysis			
χ^2-Value (Degrees of Freedom):	3.11 (2)	χ^2-Value/Degrees of Freedom:	1.56
p Value:	0.21	RMSEA:	0.05
SRMR:	–*	CFI:	1.00
GFI:	1.00	AGFI:	0.98
Factor reliability:	0.83	Average variance explained:	0.55

*Not available

References

***Sandt, J.* (2004): Management mit Kennzahlen und Kennzahlensystemen. Bestandsaufnahme, Determinanten und Erfolgswirkungen, Wiesbaden 2004, pp. 167-169.**

Simons, R. (1995): Levers of Control, Boston 1995.

47. Distribution of Information [Informationsverteilung]

Scale Description

The scale measures the extent to which relevant information is equally and timely distributed among controlling staff.

Origin

The scale was newly developed by Spillecke (2006).

Samples

Survey data were collected by questionnaire, administered via e-mail to 3,312 German managers of companies with at least 200 employees. The companies were from different industrial sectors. A total of 415 usable questionnaires (12.5%) were returned.

Scale Indicators and Reliability / Validity Parameters

Scale: from 1 (definitely false) to 5 (definitely true)

Information on individual indicators regarding "Distribution of Information [Informationsverteilung]"			
Description of indicators	*Item to Total-Correlation*	*Indicator-Reliability*	*t statistic*
1. Der Informationsfluss zwischen den Controllern ist meines Erachtens sehr gut.	0.80	0.74	-
2. Wenn ein Controller etwas Wichtiges über den Bedarf des Managers in Erfahrung bringt, sind in kürzester Zeit alle Controller informiert.	0.79	0.70	21.46
3. Es passiert sehr selten, dass zwei Controller die gleichen Sachverhalte erfragen bzw. die gleichen Fragen stellen.	0.63	0.44	15.27
4. Wenn ein neuer/ungewöhnlicher Informationsbedarf im Management besteht, wissen alle Controller in kürzester Zeit darüber Bescheid.	0.74	0.62	19.43
5. Die Controller sind meines Erachtens untereinander gut „vernetzt".	0.86	0.87	25.22

Information on scale "Distribution of Information [Informationsverteilung]"			
Descriptive Statistics		*Result of Exploratory Factor Analysis*	
Cronbach's alpha:	0.91	Total variance explained:	0.67
Results of Confirmatory Factor Analysis			
χ^2-Value (Degrees of Freedom):	5.93 (5)	χ^2-Value/Degrees of Freedom:	1.19
p Value:	0.31	RMSEA:	0.02
SRMR:	–*	CFI:	1.00
GFI:	1.00	AGFI:	0.98
Factor reliability:	0.91	Average variance explained:	0.67

*Not feasible

References

Spillecke, D. (2006): Interne Kundenorientierung des Controllerbereichs. Messung – Erfolgsauswirkungen – Determinanten, Wiesbaden 2006, pp. 116-118.

48. Divisional Dependence

Scale Description

The scale measures the dependence of subsidiaries on another for product and production development. The CEO of each subsidiary estimated the dependence.

Origin

Developed by Andersson et al. (2001).

Samples

Andersson et al. (2001) collected data from 98 subsidiaries belonging to 20 international divisions within 15 Swedish MNCs. The division headquarters were all located in Sweden. The majority of the subsidiaries were located in Europe and a few (five) in North America. The sample was chosen to represent a wide spectrum of the Swedish industry and involves large and well-known companies in industries such as pulp and paper, telecommunications equipment, petrochemicals, power distribution, hard metal tools, saws and chains, gas applications, transportation, software, management training and industrial equipment.

Scale Indicators and Reliability / Validity Parameters

Scale: from 1 (very low) to 5 (very high)

Information on individual indicators regarding "Divisional Dependence"			
Description of indicators	*Item to Total-Correlation*	*Indicator-Reliability*	*t statistic*
1. To what extent is this subsidiary important to other divisional units' product development?	–*	0.51	3.85
2. To what extent is this subsidiary important to other divisional units' production development?	–*	0.87	4.59

Information on scale "Divisional Dependence"			
Descriptive Statistics		*Result of Exploratory Factor Analysis*	
Cronbach's alpha:	–*	Total variance explained:	–*

*Not available

References

***Andersson, U./Forsgren, M./Pedersen, T.* (2001): Subsidiary Performance in Multinational Corporations: The Importance of Technology Embeddedness, in: International Business Review, Vol. 10, pp. 3-23.**

49. Dysfunctional Behavior

Scale Description

The scale measures the extent to which managers engage in dysfunctional behaviors. The scale comprises four dimensions: gaming, focusing, smoothing and invalid reporting.

Origin

The 6-item scale was developed by Jaworski and MacInnis (1989).

Samples

Survey data were collected by questionnaire, administered to 500 senior marketing executives (i.e. marketing managers, directors of marketing, vice-presidents) drawn randomly from an AMA roster. A total of 379 usable questionnaires (76%) were returned.

Comments

The dysfunctional behavior measure from Jaworski and MacInnis (1989) has been used by Ramaswami (1996), who found good reliability coefficients (Cronbach's alpha = 0.78). Ramaswami (1996) reported a mean of 2.45 and a standard deviation of 0.75.

Scale Indicators and Reliability / Validity Parameters

Scale: from 1 (never) to 5 (always)

Information on individual indicators regarding "Dysfunctional Behavior"			
Description of indicators			
1. I tend to ignore certain job related activities simply because they are not monitored by the division.			
2. I work on unimportant activities simply because they are evaluated by upper management.			
3. Even if my productivity is inconsistent, I still try to make it appear consistent.			
4. I have adjusted marketing data to make my performance appear more in line with division goals.			
5. When presenting data to upper management, I try to emphasize data that reflect favorably upon me.			
6. When presenting data to upper management, I try to avoid being the bearer of bad news.			
Information on scale "Dysfunctional Behavior"			
Descriptive Statistics		*Result of Exploratory Factor Analysis*	
Cronbach's alpha:	0.75	Total variance explained:	–*

*Not available

References

***Jaworski, B. J./MacInnis, D. J.* (1989): Marketing Jobs and Management Controls: Toward a Framework, in: Journal of Marketing Research, Vol. 26, pp. 406-419.**

Ramaswami, S. N. (1996): Marketing Controls and Dysfunctional Employee Behaviors: A Test of Traditional and Contingency Theory Postulates, in: Journal of Marketing, Vol. 60, pp. 105-120.

50. Dysfunctional Behavior [Dysfunktionales Verhalten]

Scale Description

The scale measures the extent to which managers engage in dysfunctional behaviors. The scale comprises three dimensions: propensity to create budgetary slack, neglect of non-controlled areas and data manipulation.

Origin

Künkele and Schäffer (2007) developed the scale by combining the means of the scales of propensity to create budgetary slack, neglect of non-controlled areas and data manipulation as indicators. The scale of propensity to create budgetary slack was developed by Onsi (1973), the scale of neglect of non-controlled areas contains indicators from the scale of dysfunctional behavior developed by Jaworski and MacInnis (1989). The scale of manipulation is a combination of indicators of the scales of Jaworski and MacInnis (1989) and Merchant (1990).

Samples

Survey data were collected by questionnaire, administered to business unit leaders and the responsible controllers of these business units of 1,120 German companies from 500 to 5,000 employees. The companies were from services and industrial sectors. A total of 140 usable pairs of questionnaires (12.5%) were returned.

Comments

Merchant (1985) used the measure of propensity to create budgetary slack of Onsi (1973). Merchant (1990) found good reliability measures (Cronbach's alpha = 0.70). The measure of dysfunctional behavior of Jaworski and MacInnis (1989) has been used by Ramaswami (1996), who has also found good reliability coefficients (Cronbach's alpha = 0.78).

Scale Indicators and Reliability / Validity Parameters

Scale: from 1 (definitely false) to 5 (definitely true)

Information on individual indicators regarding "Dysfunctional Behavior [Dysfunktionales Verhalten]"			
Description of indicators	*Item to Total-Correlation*	*Indicator-Reliability*	*t statistic*
1. Pufferbildung	0.40	0.27	7.04
2. Vernachlässigung nicht-kontrollierter Bereiche	0.48	0.49	8.37
3. Datenmanipulation	0.44	0.35	7.62

Information on scale "Dysfunctional Behavior [Dysfunktionales Verhalten]"			
Descriptive Statistics		*Result of Exploratory Factor Analysis*	
Cronbach's alpha:	0.63	Total variance explained:	0.57
Results of Confirmatory Factor Analysis			
Factor reliability:	0.63	Average variance explained:	0.37

References

***Künkele, J./Schäffer, U.* (2007): Zur erfolgreichen Gestaltung der Budgetkontrolle, in: Die Betriebswirtschaft, Vol. 67, pp. 75-92.**

Jaworski, B. J./MacInnis, D. J. (1989): Marketing Jobs and Management Controls: Toward a Framework, in: Journal of Marketing Research, Vol. 26, pp. 406-419.

Merchant, K. A. (1985): Budgeting and the Propensity to Create Budgetary Slack, in: Accounting, Organizations and Society, Vol. 10, pp. 201-210.

Merchant, K. A. (1990): The Effects of Financial Controls on Data Manipulation and Management Myopia, in: Accounting, Organizations and Society, Vol. 15, pp. 297-313.

Onsi, M. (1973): Factor Analysis of Behavioral Variables Affecting Budgetary Slack, in: The Accounting Review, Vol. 48, pp. 535-548.

Ramaswami, S. N. (1996): Marketing Controls and Dysfunctional Employee Behaviors: A Test of Traditional and Contingency Theory Postulates, in: Journal of Marketing, Vol. 60, pp. 105-120.

51. Economic Performance (Return on Sales) [Wirtschaftlicher Erfolg – Umsatzrendite]

Scale Description

The scale measures managers' assessment of the company's performance in terms of the development of the profit margin compared to competitors.

Origin

The scale was newly developed by Spillecke (2006) based on items by Schäffer/Willauer (2002) and Sandt (2004).

Samples

Survey data were collected by questionnaire, administered via e-mail to 3,312 German managers of companies with at least 200 employees. The companies were from different industrial sectors. A total of 415 usable questionnaires (12.5%) were returned.

Scale Indicators and Reliability / Validity Parameters

Scale: from 1 (very bad) to 5 (very good)

Information on individual indicators regarding "Economic Performance (Return on Sales) [Wirtschaftlicher Erfolg – Umsatzrendite]"			
Description of indicators	*Item to Total-Correlation*	*Indicator-Reliability*	*t statistic*
1. Unsere Umsatzrendite war im letzten Geschäftsjahr im Vergleich zu unseren Wettbewerbern...	0.82	0.83	–
2. Unsere Umsatzrendite war im Durchschnitt der letzten drei Geschäftsjahre im Vergleich zu unseren Wettbewerbern...	0.80	0.75	22.14
3. Die Entwicklung unserer Umsatzrendite war in den letzten drei Geschäftsjahren im Vergleich zu unseren Wettbewerbern...	0.75	0.63	19.91

Information on scale "Economic Performance (Return on Sales) [Wirtschaftlicher Erfolg – Umsatzrendite]"			
Descriptive Statistics		*Result of Exploratory Factor Analysis*	
Cronbach's alpha:	0.89	Total variance explained:	0.74
Results of Confirmatory Factor Analysis			
Factor reliability:	0.90	Average variance explained:	0.74

*Not feasible

References

***Spillecke, D.* (2006): Interne Kundenorientierung des Controllerbereichs. Messung – Erfolgsauswirkungen – Determinanten, Wiesbaden 2006, pp. 168-169.**

Sandt, J. (2004): Management mit Kennzahlen und Kennzahlensystemen. Bestandsaufnahme, Determinanten und Erfolgswirkungen 2004, Wiesbaden.

Schäffer, U./Willauer, B. (2002): Kontrolle, Effektivität der Planung und Erfolg von Geschäftseinheiten - Ergebnisse einer empirischen Erhebung, in: Zeitschrift für Planung, Vol. 13, pp. 73-97.

52. Education of Cost Accounting Staff [Ausbildung Kostenrechner]

Scale Description

The scale measures the education level of the accounting staff.

Origin

The scale was newly developed by Hunold (2003) following an approach of Christiaens (1999).

Samples

Survey data were collected by questionnaire administered to treasurers and accountants of 1,520 German municipalities as part of a dyadic research design. A total of 201 usable dyads (13.22%) were returned.

Scale Indicators and Reliability / Validity Parameters

Scale: from 1 (definitely false) to 5 (definitely true)

Information on individual indicators regarding "Education of Cost Accounting Staff [Ausbildung Kostenrechner]"			
Description of indicators	*Item to Total-Correlation*	*Indicator-Reliability*	*t statistic*
1. Der Anteil der Kostenrechnungsmitarbeiter mit betriebswirtschaftlicher Ausbildung ist hoch.	0.62	0.81	7.12
2. Der Ausbildungsstand der Kostenrechner im Bereich Kostenrechnung ist gut.	0.63	0.64	7.12
3. Der weitere Bedarf zur Fortbildung der Kostenrechner ist groß. (R)	0.37	0.21	7.12

Information on scale "Education of Cost Accounting Staff [Ausbildung Kostenrechner]"			
Descriptive Statistics		*Result of Exploratory Factor Analysis*	
Cronbach's alpha:	0.70	Total variance explained:	0.63
Results of Confirmatory Factor Analysis			
Factor reliability:	0.78	Average variance explained:	0.55

References

***Hunold, C.* (2003): Kommunale Kostenrechnung. Gestaltung, Nutzung und Erfolgsfaktoren, Wiesbaden 2003, pp. 149-151.**

Christiaens, J. (1999): Financial Accounting Reform in Flemish Municipalities: An Empirical Investigation, in: Financial Accountability & Management, Vol. 15, pp. 21-40.

53. Effectiveness of Budgetary Monitoring [Effektivität der Budgetkontrolle]

Scale Description

The scale measures the extent to which the goals of budgetary control are reached. The scale comprises three dimensions: realization of deviations, analysis of reasons for deviations and initiation of corrective action.

Origin

The scale was newly developed by Künkele and Schäffer (2007).

Samples

Survey data were collected by questionnaire, administered to business unit leaders and the responsible controllers of these business units of 1,120 German companies from 500 to 5,000 employees. The companies were from services and industrial sectors. A total of 140 usable pairs of questionnaires (12.5%) were returned.

Scale Indicators and Reliability / Validity Parameters

Scale: from 1 (definitely false) to 5 (definitely true)

Information on individual indicators regarding "Effectiveness of Budgetary Monitoring [Effektivität der Budgetkontrolle]"			
Description of indicators	*Item to Total-Correlation*	*Indicator-Reliability*	*t statistic*
1. Zufriedenheit mit dem Erkennen von Abweichungen.	0.63	0.51	11.91
2. Zufriedenheit mit der Analyse von Abweichungsursachen.	0.66	0.76	14.55
3. Zufriedenheit mit der Initiierung von Korrekturmaßnahmen an Budgetplänen und/oder Aktionsplänen für die aktuelle oder kommende Periode.	0.57	0.43	10.69

Information on scale "Effectiveness of Budgetary Monitoring [Effektivität der Budgetkontrolle]"			
Descriptive Statistics		*Result of Exploratory Factor Analysis*	
Cronbach's alpha:	0.78	Total variance explained:	0.70
Results of Confirmatory Factor Analysis			
Factor reliability:	0.79	Average variance explained:	0.56

References

***Künkele, J./Schäffer, U.* (2007): Zur erfolgreichen Gestaltung der Budgetkontrolle, in: Die Betriebswirtschaft, Vol. 67, pp. 75-92.**

54. Effectiveness of Operational Monitoring [Effektivität der operativen Kontrolle]

Scale Description

The scale measures the effectiveness of the operational control activities of subsidiaries.The effectiveness of operational control is operationalized by the achievement of objectives of the subsidiary, the speed of recognizing deviations and the effectiveness of corrective measures.

Origin

Developed by Eckey and Schäffer (2006).

Samples

Eckey and Schäffer (2006) collected data using a survey questionnaire sent to a total of 51 group controlling departments of management holdings listed in the German Prime Standard. The sample of companies represented a variety of industries. 37 usable responses were received, yielding a response rate of 72.5%.

Comments

Eckey and Schäffer (2006) reported a mean of 5.53 and standard deviation of 0.80 on a theoretical range of 1-7.

Scale Indicators and Reliability / Validity Parameters

Scale: from 1 (strongly disagree) to 7 (strongly agree)

Information on individual indicators regarding "Effectiveness of Operational Monitoring [Effektivität der operativen Kontrolle]"			
Description of indicators	*Item to Total-Correlation*	*Indicator-Reliability*	*t statistic*
1. Die der Tochtergesellschaft vorgegebenen operativen Ziele (z.B. Rendite von x%) werden stets erreicht.	0.55	0.25	2.86
2. Im Rahmen der laufenden Kontrolle erkennen wir früh Abweichungen vom Soll-Wert.	0.59	0.51	4.31
3. Bei signifikanten Abweichungen werden wirksame Korrekturmaßnahmen getroffen.	0.65	0.75	5.27
4. Die Tochtergesellschaft verfehlt immer die gesetzten Ziele. (R)	0.64	0.43	3.92

Information on scale "Effectiveness of Operational Monitoring [Effektivität der operativen Kontrolle]"			
Descriptive Statistics		*Result of Exploratory Factor Analysis*	
Cronbach's alpha:	0.80	Total variance explained:	0.62
Results of Confirmatory Factor Analysis			
χ^2-Value (Degrees of Freedom):	0.76 (1)	χ^2-Value/Degrees of Freedom:	0.76
p-value:	0.38	RMSEA:	0.00
NFI:	0.99	NNFI:	1.03
SRMR:	0.02	CFI:	1.00
GFI:	0.99	AGFI:	0.90
Factor reliability:	0.78	Average variance explained:	0.48

References

Eckey, M./Schäffer, U. (2006): Kontrolle von Mehrheitsbeteiligungen in börsennotierten Management-Holdings, in: Zeitschrift für Planung & Unternehmenssteuerung, Vol. 17, pp. 251-280.

55. Effectiveness of Strategic Monitoring [Effektivität der strategischen Kontrolle]

Scale Description

The scale measures the effectiveness of the strategic control activities of the subsidiaries. The effectiveness of strategic control is operationalized by the speed of recognizing deviations and the adaptability to new market conditions.

Origin

Developed by Eckey and Schäffer (2006).

Samples

Eckey and Schäffer (2006) collected data using a survey questionnaire sent to a total of 51 group controlling departments of management holdings listed in the German Prime Standard. The sample of companies represented a variety of industries. 37 usable responses were received, yielding a response rate of 72.5%.

Scale Indicators and Reliability / Validity Parameters

Scale: from 1 (strongly disagree) to 7 (strongly agree)

Information on individual indicators regarding "Effectiveness of Strategic Monitoring [Effektivität der strategischen Kontrolle]"			
Description of indicators	*Item to Total-Correlation*	*Indicator-Reliability*	*t statistic*
1. Abweichungen von der strategischen Planung erkennen wir frühzeitig.	0.55	0.45	4.09
2. Bei Veränderungen im Markt, Wettbewerb und allgemeinem Umfeld passt sich die Tochtergesellschaft schnell den neuen Bedingungen an.	0.67	0.34	3.65
3. Neuen Marktbedingungen passt sich die Tochtergesellschaft gut an.	0.80	0.52	4.80
4. Die strategische Planung berücksichtigt die neuen Markt- und Umfeldbedingungen gut.	0.73	0.79	6.25
5. Risiken und Chancen der Tochtergesellschaft werden bei der Planung berücksichtigt.	0.73	0.71	5.90

Information on scale "Effectiveness of Strategic Monitoring [Effektivität der strategischen Kontrolle]"			
Descriptive Statistics		*Result of Exploratory Factor Analysis*	
Cronbach's alpha:	0.87	Total variance explained:	0.66
Results of Confirmatory Factor Analysis			
χ^2-Value (Degrees of Freedom):	0.50 (3)	χ^2-Value/Degrees of Freedom:	0.17
p-value:	0.92	RMSEA:	0.00
NFI:	1.00	NNFI:	1.07
SRMR:	0.01	CFI:	1.00
GFI:	1.00	AGFI:	0.97
Factor reliability:	0.86	Average variance explained:	0.56

References

Eckey, M./Schäffer, U. (2006): Kontrolle von Mehrheitsbeteiligungen in börsennotierten Management-Holdings, in: Zeitschrift für Planung & Unternehmenssteuerung, Vol. 17, pp. 251-280.

56. Effectiveness of Strategy Formulation

Scale Description

The scale measures managers' assessment of the effectiveness of the company's planning process, e.g., the assessment, if the company will reach the planned performance.

Origin

The scale was newly developed by Willauer (2005).

Samples

Survey data were collected by questionnaire, administered to managers of planning departments of 4,186 German companies from the industrial sector. A total of 298 usable questionnaires (7.1%) were returned.

Scale Indicators and Reliability / Validity Parameters

Scale: from 1 (definitely false) to 7 (definitely true)

Information on individual indicators regarding "Effectiveness of Strategy Formulation"			
Description of indicators	*Item to Total-Correlation*	*Indicator-Reliability*	*t statistic*
1. Planning shows us the right way into the future.	0.54	0.36	16.61
2. When we reach the goals set in the planning we can strengthen our market position.	0.72	0.70	20.75
3. With the measures decided in the planning our offer is competitive.	0.70	0.68	20.29
4. With the measures set in the planning we reach our profitability goals.	0.69	0.59	19.78
5. When we reach the goals set in the planning we are satisfied with our operative result.	0.56	0.41	17.42
6. With the planning we can maximize shareholder value.	0.59	0.45	18.14

Information on scale "Effectiveness of Strategy Formulation"			
Descriptive Statistics		*Result of Exploratory Factor Analysis*	
Cronbach's alpha:	0.85	Total variance explained:	0.58
Results of Confirmatory Factor Analysis			
χ^2-Value (Degrees of Freedom):	20.68 (9)	χ^2-Value/Degrees of Freedom:	2.30
p Value:	0.01	RMSEA:	0.07
SRMR:	–*	CFI:	0.99
GFI:	0.99	AGFI:	0.98
Factor reliability:	0.87	Average variance explained:	0.53

*Not available

References

Willauer, B. **(2005): Consensus as a Key Success Factor in Strategy-Making, Wiesbaden 2005, pp. 213-214.**

57. Effectiveness of Strategy Implementation

Scale Description

The scale measures manager´s judgment of the effectiveness of the company's decision-making process, e.g. the assessment of regular deviations between planned and actual performance.

Origin

The scale was newly developed by Willauer (2005) based on John/Martin (1984).

Samples

Survey data were collected by questionnaire, administered to managers of planning departments of 4,186 German companies from the industrial sector. A total of 298 usable questionnaires (7.1%) were returned.

Scale Indicators and Reliability / Validity Parameters

Scale: from 1 (definitely false) to 7 (definitely true)

Information on individual indicators regarding "Effectiveness of Strategy Implementation"			
Description of indicators	*Item to Total-Correlation*	*Indicator-Reliability*	*t statistic*
1. I think that most of the time the planning anticipates the future quite well.	0.69	0.62	16.93
2. Deviations between target and actual figures are usually quite low.	0.68	0.62	16.88
3. In my view, our planning is quite realistic.	0.77	0.80	17.63
4. In my view, our planning is never very exact.	0.63	0.53	16.30

Information on scale "Effectiveness of Strategy Implementation"			
Descriptive Statistics		*Result of Exploratory Factor Analysis*	
Cronbach's alpha:	0.85	Total variance explained:	0.70
Results of Confirmatory Factor Analysis			
χ^2-Value (Degrees of Freedom):	0.13 (2)	χ^2-Value/Degrees of Freedom:	0.07
p Value:	0.94	RMSEA:	0.00
SRMR:	–*	CFI:	1.00
GFI:	1.00	AGFI:	1.00
Factor reliability:	0.88	Average variance explained:	0.64

*Not available

References

***Willauer, B.* (2005): Consensus as a Key Success Factor in Strategy-Making, Wiesbaden 2005, pp. 213-214.**

John, G./Martin, J. (1984): Effects of Organizational Structure of Marketing Planning on credibility and Utilization of Plan Output, in: Journal of Marketing Research, Vol. 21, pp. 170-183.

58. Efficiency of Monitoring [Effizienz der Kontrolle]

Scale Description

The scale measures the degree to which the control activities of the subsidiary are cost efficient.

Origin

Developed by Eckey and Schäffer (2006).

Samples

Eckey and Schäffer (2006) collected data using a survey questionnaire sent to a total of 51 group controlling departments of management holdings listed in the German Prime Standard. The sample of companies represented a variety of industries. 37 usable responses were received, yielding a response rate of 72.5%.

Comments

Eckey and Schäffer (2006) reported a mean of 5.22 and standard deviation of 0.96 on a theoretical range of 1-7.

Scale Indicators and Reliability / Validity Parameters

Scale: from 1 (strongly disagree) to 7 (strongly agree)

Information on individual indicators regarding "Efficiency of Monitoring [Effizienz der Kontrolle]"			
Description of indicators	*Item to Total-Correlation*	*Indicator-Reliability*	*t statistic*
1. Im Rahmen der Kontrollprozesse wird bei uns Doppelarbeit vermieden.	0.69	0.51	4.91
2. Im Rahmen der Kontrolle werden diejenigen Abteilungen eingesetzt, die die Aufgaben am besten lösen können.	0.71	0.70	6.03
3. Ressourcen werden bei uns im Kontrollprozess gut eingesetzt.	0.90	0.96	7.82
4. Die Kontrolle der Tochtergesellschaft ist bei uns kosteneffizient.	0.62	0.51	4.87

Information on scale "Efficiency of Monitoring [Effizienz der Kontrolle]"			
Descriptive Statistics		*Result of Exploratory Factor Analysis*	
Cronbach's alpha:	0.87	Total variance explained:	0.73
Results of Confirmatory Factor Analysis			
Factor reliability:	0.89	Average variance explained:	0.67

References

***Eckey, M./Schäffer, U.* (2006): Kontrolle von Mehrheitsbeteiligungen in börsennotierten Management-Holdings, in: Zeitschrift für Planung & Unternehmenssteuerung, Vol. 17, pp. 251-280.**

59. Enforcement of Decisions (Ex Ante) [Durchsetzung ex ante]

Scale Description

The scale measures the extent to which managers use MAS information for influencing the process of corporate decision-making.

Origin

The first indicator stems from Karlshaus´ (2000) scale of symbolic use of information. The last two items were newly developed by Schäffer/Steiners (2004).

Samples

Survey data were collected by questionnaire, administered to business unit leaders of 3,500 German companies with 100 to 2,000 employees from the industrial sector. A total of 449 usable questionnaires (12.8%) were returned.

Scale Indicators and Reliability / Validity Parameters

Scale: from 1 (definitely false) to 5 (definitely true)

Information on individual indicators regarding "Enforcement of Decisions (Ex Ante) [Durchsetzung ex ante]"			
Description of indicators	*Item to Total-Correlation*	*Indicator-Reliability*	*t statistic*
1. Wenn ich die Zustimmung von anderen brauche, helfen mir die Informationen dabei, diese Person bzw. dieses Gremium zu beeinflussen.	0.37	0.19	8.17
2. Bei Gruppenentscheidungen präsentiere ich vor allem solche Informationen, die meinen Standpunkt unterstützen.	0.52	0.47	11.10
3. Die geeignete Interpretation der Information erlaubt es mir, Entscheidungen zu beeinflussen.	0.56	0.63	12.04

Information on scale "Enforcement of Decisions (Ex Ante) [Durchsetzung ex ante]"			
Descriptive Statistics		*Result of Exploratory Factor Analysis*	
Cronbach's alpha:	0.66	Total variance explained:	0.60
Results of Confirmatory Factor Analysis			
Factor reliability:	0.68	Average variance explained:	0.43

References

***Schäffer, U./Steiners, D.* (2004): Zur Nutzung von Controllinginformationen, in: Zeitschrift für Planung und Unternehmenssteuerung, Vol. 15, pp. 377-404.**

Karlshaus, Jan T. (2000): Die Nutzung von Kostenrechnungsinformationen im Marketing, Wiesbaden 2000.

60. Enforcement of Decisions (Ex Post) [Durchsetzung ex post]

Scale Description

The scale measures the extent to which managers use MAS information for legitimating the results of the decision-making process.

Origin

Schäffer/Steiners (2004) adapted the indicators from Karlshaus´ (2000) scale of symbolic use of information.

Samples

Survey data were collected by questionnaire, administered to business unit leaders of 3,500 German companies with 100 to 2,000 employees from the industrial sector. A total of 449 usable questionnaires (12.8%) were returned.

Scale Indicators and Reliability / Validity Parameters

Scale: from 1 (definitely false) to 5 (definitely true)

Information on individual indicators regarding "Enforcement of Decisions (Ex Post) [Durchsetzung ex post]"			
Description of indicators	*Item to Total-Correlation*	*Indicator-Reliability*	*t statistic*
1. Die Informationen helfen mir bei der Durchsetzung von bereits getroffenen Entscheidungen.	0.63	0.49	15.50
2. Ich setze die Informationen ein, um bereits getroffene Entscheidungen anderen mitzuteilen.	0.70	0.66	18.30
3. Die Informationen helfen mir bei der Begründung bereits getroffener Entscheidungen.	0.70	0.67	18.53

Information on scale "Enforcement of Decisions (Ex Post) [Durchsetzung ex post]"			
Descriptive Statistics		*Result of Exploratory Factor Analysis*	
Cronbach's alpha:	0.82	Total variance explained:	0.74
Results of Confirmatory Factor Analysis			
Factor reliability:	0.82	Average variance explained:	0.61

References

Schäffer, U./Steiners, D. **(2004): Zur Nutzung von Controllinginformationen, in: Zeitschrift für Planung und Unternehmenssteuerung, Vol. 15, pp. 377-404.**

Karlshaus, J. T. (2000): Die Nutzung von Kostenrechnungsinformationen im Marketing, Wiesbaden 2000.

61. Ethical Orientation

Scale Description

The 20-item scale measures idealism and relativism. Idealism is measured by the mean of the responses to the first 10 questions. Relativism is measured by the mean of the responses to the last 10 questions.

Origin

Developed by Forsyth (1980) to measure the two constructs idealism and relativism.

Samples

Clikeman et al. (2001) surveyed 480 individuals beginning their careers with two Big 5 accounting firms. 66 individuals did not provide demographic data or did not answer all the questions, resulting in 414 useable responses. Most of the respondents were between the ages of 21 and 25 (86%); a little over half were female (55%); most had completed a 4-year bachelor's program. Another 21% had completed a master's program, while 19 (5%) had earned a second baccalaureate.

Comments

Clikeman et al. (2001) reported a scale mean of 6.61 and a standard deviation of 1.26 for idealism (first 10 items of the scale) and a scale mean of 4.74 and a standard deviation of 1.49 for relativism (last 10 items of scale).

Scale Indicators and Reliability / Validity Parameters

Scale: from 1 (completely disagree) to 9 (completely agree)

Information on individual indicators regarding "Ethical Orientation"
Description of indicators
1. A person should make certain that their actions never intentionally harm another even to a small degree.
2. Risks to another should never be tolerated, irrespective of how small the risks might be.
3. The existence of potential harm to others is always wrong, irrespective of the benefits to be gained.
4. One should never psychologically or physically harm another person.
5. One should not perform an action which might in any way threaten the dignity and welfare of another individual.
6. If an action could harm an innocent other, then it should not be done.
7. Deciding whether or nor to perform an act by balancing the positive consequences of the act against the negative consequences of the act is immoral.
8. The dignity and welfare of people should be the most important concern in any society.
9. It is never necessary to sacrifice the welfare of others.
10. Moral actions are those which closely match ideals of the most „perfect" action.
11. There are no ethical principles that are so important that they should be a part of any code of ethics.
12. What is ethical varies from one situation and society to another.
13. Moral standards should be seen as being individualistic; what one person considers to be more moral may be judged immoral by another person.
14. Different types of moralities cannot be compared as to „rightness".

15. Questions of what is ethical for everyone can never be resolved since what is moral or immoral is up to the individual.			
16. Moral standards are simply *personal* rules which indicate how a person should behave and are not to be applied in making judgments of others.			
17. Ethical considerations in interpersonal relations are so complex that individuals should be allowed to formulate their own individual codes.			
18. Rigidly codifying an ethical position that prevents certain types of actions could stand in the way of better human relations and adjustment.			
19. No rule concerning lying can be formulated; whether a lie is permissible or nor permissible totally depends upon the situation.			
20. Whether a lie is judged to be moral or immoral depends upon the circumstances surrounding the action.			
Information on scale "Ethical Orientation"			
Descriptive Statistics		*Result of Exploratory Factor Analysis*	
Cronbach's alpha: Idealism Relativism	0.83 0.83	Total variance explained:	–*

*Not available

References

***Clikeman, P. M./Schwartz, B. N./Lathan, M. H.* (2001): The Effect of the 150-Hour Requirement on New Accountants' Professional Commitment, Ethical Orientation, and Professionalism, in: Critical Perspectives on Accounting, Vol. 12, pp. 627-645.**

Forsyth, D. R. (1980): A Taxonomy of Ethical Ideologies, in: Journal of Personality and Social Psychology, Vol. 39, pp. 175-184.

62. Evaluation (in the Context of Business Networks) [Evaluation im Kontext von Unternehmensnetzwerken]

Scale Description

The scale measures the detailedness of the evaluation of actions taken within business networks.

Origin

The scale was first used by Möller (2006).

Samples

Survey data were collected by questionnaire, administered to business unit leaders or responsible controllers of 5,717 German companies. A total of 102 questionnaires (1.9%) were returned.

Scale Indicators and Reliability / Validity Parameters

Scale: from 1 (definitely false) to 5 (definitely true)

Information on individual indicators regarding "Evaluation (in the Context of Business Networks) [Evaluation im Kontext von Unternehmensnetzwerken]"			
Description of indicators	*Item to Total-Correlation*	*Indicator-Reliability*	*t statistic*
1. Beurteilen Sie die Bedeutung der Erfolgmessung für Ihr Netzwerk.	0.41	0.18	–*
2. Wie detailliert ist die Kostenrechnung in Ihrem Netzwerk ausgestaltet?	0.78	0.88	4.11
3. Wie detailliert ist das Kostenmanagement in Ihrem Netzwerk ausgestaltet?	0.71	0.68	4.21
4. Wie detailliert ist das Risikomanagement in Ihrem Netzwerk ausgestaltet?	0.63	0.46	3.95

Information on scale "Evaluation (in the Context of Business Networks) [Evaluation im Kontext von Unternehmensnetzwerken]"			
Descriptive Statistics		*Result of Exploratory Factor Analysis*	
Cronbach's alpha:	0.78	Total variance explained:	0.49
Results of Confirmatory Factor Analysis			
Factor reliability:	0.84	Average variance explained:	0.59

*Not feasible

References

Möller, K. (2006): Unternehmensnetzwerke und Erfolg – eine empirische Analyse von Einfluss- und Gestaltungsfaktoren, in: Zeitschrift für betriebswirtschaftliche Forschung (zfbf), Vol. 58, pp. 1051-1076.

63. Expected Market Performance (of Subsidiaries)

Scale Description

The scale measures the degree of managers' perception of a subsidiary's future performance by estimating the future increase in sales and market shares for every subsidiary.

Origin

Developed by Andersson et al. (2001).

Samples

Andersson et al. (2001) collected data from 98 subsidiaries belonging to 20 international divisions within 15 Swedish MNCs. The division headquarters were all located in Sweden. The majority of the subsidiaries were located in Europe and a few (five) in North America. The sample was chosen to represent a wide spectrum of Swedish industry and involves large and well-known companies in industries such as pulp and paper, telecommunications equipment, petrochemicals, power distribution, hard metal tools, saws and chains, gas applications, transportation, software, management training and industrial equipment.

Comments

The values of the t statistic above 5.82 and factor loadings over 0.80 show that the indicators are valid representations of the expected market performance construct.

Scale Indicators and Reliability / Validity Parameters

Scale: from 1 (very small) to 5 (very high)

Information on individual indicators regarding "Expected Market Performance (of Subsidiaries)"			
Description of indicators	*Item to Total-Correlation*	*Indicator-Reliability*	*t statistic*
1. How does the HQ judge this subsidiary's future increase in sales volume?	–*	0.91	5.85
2. How does the HQ judge this subsidiary's future market share expansion?	–*	0.80	5.82

Information on scale "Expected Market Performance (of Subsidiaries)"			
Descriptive Statistics		*Result of Exploratory Factor Analysis*	
Cronbach's alpha:	–*	Total variance explained:	–*

*Not available

References

Andersson, U./Forsgren, M./Pedersen, T. **(2001): Subsidiary Performance in Multinational Corporations: The Importance of Technology Embeddedness, in: International Business Review, Vol. 10, pp. 3-23.**

64. External Significance of Logistics [Externe Bedeutung Logistik]

Scale Description

The scale measures the importance of logistics in order to generate competitive advantages.

Origin

The scale was newly developed by Blum (2006).

Samples

Survey data were collected by questionnaire, administered to logistics managers of 1,394 German companies in the manufacturing industry. A total of 316 usable questionnaires (23%) were returned.

Scale Indicators and Reliability / Validity Parameters

Scale: from 1 (definitely false) to 7 (definitely true)

Information on individual indicators regarding "External Significance of Logistics [Externe Bedeutung Logistik]"			
Description of indicators	*Item to Total-Correlation*	*Indicator-Reliability*	*t statistic*
1. Logistikkosten spielen eine wichtige Rolle zur Erzielung von Kostenvorteilen gegenüber unseren Wettbewerbern.	0.51	0.33	11.44
2. Unsere Kunden erwarten von uns sehr hohe logistische Leistungen.	0.65	0.68	11.44
3. Logistikleistungen sind in unserem Geschäft ein wichtiges Erfolgskriterium.	0.68	0.87	11.44

Information on scale "External Significance of Logistics [Externe Bedeutung Logistik]"			
Descriptive Statistics		*Result of Exploratory Factor Analysis*	
Cronbach's alpha:	0.77	Total variance explained:	0.70
Results of Confirmatory Factor Analysis			
Factor reliability:	0.83	Average variance explained:	0.63

References

Blum, H. S. **(2006): Logistik-Controlling. Kontext, Ausgestaltung und Erfolgswirkungen, Wiesbaden 2006, pp. 109-110.**

65. Feedback

Scale Description

The scale measures the frequency with which information on quality efforts made (e.g. attendance at training courses, suggestions submitted, the completion of quality projects, etc) and quality results attained (e.g. defect rates, cycle time, warranty claims, etc.) is reported to management.

Origin

A major international management consulting firm developed the construct in 1991.

Samples

Ittner and Larcker (1997) examined the use and performance consequences of strategic control systems using survey data collected by a major international management consulting firm during 1991. The survey covered the automobile and computer industries in Canada, Germany, Japan, and the United States. All automobile assemblers and a random sample of their suppliers were invited to participate. A total of 249 organizations agreed to participate, representing an 85% response rate.

Comments

The scale emerged from a principal component analysis used to reduce the dimensionality of 36 questions from a survey assessing the extent to which organizations employ strategic control practices discussed in the quality literature.

Scale Indicators and Reliability / Validity Parameters

Scale: 1 (not at all), 2 (less than annually), 3 (annually), 4 (quarterly), 5 (monthly), 6 (weekly), 7 (daily), 8 (continuously)

Information on individual indicators regarding "Feedback"
Description of indicators
1. How frequently does the management information process measure and report information to senior management on quality efforts made?
2. How frequently does the management information process measure and report information to senior management on quality results attained?
3. How frequently does the management information process measure and report information to middle management on quality efforts made?
4. How frequently does the management information process measure and report information to middle management on quality results attained?
5. How frequently does the management information process measure and report information to first-line supervisors on quality efforts made?
6. How frequently does the management information process measure and report information to first-line supervisors on quality results attained?

Information on scale "Feedback"			
Descriptive Statistics		*Result of Exploratory Factor Analysis*	
Cronbach's alpha:	0.91	Total variance explained:	–*

*Not available

References

***Ittner, C. D./Larcker, D. F.* (1997): Quality Strategy, Strategic Control Systems, and Organizational Performance, in: Accounting, Organizations and Society, Vol. 22, pp. 293-314.**

66. Feedback-seeking Behavior

Scale Description

The scale measures the degree of feedback-seeking behavior through feedback-seeking by one or both of two mutually nonexclusive strategies: feedback-seeking through monitoring and feedback-seeking through inquiry.

Origin

Adopted by Ashford (1986). Since Ashford (1986) had developed the scale for middle-level managers and lower-level employees, Gupta et al. made minor modifications in the wording to mark the items more suitable for the subsidiary presidents of MNCs.

Samples

Gupta et al. (1999) mailed questionnaires to the heads of 987 foreign subsidiaries of major MNCs headquartered in the United States, Japan, and Europe. A total of 374 subsidiaries (38%) of 74 MNCs participated in the study.

Scale Indicators and Reliability / Validity Parameters

Scale: from 1 (very infrequent) to 7 (very frequent)

Information on individual indicators regarding "Feedback-seeking Behavior"
Description of indicators
In order to find out for yourself how well you are performing in your present job, how frequently do you:
1. Observe what performance behaviors your superiors reward and use this as feedback on your own performance.
2. Compare yourself with executives at your level in the organization.
3. Pay attention to how your superiors act toward you in order to understand how they perceive and evaluate your performance.
4. Observe the characteristics of executives rewarded by your superiors and use this information.
5. Seek information from your colleagues about your work performance.
6. Seek feedback from your superiors about your work performance.
7. Seek feedback from your superiors about your potential for advancement within this corporation.

Information on scale "Feedback-seeking Behavior"			
Descriptive Statistics		*Result of Exploratory Factor Analysis*	
Cronbach's alpha (items 1-4): (items 5-7):	0.83 0.76	Total variance explained:	–*

*Not available

References

***Gupta, A. K./Govindarajan, V./Malhotra, A.* (1999): Feedback-Seeking Behavior within Multinational Corporations, in: Strategic Management Journal, Vol. 20, pp. 205-222.**

Ashford, S. J. (1986): Feedback-Seeking in Individual Adaptation: A Resource Perspective, in: Academy of Management Journal, Vol. 29, pp. 465-487.

67. Fit with Vision

Scale Description

The scale measures the extent to which a marketing strategy being implemented is perceived to fit within the broader strategic direction of the organization.

Origin

Developed by Noble and Mokwa (1999).

Samples

The survey-based study conducted by Noble and Mokwa (1999) involved sampling from two firms: One firm was a large, multinational, financial services organization. Participants were managers with extensive responsibilities for the implementation of marketing strategies. The other firm was a market share leader in the packaged goods industry. In this company, participants were regional sales managers with full responsibility for a geographic area, including discretionary budgets for promotions and responsibility for implementing corporate promotional strategies. The sample consisted of 254 managers in the financial services company and 534 managers in the packaged goods company. Usable responses were 161 from the financial service company (63% response rate) and 325 from the other company (61% response rate). The total of 486 usable responses represents an overall 62% response rate.

Scale Indicators and Reliability / Validity Parameters

Scale: from 1 (strongly agree) to 5 (strongly disagree)

Information on individual indicators regarding "Fit with Vision"			
Description of indicators	*Item to Total-Correlation*	*Indicator-Reliability*	*t statistic*
1. This strategy was part of an overall strategic plan with in the company.	–*	0.399	3.78
2. This strategy was not consistent with other things going on in the company at the time. (R)	–*	0.536	4.38
3. I understood how this strategy fit within the strategic vision of the organization.	–*	0.710	4.85

Information on scale "Fit with Vision"			
Descriptive Statistics		*Result of Exploratory Factor Analysis*	
Cronbach's alpha:	0.54	Total variance explained:	–*

*Not available

References

Noble, C. H./Mokwa, M. P. **(1999): Implementing Marketing Strategies: Developing and Testing a Managerial Theory, in: Journal of Marketing, Vol. 63, pp. 57-73.**

68. Flow Orientation of Cost Accounting [Flußorientierung der Kostenrechnung]

Scale Description

The scale measures the extent to which a company's accounting system contains abundant explicit logistics data.

Origin

The scale was newly developed by Dehler (2001).

Samples

Survey data were collected by questionnaire, administered to logistics managers of 1,394 German companies in the manufacturing industry. A total of 316 usable questionnaires (23%) were returned.

Scale Indicators and Reliability / Validity Parameters

Scale: from 1 (definitely false) to 7 (definitely true)

Information on individual indicators regarding "Flow Orientation of Cost Accounting [Flußorientierung der Kostenrechnung]"			
Description of indicators	*Item to Total-Correlation*	*Indicator-Reliability*	*t statistic*
1. Die Logistikkosten werden in unserer Kostenrechnung durch zahlreiche Kostenarten erfaßt.	0.73	0.82	19.53
2. Zur verursachungsgerechten Erfassung der Logistikkosten sind zahlreiche Kostenstellen eingerichtet.	0.66	0.65	18.93
3. Die Logistikkosten sind ein fester Bestandteil der Produktkalkulation.	0.57	0.49	17.84
4. Die Prozeßkostenrechnung findet in unserer Geschäftseinheit einen weitreichenden Einsatz.	0.50	0.31	15.79

Information on scale "Flow Orientation of Cost Accounting [Flußorientierung der Kostenrechnung]"			
Descriptive Statistics		*Result of Exploratory Factor Analysis*	
Cronbach's alpha:	0.80	Total variance explained:	0.63
Results of Confirmatory Factor Analysis			
χ^2-Value (Degrees of Freedom):	0.82 (2)	χ^2-Value/Degrees of Freedom:	0.41
p Value:	0.66	RMSEA:	0.00
SRMR:	–*	CFI:	1.00
GFI:	1.00	AGFI:	1.00
Factor reliability:	0.84	Average variance explained:	0.57

*Not available

References

Dehler, M. **(2001): Entwicklungsstand der Logistik. Messung – Determinanten – Erfolgswirkungen 2001, Wiesbaden, pp. 161-162.**

69. Flow Orientation of Monitoring [Flussorientierung der Kontrolle]

Scale Description

The scale measures the extent to which a company puts effort into controlling the tasks and processes of the logistics department.

Origin

The scale was newly developed by Dehler (2001).

Samples

Data were collected by questionnaire, administered to logistics managers of 1,394 German manufacturing companies. A total of 316 usable questionnaires (23%) were returned.

Scale Indicators and Reliability / Validity Parameters

Scale: from 1 (definitely false) to 7 (definitely true)

Information on individual indicators regarding "Flow Orientation of Monitoring [Flussorientierung der Kontrolle]"			
Description of indicators	*Item to Total-Correlation*	*Indicator-Reliability*	*t statistic*
1. Wir führen eine konsequente Kontrolle unserer Durchlaufzeiten durch.	0.68	0.60	26.29
2. Wir führen eine konsequente Kontrolle der Qualität unserer Geschäftsprozesse durch.	0.64	0.54	25.21
3. Wir führen eine konsequente Kontrolle der Kosten unserer Geschäftsprozesse durch.	0.66	0.58	25.89
4. Wir führen eine konsequente Kontrolle unserer Logistikleistung (Lieferzeit, Liefertreue, etc.) durch.	0.72	0.69	27.22
5. Wir führen eine konsequente Kontrolle unserer Bestandshöhen durch.	0.60	0.50	24.70
6. Wir führen eine konsequente Kontrolle unserer Logistikkosten durch.	0.65	0.54	25.52

Information on scale "Flow Orientation of Monitoring [Flussorientierung der Kontrolle]"			
Descriptive Statistics		*Result of Exploratory Factor Analysis*	
Cronbach's alpha:	0.86	Total variance explained:	0.60
Results of Confirmatory Factor Analysis			
χ^2-Value (Degrees of Freedom):	26.05 (9)	χ^2-Value/Degrees of Freedom:	2.89
p Value:	0.00	RMSEA:	0.06
SRMR:	–*	CFI:	0.99
GFI:	0.99	AGFI:	0.98
Factor reliability:	0.89	Average variance explained:	0.57

*Not available

References

Dehler, M. **(2001): Entwicklungsstand der Logistik. Messung – Determinanten – Erfolgswirkungen, Wiesbaden 2001, pp. 161-162.**

70. Flow Orientation of the Metrics System [Flußorientierung des Kennzahlensystems]

Scale Description

The scale measures the extent to which a company's metrics contain a lot of explicit logistics data.

Origin

The scale was newly developed by Dehler (2001).

Samples

Survey data were collected by questionnaire, administered to logistics managers of 1,394 German companies in the manufacturing industry. A total of 316 usable questionnaires (23%) were returned.

Scale Indicators and Reliability / Validity Parameters

Scale: from 1 (definitely false) to 7 (definitely true)

Information on individual indicators regarding "Flow Orientation of the Metrics System [Flußorientierung des Kennzahlensystems]"			
Description of indicators	*Item to Total-Correlation*	*Indicator-Reliability*	*t statistic*
1. Wir erheben zahlreiche prozeßorientierte Kennzahlen zur Erfassung der Dauer unserer Geschäftsprozesse (z.B. Durchlaufzeiten).	0.76	0.75	22.67
2. Wir erheben zahlreiche Kennzahlen zur Erfassung unserer Prozeßqualität (z.B. first-pass-yield, Direktläuferanteil, Anzahl Nacharbeiten, etc.).	0.71	0.67	22.27
3. Wir erheben zahlreiche Kennzahlen zur Messung unserer Logistikleistung (z.B. Lieferzeit, Liefertreue).	0.74	0.71	22.23
4. Unsere Bestandshöhen werden durch zahlreiche Kennzahlen ermittelt.	0.66	0.58	21.51

Information on scale "Flow Orientation of the Metrics System [Flußorientierung des Kennzahlensystems]"			
Descriptive Statistics		*Result of Exploratory Factor Analysis*	
Cronbach's alpha:	0.87	Total variance explained:	0.72
Results of Confirmatory Factor Analysis			
χ^2-Value (Degrees of Freedom):	6.45 (2)	χ^2-Value/Degrees of Freedom:	3.22
p Value:	0.04	RMSEA:	0.07
SRMR:	–*	CFI:	1.00
GFI:	1.00	AGFI:	0.99
Factor reliability:	0.89	Average variance explained:	0.68

*Not available

References

Dehler, M. (2001): Entwicklungsstand der Logistik. Messung – Determinanten – Erfolgswirkungen, Wiesbaden 2001, pp. 161-162.

71. Focus of Operative Monitoring – Analysis [Fokussierung der operativen Kontrolle – Analyse]

Scale Description

The scale measures the extent to which operational control is focused within the context of the control activities of the parent company. The scale is operationalized by focusing on significant deviations only.

Origin

Developed by Eckey and Schäffer (2006).

Samples

Eckey and Schäffer (2006) collected data using a survey questionnaire sent to a total of 51 group controlling departments of management holdings listed in the German Prime Standard. The sample of companies represented a variety of industries. 37 usable responses were received, yielding a response rate of 72.5%.

Comments

Eckey and Schäffer (2006) reported a mean of 4.51 and standard deviation of 1.49 on a theoretical range of 1-7.

Scale Indicators and Reliability / Validity Parameters

Scale: from 1 (strongly disagree) to 7 (strongly agree)

Information on individual indicators regarding "Focus of Operative Monitoring – Analysis [Fokussierung der operativen Kontrolle - Analyse]"			
Description of indicators	*Item to Total-Correlation*	*Indicator-Reliability*	*t statistic*
1. Lediglich bei signifikanten Planabweichungen im Rahmen der operativen Kontrolle führt das zentrale Controlling eine Abweichungsanalyse durch. (R)	0.58	0.36	3.83
2. Bei der operativen Kontrolle untersuchen wir alles detailliert.	0.84	0.91	7.43
3. Im Rahmen der operativen Kontrolle stellen wir sicher, dass die Kontrollintensität überall gleich hoch ist.	0.74	0.63	5.61
4. Wir gehen bei der operativen Kontrolle stets in die Tiefe, indem wir auch geringe Abweichungen analysieren.	0.78	0.73	6.24

Information on scale "Focus of Operative Monitoring – Analysis [Fokussierung der operativen Kontrolle - Analyse]"			
Descriptive Statistics		*Result of Exploratory Factor Analysis*	
Cronbach's alpha:	0.88	Total variance explained:	0.73
Results of Confirmatory Factor Analysis			
χ^2-Value (Degrees of Freedom):	0.25 (2)	χ^2-Value/Degrees of Freedom:	0.13
p-value:	0.88	RMSEA:	0.00
NFI:	1.00	NNFI:	1.06
GFI:	1.00	AGFI:	0.98
Factor reliability:	0.88	Average variance explained:	0.66

References

Eckey, M./Schäffer, U. **(2006): Kontrolle von Mehrheitsbeteiligungen in börsennotierten Management-Holdings, in: Zeitschrift für Planung & Unternehmenssteuerung, Vol. 17, pp. 251-280.**

72. Focus of Operative Monitoring – Corrective Action [Fokussierung der operativen Kontrolle – Maßnahme]

Scale Description

The scale measures the extent to which operational control is focused within the context of the control activities of the parent company. The scale is operationalized by focusing on significant corrective action only.

Origin

Developed by Eckey and Schäffer (2006).

Samples

Eckey and Schäffer (2006) collected data using a survey questionnaire sent to a total of 51 group controlling departments of management holdings listed in the German Prime Standard. The sample of companies represented a variety of industries. 37 usable responses were received, yielding a response rate of 72.5%.

Scale Indicators and Reliability / Validity Parameters

Scale: from 1 (strongly disagree) to 7 (strongly agree)

Information on individual indicators regarding "Focus of Operative Monitoring – Corrective Action [Fokussierung der operativen Kontrolle - Maßnahme]"			
Description of indicators	*Item to Total-Correlation*	*Indicator-Reliability*	*t statistic*
1. Das Erarbeiten von Korrekturmaßnahmen bei Abweichungen im Rahmen der operativen Kontrolle obliegt stets dem zentralen Controlling. (R)	0.69	0.76	5.21
2. Lediglich bei signifikanten Abweichungen im Rahmen der operativen Kontrolle greift das zentrale Controlling beim Erarbeiten von Korrekturmaßnahmen ein.	0.66	0.65	4.82
3. Die Verantwortung für Korrekturmaßnahmen liegt stets beim dezentralen Controlling.	0.50	0.30	3.32

Information on scale "Focus of Operative Monitoring – Corrective Action [Fokussierung der operativen Kontrolle - Maßnahme]"			
Descriptive Statistics		*Result of Exploratory Factor Analysis*	
Cronbach's alpha:	0.78	Total variance explained:	0.70
Results of Confirmatory Factor Analysis			
Factor reliability:	0.80	Average variance explained:	0.57

*Not available

References

Eckey, M./Schäffer, U. **(2006): Kontrolle von Mehrheitsbeteiligungen in börsennotierten Management-Holdings, in: Zeitschrift für Planung & Unternehmenssteuerung, Vol. 17, pp. 251-280.**

73. Formalization [Formalisierung]

Scale Description

The scale measures the extent to which the process of decision-making within a firm is based on strict rules and regulations.

Origin

The scale is based on a scale developed by Menon et al. (1999). Similar items were used by Spieker (2004).

Samples

Survey data were collected by questionnaire, administered to business unit leaders of 3,500 German companies with 100 to 2,000 employees from the industrial sector. A total of 449 usable questionnaires (12.8%) were returned.

Scale Indicators and Reliability / Validity Parameters

Scale: from 1 (definitely false) to 5 (definitely true)

Information on individual indicators regarding "Formalization [Formalisierung]"			
Description of indicators	*Item to Total-Correlation*	*Indicator-Reliability*	*t statistic*
1. Der Ablauf wichtiger Entscheidungsprozesse ist bei uns klar definiert.	0.52	0.40	12.19
2. Entscheidungsprozesse sind bei uns weitgehend standardisiert.	0.60	0.63	14.74
3. Für die meisten Dinge gibt es bei uns Regeln und Arbeitsanweisungen.	0.54	0.42	12.60

Information on scale "Formalization [Formalisierung]"			
Descriptive Statistics		*Result of Exploratory Factor Analysis*	
Cronbach's alpha:	0.73	Total variance explained:	0.65
Results of Confirmatory Factor Analysis			
Factor reliability:	0.73	Average variance explained:	0.48

References

Schäffer, U./Steiners, D. (2004): Zur Nutzung von Controllinginformationen, in: Zeitschrift für Planung und Unternehmenssteuerung, Vol. 15, pp. 377-404.

Menon, A./Bharadwaj, S./Adidam, P. T./Edison, S. W. (1999): Antecedents and Consequences of Marketing Strategy Making: A Model and a Test, in: Journal of Marketing, Vol. 63, pp. 18-40.

Spieker, M. (2004): Entscheidungen in Gründerteams. Determinanten – Parameter – Erfolgsauswirkungen, Wiesbaden 2004, pp. 237-238.

74. Formalization (of Strategic Planning) [Formalisierung der Strategischen Planung]

Scale Description

The scale measures the extent to which the process of strategic planning within a firm is based on strict rules and regulations.

Origin

The scale was newly developed by Willauer as part of a doctoral research project. Results were published in Weber/Schäffer/Willauer (2003).

Samples

Survey data were collected by questionnaire, administered to managers of planning departments of 4,186 German companies from the industrial sector. A total of 298 usable questionnaires (7.1%) were returned.

Scale Indicators and Reliability / Validity Parameters

Scale: from 1 (definitely false) to 7 (definitely true)

Information on individual indicators regarding "Formalization (of Strategic Planning) [Formalisierung der Strategischen Planung]"			
Description of indicators	*Item to Total-Correlation*	*Indicator-Reliability*	*t statistic*
1. Der Ablauf der strategischen/langfristigen Planung ist in Handbüchern umfassend dargestellt.	0.52	0.39	14.33
2. Im Rahmen der strategischen/langfristigen Planung gibt es bei uns für alles ein Formular oder eine Bildschirmmaske.	0.70	0.69	16.40
3. Im Rahmen der strategischen/langfristigen Planung gibt es bei uns umfassende Regelungen über Inhalt, Umfang und äußere Form von Planungsunterlagen.	0.76	0.78	16.86
4. Im Rahmen der strategischen/langfristigen Planung ist das Vorgehen im Planungsprozess bei uns weitgehend standardisiert.	0.72	0.72	16.85

Information on scale "Formalization (of Strategic Planning) [Formalisierung der Strategischen Planung]"			
Descriptive Statistics		*Result of Exploratory Factor Analysis*	
Cronbach's alpha:	0.84	Total variance explained:	0.58
Results of Confirmatory Factor Analysis			
χ^2-Value (Degrees of Freedom):	1.53 (2)	χ^2-Value/Degrees of Freedom:	0.77
p Value:	0.46	RMSEA:	0.00
SRMR:	–*	CFI:	1.00
GFI:	1.00	AGFI:	0.99
Factor reliability:	0.88	Average variance explained:	0.65

*Not available

References

Weber, J /Schäffer, U./Willauer, B. **(2003): Skalenübersicht, in: Weber, J./Kunz, J. (Ed.): Empirische Controllingforschung: Begründung, Beispiele, Ergebnisse, Wiesbaden 2003, pp. 385-467.**

75. Functional Integration [Funktionale Integration]

Scale Description

The scale measures the extent to which all of a firm's functional departments take part in the strategic planning process.

Origin

The scale was newly developed by Willauer as part of a doctoral research project. Results were published in Weber/Schäffer/Willauer (2003).

Samples

Data were collected by questionnaire, administered to planning department managers of 4,186 German industrial companies. A total of 298 usable questionnaires (7.1%) were returned.

Scale Indicators and Reliability / Validity Parameters

Scale: from 1 (definitely false) to 7 (definitely true)

Information on individual indicators regarding "Functional Integration [Funktionale Integration]"			
Description of indicators	*Item to Total-Correlation*	*Indicator-Reliability*	*t statistic*
1. Im Rahmen der strategischen/langfristigen Planung sind alle Funktionsbereiche (Marketing, Vertrieb, Finanzen/ Controlling. F & E, Produktion, etc.) beteiligt.	0.79	0.80	20.15
2. Im Planungsprozess/-team sind alle betroffenen Abteilungen adäquat vertreten.	0.80	0.80	20.26
3. In der strategischen/langfristigen Planung haben alle Funktionsbereiche (Marketing, Vertrieb, Finanzen/Controlling, F & E, Produktion, etc.) das gleiche Sagen.	0.73	0.69	19.56
4. Im Planungsprozess/-team werden die unterschiedlichen Sichten der Funktionsbereiche (Marketing, Vertrieb, Finanzen/ Controlling. F & E, Produktion, etc.) berücksichtigt.	0.77	0.73	19.89

Information on scale "Functional Integration [Funktionale Integration]"			
Descriptive Statistics		*Result of Exploratory Factor Analysis*	
Cronbach's alpha:	0.90	Total variance explained:	0.77
Results of Confirmatory Factor Analysis			
χ^2-Value (Degrees of Freedom):	0.88 (2)	χ^2-Value/Degrees of Freedom:	0.44
p Value:	0.00	RMSEA:	0.00
SRMR:	–*	CFI:	1.00
GFI:	1.00	AGFI:	1.00
Factor reliability:	0.92	Average variance explained:	0.76

*Not available

References

Weber, J /Schäffer, U./Willauer, B. (2003): Skalenübersicht, in: Weber, J./Kunz, J. (Ed.): Empirische Controllingforschung: Begründung, Beispiele, Ergebnisse, Wiesbaden 2003, pp. 385-467.

76. Generation of Information (formal) [Formelle Informationsgenerierung]

Scale Description

The scale measures the extent to which controllers use formal ways and methods for assessing the need for information of their managers.

Origin

The indicators are based on scales by Jaworski/Kohli (1993) and Lings/Greenley (2005).

Samples

Survey data were collected by questionnaire, administered via e-mail to 3,312 German managers of companies with at least 200 employees. The companies were from different industrial sectors. A total of 415 usable questionnaires (12.5%) were returned.

Scale Indicators and Reliability / Validity Parameters

Scale: from 1 (definitely false) to 5 (definitely true)

Information on individual indicators regarding "Generation of Information (formal) [Formelle Informationsgenerierung]"			
Description of indicators	*Item to Total-Correlation*	*Indicator-Reliability*	*t statistic*
1. Unsere Controller erkennen Veränderungen im Informationsbedarf der Manager sehr schnell.	0.72	0.62	-
2. Unserer Controller treffen sich regelmäßig mit dem Management, um herauszufinden, welche Controllingleistungen in Zukunft benötigt werden.	0.68	0.54	15.10
3. Unsere Controller versuchen, aktiv die Informationsbedürfnisse des Managements zu verstehen.	0.75	0.70	17.23
4. Unsere Controller treten häufig direkt mit dem Management in Kontakt, um zu verstehen, wie die Zufriedenheit mit dem Controlling weiter gesteigert werden kann.	0.74	0.66	16.78

Information on scale "Generation of Information (formal) [Formelle Informationsgenerierung]"			
Descriptive Statistics		*Result of Exploratory Factor Analysis*	
Cronbach's alpha:	0.87	Total variance explained:	0.63
Results of Confirmatory Factor Analysis			
χ^2-Value (Degrees of Freedom):	4.19 (2)	χ^2-Value/Degrees of Freedom:	2.09
p Value:	0.15	RMSEA:	0.08
SRMR:	–*	CFI:	0.99
GFI:	0.99	AGFI:	0.95
Factor reliability:	0.87	Average variance explained:	0.63

*Not available

References

Spillecke, D. **(2006): Interne Kundenorientierung des Controllerbereichs. Messung – Erfolgsauswirkungen – Determinanten, Wiesbaden 2006, pp. 114-115.**

Jaworski, B. J./Kohli, A.K. (1993): Market Orientation: Antecedents and Consequences, in: Journal of Marketing, Vol. 57, pp. 53-70.

Lings, I. N./Greenley, G. E. (2005): Measuring Internal Market Orientation, in: Journal of Service Research, Vol. 7, pp. 290-305.

77. Generation of Information (informal) [Informelle Informationsgenerierung]

Scale Description

The scale measures the extent to which controllers use informal ways and methods for assessing the need for information of their managers.

Origin

The indicators are based on scales created by Jaworski/Kohli (1993) and Lings/Greenley (2005).

Samples

Survey data were collected by questionnaire, administered via e-mail to 3,312 German managers of companies with at least 200 employees. The companies were from different industrial sectors. A total of 415 usable questionnaires (12.5%) were returned.

Scale Indicators and Reliability / Validity Parameters

Scale: from 1 (definitely false) to 5 (definitely true)

Information on individual indicators regarding "Generation of Information (informal) [Informelle Informationsgenerierung]"			
Description of indicators	*Item to Total-Correlation*	*Indicator-Reliability*	*t statistic*
1. Unserer Controller sprechen auch informell regelmäßig mit den Managern, um ihre Bedürfnisse zu verstehen.	0.62	0.44	-
2. Unsere Controller diskutieren oftmals außerhalb der offiziellen Treffen (z.B. abends bei einem Bier/auf dem Flur) mit dem Management über aktuelle Themen.	0.78	0.72	14.53
3. Unsere Controller nutzen auch informelle Treffen, um die Fragestellungen des Managements besser zu verstehen (z.B. während des Mittagessens).	0.80	0.77	14.78
4. Unsere Controller beteiligen sich sehr aktiv an Flurgesprächen mit Managern, die sich auf aktuelle Probleme des Unternehmens beziehen.	0.76	0.68	14.18

Information on scale "Generation of Information (informal) [Informelle Informations-generierung]"			
Descriptive Statistics		*Result of Exploratory Factor Analysis*	
Cronbach's alpha:	0.88	Total variance explained:	0.65
Results of Confirmatory Factor Analysis			
χ^2-Value (Degrees of Freedom):	0.56 (2)	χ^2-Value/Degrees of Freedom:	0.28
p Value:	0.75	RMSEA:	0.00
SRMR:	–*	CFI:	1.00
GFI:	0.99	AGFI:	0.99
Factor reliability:	0.89	Average variance explained:	0.67

*Not available

References

Spillecke, D. (2006): Interne Kundenorientierung des Controllerbereichs. Messung – Erfolgsauswirkungen – Determinanten, Wiesbaden 2006, pp. 136-137.

Jaworski, B. J./Kohli, A.K. (1993): Market Orientation: Antecedents and Consequences, in: Journal of Marketing, Vol. 57, pp. 53-70.

Lings, I. N./Greenley, G. E. (2005): Measuring Internal Market Orientation, in: Journal of Service Research, Vol. 7, pp. 290-305.

78. Goal Congruence of Incentive System [Anreizkompatibilität der Incentivierung]

Scale Description

The scale measures the degree to which the target to the subsidiary and the reference parameter of the variable compensation of the management of the subsidiary are identical.

Origin

Developed by Eckey and Schäffer (2006).

Samples

Eckey and Schäffer (2006) collected data using a survey questionnaire sent to a total of 51 group controlling departments of management holdings listed in the German Prime Standard. The sample of companies represented a variety of industries. 37 usable responses were received, yielding a response rate of 72.5%.

Comments

Eckey and Schäffer (2006) reported a mean of 5.95 and standard deviation of 0.96 on a theoretical range of 1-7.

Scale Indicators and Reliability / Validity Parameters

Scale: from 1 (strongly disagree) to 7 (strongly agree)

Information on individual indicators regarding "Goal Congruence of Incentive System [Anreizkompatibilität der Incentivierung]"			
Description of indicators	*Item to Total-Correlation*	*Indicator-Reliability*	*t statistic*
1. Die Zielvorgabe an die Tochtergesellschaft (z.B. EVA) und die Bezugsgröße der variablen Vergütung des Managements der Tochtergesellschaft sind identisch.	0.83	0.73	6.37
2. Das variable Gehalt des Managements der Tochtergesellschaft ist in hohem Maße vom Zielerreichungsgrad der Tochtergesellschaft abhängig.	0.60	0.36	3.91
3. Der Zielerreichungsgrad der Tochtergesellschaft und die Bezugsgröße der variablen Entlohnung des dezentralen Managements sind bei uns entkoppelt. (R)	0.86	0.87	7.29
4. Das variable Gehalt des Managements der Tochtergesellschaft richtet sich nicht nach dem Zielerreichungsgrad der Ziele an die Tochtergesellschaft, sondern ist von anderen Größen abhängig. (R)	0.87	0.91	7.59

Information on scale "Goal Congruence of Incentive System [Anreizkompatibilität der Incentivierung]"			
Descriptive Statistics		*Result of Exploratory Factor Analysis*	
Cronbach's alpha:	0.91	Total variance explained:	0.78
Results of Confirmatory Factor Analysis			
χ^2-Value (Degrees of Freedom):	0.76 (2)	χ^2-Value/Degrees of Freedom:	0.38
p-value:	0.68	RMSEA:	0.00
NFI:	0.99	NNFI:	1.04
SRMR:	0.02	CFI:	1.00
GFI:	0.99	AGFI:	0.85
Factor reliability:	0.91	Average variance explained:	0.72

References

Eckey, M./Schäffer, U. (2006): Kontrolle von Mehrheitsbeteiligungen in börsennotierten Management-Holdings, in: Zeitschrift für Planung & Unternehmenssteuerung, Vol. 17, pp. 251-280.

79. Goal Setting [Zielfindung und -formulierung]

Scale Description

The scale indicates manager´s perception of the controlling staff's involvement and scope of activities in the process of finding and formulating organizational goals.

Origin

The scale was newly developed by Bauer (2002).

Samples

Survey data were collected by questionnaire, administered via mail to 2,527 German companies. A total of 347 companies sent usable answers, yielding a 14.8% return rate.

Comments

The study used a dyadic design approach, where a manager and a controller of the same company were questioned. The data for this scale solely stem from the answers of the managers.

Scale Indicators and Reliability / Validity Parameters

Scale: from 1 (definitely false) to 7 (definitely true)

Information on individual indicators regarding "Goal Setting [Zielfindung und -formulierung]"			
Description of indicators	*Item to Total-Correlation*	*Indicator-Reliability*	*t statistic*
1. Der Controller setzt auch Zero Base Analysen ein, um Ziele zu bestimmen.	0.56	0.51	17.7
2. Benchmarking wird vom Controller ebenfalls zur Zielfindung eingesetzt	0.55	0.47	17.5
3. Sehr anspruchsvolle Ziele werden zusammen mit dem Controller als „Stretch Targets" entwickelt und konkretisiert.	0.60	0.59	17.9
4. An der Zielfindung und –formulierung ist der Controller i.d.R. nicht beteiligt. (R)	0.38	0.22	14.1

Information on scale "Goal Setting [Zielfindung und -formulierung]"			
Descriptive Statistics		*Result of Exploratory Factor Analysis*	
Cronbach's alpha:	0.73	Total variance explained:	0.55
Results of Confirmatory Factor Analysis			
χ^2-Value (Degrees of Freedom):	4.83 (2)	χ^2-Value/Degrees of Freedom:	2.42
p Value:	0.1	RMSEA:	0.05
NFI:	0.99	NNFI:	–*
SRMR:	–*	CFI:	1.00
GFI:	1.00	AGFI:	0.99
Factor reliability:	0.76	Average variance explained:	0.45

*Not available

References

Bauer, M. **(2002): Controllership in Deutschland. Zur erfolgreichen Zusammenarbeit von Controllern und Managern, Wiesbaden 2002, pp. 190-192.**

80. Headquarter Control

Scale Description

The scale measures the degree of headquarter control over the subsidiary.

Origin

Developed by Birkinshaw et al. (2000).

Samples

Birkinshaw et al. (2000) collected data on a total of 100 HQ-subsidiary dyads. The MNCs operate in a wide variety of industries, though with an emphasis in manufacturing (hard materials, paper, power, retailing, transportation services and telecommunications). A total of 19 MNC divisions participated in the study, all but one were headquartered in Sweden. The sample of subsidiaries was selected through discussion with HQ managers in the 19 MNC divisions. Between 3 and 10 subsidiaries in each MNC division were selected.

Scale Indicators and Reliability / Validity Parameters

Scale: from 1 (totally agree) to 5 (totally agree)

Information on individual indicators regarding "Headquarter Control"			
Description of indicators	*Item to Total-Correlation*	*Indicator-Reliability*	*t statistic*
1. The subsidiary can choose its suppliers without consulting the global divisional management.	–*	0.83	5.63
2. The subsidiary can change its organization without consulting the global division management.	–*	0.66	5.26
Information on scale "Headquarter Control"			
Descriptive Statistics		*Result of Exploratory Factor Analysis*	
Cronbach's alpha:	–*	Total variance explained:	–*

*Not available

References

***Birkinshaw, J./Holm, U./Thilenius, P./Arvidsson, N.* (2000): Consequences of Perception Gaps in the Headquarters-Subsidiary Relationship, in: International Business Review, Vol. 9, pp. 321-344.**

81. Headquarter-Subsidiary Centralization

Scale Description

The scale measures the degree of headquarter-subsidiary centralization by asking for the typical influence that subsidiaries had in affecting the outcome of decisions.

Origin

Adapted from Vancil and Buddrus (1980).

Samples

Gupta et al. (1999) mailed questionnaires to the heads of 987 foreign subsidiaries of major MNCs headquartered in the United States, Japan, and Europe. A total of 374 subsidiaries (38%) of 74 MNCs participated in the study.

Scale Indicators and Reliability / Validity Parameters

Scale: 1 (proposal by you, followed by consultation with superior, with your opinion prevailing), 2 (proposal by you, decision made jointly by you and your superior), 3 (proposal by superior, your opinion is asked and it carries a lot of weight), 4 (proposal by superior, your opinion is asked and it carries little weight), 5 (your opinion not asked but decision is explained to you)

Information on individual indicators regarding "Headquarter-Subsidiary Centralization"
Description of indicators
For each of the following decisions, each respondent was asked to indicate the typical influence that they had in affecting the outcome of the decision:
1. Formulation of your subsidiary's annual budget.
2. Discontinuing a major existing product or product line.
3. Investing in major plant and equipment to expand capacity for existing products.
4. Developing a major new product line.
5. Increasing (beyond budget) the level of expenditure for advertising and promotion.
6. Changing the selling price on a major product or product line.
7. Increasing (beyond budget) the level of expenditure for research and development.
8. Buying from an outside vendor when the items required could be supplied by another unit of the company.
9. Increasing (beyond budget) the number of personnel employed by your subsidiary.

Information on scale "Headquarter-Subsidiary Centralization"			
Descriptive Statistics		*Result of Exploratory Factor Analysis*	
Cronbach's alpha:	0.86	Total variance explained:	–*

*Not available

References

Gupta, A. K./Govindarajan, V./Malhotra, A. **(1999): Feedback-Seeking Behavior within Multinational Corporations, in: Strategic Management Journal, Vol. 20, pp. 205-222.**

Vancil, R. F./Buddrus, L. E. (1980): Decentralization: Managerial Ambiguity by Design, Homewood, Ill. 1980.

82. Headquarter-Subsidiary Communication

Scale Description

The scale measures the degree of communication for different modes of communication (face-to-face, over the telephone, routine and periodic formal reports, and electronic or paper-based letters or memos).

Origin

Adapted from Van de Ven and Ferry (1980).

Samples

Gupta et al. (1999) mailed questionnaires to the heads of 987 foreign subsidiaries of major MNCs headquartered in the United States, Japan, and Europe. A total of 374 subsidiaries (38%) of 74 MNCs participated in the study.

Comments

Gupta et al. (1999) reported a scale mean of 4.71 and a standard deviation of 1.02.

Scale Indicators and Reliability / Validity Parameters

Scale: from 1 (daily) to 7 (less often than once a year)

Information on individual indicators regarding "Headquarter-Subsidiary Communication"			
Description of indicators			
Please indicate the frequency of communication between yourself and executives from the parent corporation for each of four models of communication:			
1. face-to-face			
2. over the telephone			
3. routine and periodic formal reports			
4. electronic or paper-based letters or memos			
Information on scale "Headquarter-Subsidiary Communication"			
Descriptive Statistics		*Result of Exploratory Factor Analysis*	
Cronbach's alpha:	0.80	Total variance explained:	–*

*Not available

References

***Gupta, A. K./Govindarajan, V./Malhotra, A.* (1999): Feedback-Seeking Behavior within Multinational Corporations, in: Strategic Management Journal, Vol. 20, pp. 205-222.**

Van de Ven, A. H./Ferry, D. L. (1980): Measuring and Assessing Organizations, New York 1980.

83. Headquarter-Subsidiary Cooperation

Scale Description

The scale measures the degree of headquarter-subsidiary cooperation.

Origin

Developed by Birkinshaw et al. (2000).

Samples

Birkinshaw et al. (2000) collected data on a total of 100 HQ-subsidiary dyads. The MNCs operate in a wide variety of industries, though with an emphasis in manufacturing (hard materials, paper, power, retailing, transportation services and telecommunications). A total of 19 MNC divisions participated in the study, all but one were headquartered in Sweden. The sample of subsidiaries was selected through discussion with HQ managers in the 19 MNC divisions. Between 3 and 10 subsidiaries in each MNC division were selected.

Scale Indicators and Reliability / Validity Parameters

Scale: from 1 (totally agree) to 5 (totally agree)

Information on individual indicators regarding "Headquarter-Subsidiary Cooperation"			
Description of indicators	*Item to Total-Correlation*	*Indicator-Reliability*	*t statistic*
1. The global divisional management's and subsidiary's interests are usually identical when it concerns size and direction of subsidiary investments.	–*	0.47	4.00
2. The global divisional management's and subsidiary's interest are usually identical when it concerns purchasing.	–*	0.74	4.81
3. The subsidiary and the global divisional management fully agree about the subsidiary role in the relationship.	–*	0.56	4.2

Information on scale "Headquarter-Subsidiary Cooperation"			
Descriptive Statistics		*Result of Exploratory Factor Analysis*	
Cronbach's alpha:	–*	Total variance explained:	–*

*Not available

References

Birkinshaw, J./Holm, U./Thilenius, P./Arvidsson, N. **(2000): Consequences of Perception Gaps in the Headquarters-Subsidiary Relationship, in: International Business Review, Vol. 9, pp. 321-344.**

84. Horizontal Coordination [Horizontale Koordination]

Scale Description

The scale measures the extent to which the strategic planning process of a firm's different business units is connected.

Origin

The scale was newly developed by Willauer as part of a doctoral research project. Results were published in Weber/Schäffer/Willauer (2003).

Samples

Survey data were collected by questionnaire, administered to managers of planning departments of 4,186 German companies from the industrial sector. A total of 298 usable questionnaires (7.1%) were returned.

Scale Indicators and Reliability / Validity Parameters

Scale: from 1 (definitely false) to 7 (definitely true)

Information on individual indicators regarding "Horizontal Coordination [Horizontale Koordination]"			
Description of indicators	*Item to Total-Correlation*	*Indicator-Reliability*	*t statistic*
1. Die strategische/langfristige Planung unserer Geschäftseinheit ist mit der strategischen/langfristigen Planung der anderen Geschäftseinheiten eng verknüpft.	0.82	0.79	20.14
2. Die strategische/langfristige Planung unserer Geschäftseinheit ist auf die strategische/langfristige Planung der anderen Geschäftseinheiten abgestimmt (z.B. bzgl. der Art der Führerschaft).	0.77	0.72	19.85
3. Die operative Planung unserer Geschäftseinheit ist mit der Planung der anderen Geschäftseinheiten eng verknüpft.	0.81	0.77	20.22
4. Die operative Planung unserer Geschäftseinheit ist auf die operative Planung anderer Geschäftseinheiten abgestimmt (z.B. bei der Aufteilung gemeinsam genutzter Ressourcen.	0.83	0.79	20.25

Information on scale "Horizontal Coordination [Horizontale Koordination]"			
Descriptive Statistics		*Result of Exploratory Factor Analysis*	
Cronbach's alpha:	0.91	Total variance explained:	0.80
Results of Confirmatory Factor Analysis			
χ^2-Value (Degrees of Freedom):	8.10 (2)	χ^2-Value/Degrees of Freedom:	4.05
p Value:	0.02	RMSEA:	0.10
SRMR:	–*	CFI:	0.99
GFI:	1.00	AGFI:	0.98
Factor reliability:	0.93	Average variance explained:	0.77

*Not available

References

Weber, J /Schäffer, U./Willauer, B. (2003): Skalenübersicht, in: Weber, J./Kunz, J. (Ed.): Empirische Controllingforschung: Begründung, Beispiele, Ergebnisse, Wiesbaden 2003, pp. 385-467.

85. Implementation Success

Scale Description

The scale measures the extent to which an implementation effort is considered successful by the organization.

Origin

Developed by Noble and Mokwa (1999).

Samples

The survey-based study conducted by Noble and Mokwa (1999) involved sampling from two firms: One firm was a large, multi state, financial services organization. Subjects were managers with extensive responsibilities for the implementation of marketing strategies. The other firm was a market share leader in the packaged goods industry. In this company, participants were regional sales managers with full responsibility for a geographic area, including discretionary budgets for promotions and responsibility for implementing corporate promotional strategies. The sample consisted of 254 managers in the financial services company and 534 managers in the packaged goods industry. Usable responses were 161 from the financial service company (63% response rate) and 325 from the other company (61% response rate). The total of 486 usable responses represents an overall 62% response rate.

Scale Indicators and Reliability / Validity Parameters

Scale: from 1 (strongly agree) to 5 (strongly disagree)

Information on individual indicators regarding "Implementation Success"			
Description of indicators	*Item to Total-Correlation*	*Indicator-Reliability*	*t statistic*
1. The strategy was an example of effective strategy implementation.	–*	0.745	–*
2. The organization's implementation effort on this strategy was disappointing. (R)	–*	0.772	–*
3. The implementation of the strategy was generally considered a great success in the organization.	–*	0.813	–*
4. I personally think the implementation of the strategy was a success.	–*	0.869	–*
5. The implementation of the strategy was considered a success in my area.	–*	0.820	–*

Information on scale "Implementation Success"			
Descriptive Statistics		*Result of Exploratory Factor Analysis*	
Cronbach's alpha:	–*	Total variance explained:	–*

*Not available

References

Noble, C. H./Mokwa, M. P. **(1999): Implementing Marketing Strategies: Developing and Testing a Managerial Theory, in: Journal of Marketing, Vol. 63, pp. 57-73.**

86. Importance of a Strategy

Scale Description

The scale measures the extent to which a strategy is perceived as having potentially significant organizational consequences.

Origin

Developed by Noble and Mokwa (1999).

Samples

The survey-based study conducted by Noble and Mokwa (1999) involved sampling from two firms: One firm was a large, multi state, financial services organization. Subjects were managers with extensive responsibilities for the implementation of marketing strategies. The other firm was a market share leader in the packaged goods industry. In this company, participants were regional sales managers with full responsibility for a geographic area, including discretionary budgets for promotions and responsibility for implementing corporate promotional strategies. The sample consisted of 254 managers in the financial services company and 534 managers in the packaged goods industry. Usable responses were 161 from the financial service company (63% response rate) and 325 from the other company (61% response rate). The total of 486 usable responses represents an overall 62% response rate.

Scale Indicators and Reliability / Validity Parameters

Scale: from 1 (strongly agree) to 5 (strongly disagree)

Information on individual indicators regarding "Importance of a Strategy"			
Description of indicators	*Item to Total-Correlation*	*Indicator-Reliability*	*t statistic*
1. This strategy will influence the company for years to come.	–*	0.512	5.41
2. The strategy was extremely important.	–*	0.396	4.32
3. The strategy was pretty minor in the overall mission of the company. (R)	–*	0.420	4.56
4. The success of the strategy was expected to significantly affect the future of the company.	–*	0.859	7.59

Information on scale "Importance of a Strategy"			
Descriptive Statistics		*Result of Exploratory Factor Analysis*	
Cronbach's alpha:	0.62	Total variance explained:	–*

*Not available

References

Noble, C. H./Mokwa, M. P. **(1999): Implementing Marketing Strategies: Developing and Testing a Managerial Theory, in: Journal of Marketing, Vol. 63, pp. 57-73.**

87. Importance of Costs

Scale Description

The scale measures the degree to which a firm can actually utilize better cost information in its decision-making process. Besides competitive environment, other factors affecting the decision usefulness of cost information include the firm's use of cost data in pricing decisions, cost reduction efforts, need for special cost studies, strategic focus, and average profit margin (Estrin et al. (1994)).

Origin

Adapted from Estrin et al. (1994) and used by Krumwiede (1996, 1998).

Samples

A questionnaire was distributed to 1,058 internal auditing professionals. 204 completed usable responses were received. 134 are from the first and 67 from the second mailings, yielding a response rate of 21.2%. 65 responses (31.8%) indicate some use of ABC. The remaining 139 responses serve as a non-using control group.

Comments

Two items were deleted.

Scale Indicators and Reliability / Validity Parameters

Scale: from 1 (strongly disagree) to 5 (strongly agree)

Information on individual indicators regarding "Importance of Costs"			
Description of indicators			
Regarding the use of cost data within your business unit:			
1. Product costs must be accurate to compete in your market.			
2. Cost data are important because of your cost reduction efforts.			
3. Cost data are an important factor in pricing considerations.			
4. The business unit performs many special cost studies.			
5. Capital expenditures are based on 'strategic reasons' instead of cost issues.			
6. Price competition in your industry is intense.			
Information on scale "Importance of Costs"			
Descriptive Statistics		*Result of Exploratory Factor Analysis*	
Cronbach's alpha:	0.54	Total variance explained:	–*
Results of Confirmatory Factor Analysis			
χ^2-Value (Degrees of Freedom):	10.71 (1)	χ^2-Value/Degrees of Freedom:	10.71
p Value:	0.00	RMSEA:	0.082
NFI:	0.91	NNFI:	–*
GFI:	0.97	AGFI:	0.80
Factor reliability:	–*	Average variance explained:	–*

*Not available

References

***Cagwin, D./Bouwman, M. J.* (2002): The Association between Activity-Based Costing and Improvement in Financial Performance, in: Management Accounting Research, Vol. 13, pp. 1-39.**

Estrin, T. L./Kantor, J./Albers, D. C. (1994): Is ABC Suitable for Your Company?, in: Management Accounting, Vol. 75, pp. 40-45.

Krumwiede, K. R. (1996): An Empirical Examination of Factors Affecting the Adoption and Infusion of Activity-Based Costing, Dissertation University of Tennessee 1996.

Krumwiede, K. R. (1998): The Implementation Stages of Activity-Based Costing and the Impact of Contextual and Organizational Factors, in: Journal of Management Accounting Research, Vol. 10, pp. 239-277.

88. Importance of Strategic Action Plans

Scale Description

The scale measures the importance of strategic action plans and targets in the strategic planning process.

Origin

A major international management consulting firm developed the construct in 1991.

Samples

Ittner and Larcker (1997) examined the use and performance consequences of strategic control systems using survey data collected by a major international management consulting firm during 1991. The survey covered the automobile and computer industries in Canada, Germany, Japan, and the United States. All automobile assemblers and a random sample of their suppliers were invited to participate. A total of 249 organizations agreed to participate, representing an 85% response rate.

Comments

The scale emerged from a principal component analysis used to reduce the dimensionality of 36 questions from a survey assessing the extent to which organizations employ strategic control practices discussed in the quality literature.

Scale Indicators and Reliability / Validity Parameters

Scale: from 1 (slight or not at all) to 4 (primary or dominant concern)

Information on individual indicators regarding "Importance of Strategic Action Plans"
Description of indicators
How important are these elements in the planning process and in the resulting strategic plan?
1. Improvement actions and targets
2. Targeted results
3. Action plans to target
4. Action plans by individual organizational entities

Information on scale "Importance of Strategic Action Plans"			
Descriptive Statistics		*Result of Exploratory Factor Analysis*	
Cronbach's alpha:	0.78	Total variance explained:	–*

*Not available

References

***Ittner, C. D./Larcker, D. F.* (1997): Quality Strategy, Strategic Control Systems, and Organizational Performance, in: Accounting, Organizations and Society, Vol. 22, pp. 293-314.**

89. Indirect Enforcement [Mittelbare Durchsetzung]

Scale Description

The scale measures the extent to which managers use MAS information for indirect enforcement of decisions (information which is not instantly relevant but could be in the future).

Origin

The scale was newly developed by Schäffer/Steiners (2004).

Samples

Survey data were collected by questionnaire, administered to business unit leaders of 3,500 German companies with 100 to 2,000 employees from the industrial sector. A total of 449 usable questionnaires (12.8%) were returned.

Comments

Scale Indicators and Reliability / Validity Parameters

Scale: from 1 (definitely false) to 5 (definitely true)

Information on individual indicators regarding "Indirect Enforcement [Mittelbare Durchsetzung]"			
Description of indicators	*Item to Total-Correlation*	*Indicator-Reliability*	*t statistic*
1. Je besser ich die Informationen kenne, desto größer ist mein Einfluss auf Entscheidungen.	0.63	0.55	15.88
2. Eine genaue Kenntnis der Informationen hilft mir dabei, mich gegenüber anderen durchzusetzen.	0.67	0.67	17.60
3. Je mehr andere davon überzeugt sind, dass meinen Entscheidungen viele Informationen zu Grunde liegen, desto eher kann ich meine Meinung durchsetzen.	0.61	0.49	14.94

Information on scale "Indirect Enforcement [Mittelbare Durchsetzung]"			
Descriptive Statistics		*Result of Exploratory Factor Analysis*	
Cronbach's alpha:	0.79	Total variance explained:	0.71
Results of Confirmatory Factor Analysis			
Factor reliability:	0.80	Average variance explained:	0.57

References

***Schäffer, U./Steiners, D.* (2004): Zur Nutzung von Controllinginformationen, in: Zeitschrift für Planung und Unternehmenssteuerung, Vol. 15, pp. 377-404.**

90. Influence (of Controlling Department) [Einfluss der Controlling-Abteilung]

Scale Description

The scale measures the extent of the controlling department's influence on the process of organisational decision-making as perceived by the management.

Origin

The first items were newly developed by Spillecke (2006). The last item was taken from Bauer (2002).

Samples

Survey data were collected by questionnaire, administered via e-mail to 3,312 German managers of companies with at least 200 employees. The companies were from different industrial sectors. A total of 415 usable questionnaires (12.5%) were returned.

Scale Indicators and Reliability / Validity Parameters

Scale: from 1 (definitely false) to 5 (definitely true)

Information on individual indicators regarding "Influence (of Controlling Department) [Einfluss der Controlling-Abteilung]"			
Description of indicators	*Item to Total-Correlation*	*Indicator-Reliability*	*t statistic*
1. Das Controlling spielt eine sehr wichtige Rolle bei der Entscheidungsfindung in unserer Organisation.	0.74	0.62	–
2. Ich lege großen Wert auf die Meinung des Controllings bei der Entscheidungsfindung.	0.83	0.85	19.49
3. Das Controlling hat einen starken Einfluss auf die Entscheidungen des Managements in unserer Geschäftseinheit.	0.78	0.71	18.76

Information on scale "Influence (of Controlling Department) [Einfluss der Controlling-Abteilung]"			
Descriptive Statistics		*Result of Exploratory Factor Analysis*	
Cronbach's alpha:	0.89	Total variance explained:	0.73
Results of Confirmatory Factor Analysis			
Factor reliability:	0.89	Average variance explained:	0.73

References

***Spillecke, D.* (2006): Interne Kundenorientierung des Controllerbereichs. Messung – Erfolgsauswirkungen – Determinanten, Wiesbaden 2006, pp. 161-164.**

Bauer, M. (2002): Controllership in Deutschland. Zur erfolgreichen Zusammenarbeit von Managern und Controllern, Wiesbaden 2002.

91. Informal Reporting [Informelles Berichtswesen]

Scale Description

The scale measures the operability of an informal reporting system. It comprises three dimensions: increased relevance to current situations, increased scope of information compared to the formal reporting system as well as the integration into an informal network.

Origin

Developed by Eckey and Schäffer (2006).

Samples

Eckey and Schäffer (2006) collected data using a survey questionnaire sent to a total of 51 group controlling departments of management holdings listed in the German Prime Standard. The sample of companies represented a variety of industries. 37 usable responses were received, yielding a response rate of 72.5%.

Scale Indicators and Reliability / Validity Parameters

Scale: from 1 (strongly disagree) to 7 (strongly agree)

Information on individual indicators regarding "Informal Reporting [Informelles Berichtswesen]"			
Description of indicators	*Item to Total-Correlation*	*Indicator-Reliability*	*t statistic*
1. Wichtige Dinge erfahre ich, bevor der formale Bericht eingeht.	0.61	0.49	4.48
2. Überraschungen im Berichtswesen kommen bei uns selten vor.	0.64	0.52	4.60
3. Selbst wenn ich bedeutende Sachverhalte nicht über direkte Kommunikation mit der betreffenden Person mitbekomme, erfahre ich sie aus anderen Quellen im Konzern.	0.49	0.29	3.04
4. Informationen entnehme ich ausschließlich dem Berichtswesen (R).	0.74	0.81	6.07

Information on scale "Informal Reporting [Informelles Berichtswesen]"			
Descriptive Statistics		*Result of Exploratory Factor Analysis*	
Cronbach's alpha:	0.80	Total variance explained:	0.63
Results of Confirmatory Factor Analysis			
χ^2-Value (Degrees of Freedom):	0.18 (2)	χ^2-Value/Degrees of Freedom:	0.09
p-value:	0.91	RMSEA:	0.00
NFI:	1.00	CFI:	1.00
GFI:	1.00	AGFI:	0.99
Factor reliability:	0.81	Average variance explained:	0.53

References

Eckey, M./Schäffer, U. **(2006): Kontrolle von Mehrheitsbeteiligungen in börsennotierten Management-Holdings, in: Zeitschrift für Planung & Unternehmenssteuerung, Vol. 17, pp. 251-280.**

92. Information Technology Sophistication (for Activity Based Costing)

Scale Description

The scale describes the sophistication of information technology needed by activity-based costing.

Origin

Developed based on Reeve (1996), modified by Krumwiede (1996, 1998).

Samples

Cagwin and Bouwman (2002) distributed questionnaire to 1,058 internal auditing professionals. They received 204 usable responses, yielding a response rate of 21.2%. 65 responses (31.8%) indicate some use of ABC. The remaining 139 responses serve as a non-using control group.

Comments

According to Cagwin and Bouwman (2002), an information system providing detailed historical data and easy access to users may provide much of the driver information. Reeve (1996) suggests that an integrated ABC system pre-supposes a relatively high level of information sophistication with real-time activity driver information. Cagwin and Bouwman (2002) mention that SAP, PeopleSoft and Oracle have recently acquired ABC software companies or partnered to develop ABC modules.

Scale Indicators and Reliability / Validity Parameters

Scale: from 1 (strongly disagree) to 5 (strongly agree)

Information on individual indicators regarding "Information Technology Sophistication (for Activity Based Costing)"			
Description of indicators			
1. The business unit's information systems (e.g. sales, manufacturing, etc.) are integrated with each other.			
2. The information system offers user-friendly query capability.			
3. The past year's detailed sales and operating data are available.			
4. Many perspectives of cost and performance data are available.			
5. Operating data are updated 'real time'.			
6. The quality of your cost management system is excellent.			
Information on scale "Information Technology Sophistication (for Activity Based Costing)"			
Descriptive Statistics		*Result of Exploratory Factor Analysis*	
Cronbach's alpha:	0.84	Total variance explained:	–*
Results of Confirmatory Factor Analysis			
χ^2-Value (Degrees of Freedom):	3.93 (4)	χ^2-Value/Degrees of Freedom:	0.98
p Value:	0.42	RMSEA:	0.016
NFI:	0.99	NNFI:	–*
GFI:	0.99	AGFI:	0.97
Factor reliability:	–*	Average variance explained:	–*

*Not available

References

***Cagwin, D./Bouwman, M. J.* (2002): The Association between Activity-Based Costing and Improvement in Financial Performance, in: Management Accounting Research, Vol. 13, pp. 1-39.**

Krumwiede, K. R. (1996): An Empirical Examination of Factors Affecting the Adoption and Infusion of Activity-Based Costing, Dissertation University of Tennessee 1996.

Krumwiede, K. R. (1998): The Implementation Stages of Activity-Based Costing and the Impact of Contextual and Organizational Factors, in: Journal of Management Accounting Research, Vol. 10, pp. 239-277.

Reeve, J. M. (1996): Projects, Models, and Systems - Where Is ABM Headed?, in: Journal of Cost Management, Vol. 10, pp. 5-16.

93. Information Supply and Preparation [Informationsversorgung und -aufbereitung]

Scale Description

The scale indicates manager's perception of the controlling staff's involvement in the process of supplying and preparing relevant business data.

Origin

The scale was newly developed by Bauer (2002).

Samples

Survey data were collected by questionnaire, administered via mail to 2,527 German companies. A total of 347 companies sent usable answers, yielding a 14.8% return rate.

Comments

The study used a dyadic design approach, where a manager and a controller of the same company were questioned. The data for this scale solely stem from the answers of the managers.

Scale Indicators and Reliability / Validity Parameters

Scale: from 1 (definitely false) to 7 (definitely true)

Information on individual indicators regarding "Information Supply and Preparation [Informationsversorgung und -aufbereitung]"			
Description of indicators	*Item to Total-Correlation*	*Indicator-Reliability*	*t statistic*
1. Unser Controller sorgt für die systematische Erfassung von Ist-Daten über die wichtigen Größen unseres Geschäfts.	0.66	–*	–*
2. Es werden zur Entscheidungsfindung möglichst viele verschiedene Informationen herangezogen.	0.66	–*	–*

Information on scale "Information Supply and Preparation [Informationsversorgung und –aufbereitung]"			
Descriptive Statistics		*Result of Exploratory Factor Analysis*	
Cronbach's alpha:	0.80	Total variance explained:	0.83

*Not feasible

References

Bauer, M. **(2002): Controllership in Deutschland. Zur erfolgreichen Zusammenarbeit von Controllern und Managern, Wiesbaden 2002, pp. 194-195.**

94. Information Tool (Cost Accounting) [Kostenrechnung als Auskunftsapparat]

Scale Description

The scale measures the extent to which the primary clients of accounting information use these data as a means of gaining knowledge about their business in the decision-making process.

Origin

The scale was newly developed by Aust (1999).

Samples

The scale stems from a questionnaire sent to 1,163 German industrial companies, of which 143 participated, yielding a return rate of 12.3%. The study used a triadic design approach, where the general manager, the marketing or sales director and an accountant of the same company were questioned. Altogether, 105 usable triads were returned.

Scale Indicators and Reliability / Validity Parameters

Scale: from 1 (definitely false) to 5 (definitely true)

Information on individual indicators regarding "Information Tool (Cost Accounting) [Kostenrechnung als Auskunftsapparat]"			
Description of indicators	*Item to Total-Correlation*	*Indicator-Reliability*	*t statistic*
1. Ohne die Kostenrechnungsinformationen würden meine Entscheidungen zumeist anders ausfallen.	0.49	0.28	7.84
2. Die Kostenrechnungsinformationen lenken meine Aufmerksamkeit auf Aspekte meiner Entscheidungen, die ich sonst nicht beachten würde.	0.48	0.29	7.98
3. Für meine Entscheidungen benötige ich eigentlich kaum Informationen aus der Kostenrechnung. (R)	0.58	0.62	12.45
4. Bei konkreten Entscheidungen nutze ich im Wesentlichen andere Informationen als die Kostenrechnung. (R)	0.45	0.38	9.31
5. Die meisten Kostenrechnungsinformationen lösen bei mir unmittelbare Handlungen aus.	0.42	0.30	8.09
6. Kostenrechnungsinformationen helfen mir bei der Überwachung der Aktivitäten in meinem Verantwortungsbereich.	0.46	0.34	8.66

Information on scale "Information Tool (Cost Accounting) [Kostenrechnung als Auskunftsapparat]"			
Descriptive Statistics		*Result of Exploratory Factor Analysis*	
Cronbach's alpha:	0.74	Total variance explained:	0.44
Results of Confirmatory Factor Analysis			
Factor reliability:	0.77	Average variance explained:	0.37

References

***Aust, R.* (1999): Kostenrechnung als unternehmensinterne Dienstleistung, Wiesbaden 1999, pp. 102-103.**

95. Instrumental Use of Controlling Information [Instrumentelle Nutzung von Controlling-Informationen]

Scale Description

The scale measures the extent, to which managers use controlling information as input in the immediate decision-making process. Here the controlling information is used as a means to finding the right conclusion to a specific business problem.

Origin

The scale was newly developed by Bauer (2002), adapting items from Karlshaus (2000).

Samples

Survey data were collected by questionnaire, administered via mail to 2,527 German companies. A total of 347 companies sent usable answers, yielding a 14.8% return rate.

Comments

The study used a dyadic design approach, where a manager and a controller of the same company were questioned. The data for this scale sole stem from the answers of the managers. Four items had to be eliminated due to a lack of Item-to-Total Correlation.

Scale Indicators and Reliability / Validity Parameters

Scale: from 1 (definitely false) to 7 (definitely true)

Information on individual indicators regarding "Instrumental Use of Controlling Information [Instrumentelle Nutzung von Controlling-Informationen]"			
Description of indicators	*Item to Total-Correlation*	*Indicator-Reliability*	*t statistic*
1. Ohne unser Controlling würden meine Entscheidungen zumeist anders ausfallen.	0.56	–*	–*
2. Der Controller lenkt meine Aufmerksamkeit auf Aspekte meiner Entscheidungen, die ich sonst nicht beachten würde.	0.56	–*	–*

Information on scale "Instrumental Use of Controlling Information [Instrumentelle Nutzung von Controlling-Informationen]"			
Descriptive Statistics		*Result of Exploratory Factor Analysis*	
Cronbach's alpha:	0.72	Total variance explained:	0.78

*Not feasible

References

***Bauer, M.* (2002): Controllership in Deutschland. Zur erfolgreichen Zusammenarbeit von Controllern und Managern, Wiesbaden 2002, pp. 204-205.**

Karlshaus, J. T. (2000): Die Nutzung von Kostenrechnungsinformationen im Marketing 2000, Wiesbaden.

96. Instrumental Use of Metrics [Instrumentelle Nutzung von Kennzahlen]

Scale Description

The scale measures the extent, to which managers use metrics as input in the immediate decision-making process. Here, metrics are used as a means to finding the right conclusion to a specific business problem.

Origin

The scale was adopted by Sandt (2004) from Karlshaus (2000). A similar approach concerning accounting data was used by Hunold (2003).

Samples

The questionnaire was sent to 2,386 German upper level managers. 254 responses could be integrated into the analysis, yielding a response rate of 11.1%.

Scale Indicators and Reliability / Validity Parameters

Scale: from 1 (definitely false) to 5 (definitely true)

Information on individual indicators regarding "Instrumental Use of Metrics [Instrumentelle Nutzung von Kennzahlen]"			
Description of indicators	*Item to Total-Correlation*	*Indicator-Reliability*	*t statistic*
1. Ohne die Kennzahlen würden meine Entscheidungen zumeist anders ausfallen.	0.64	0.70	9.4
2. Die Kennzahlen lenken meine Aufmerksamkeit auf Aspekte meiner Entscheidung, die ich sonst nicht beachten würde.	0.59	0.54	9.4
3. Für meine Entscheidungen benötige ich die Kennzahlen eigentlich kaum. (R)	0.50	0.38	9.4

Information on scale "Instrumental Use of Metrics [Instrumentelle Nutzung von Kennzahlen]"			
Descriptive Statistics		*Result of Exploratory Factor Analysis*	
Cronbach's alpha:	0.75	Total variance explained:	0.66
Results of Confirmatory Factor Analysis			
Factor reliability:	0.77	Average variance explained:	0.54

References

***Sandt, J.* (2004): Management mit Kennzahlen und Kennzahlensystemen. Bestandsaufnahme, Determinanten und Erfolgswirkungen, Wiesbaden 2004, pp. 162-163.**

Hunold, C. (2003): Kommunale Kostenrechnung. Gestaltung, Nutzung und Erfolgsfaktoren, Wiesbaden 2003.

Karlshaus, J. T. (2000): Die Nutzung von Kostenrechnungsinformationen im Marketing, Wiesbaden 2000.

97. Intensity of Monitoring [Kontrollintensität]

Scale Description

The scale measures the extent to which deviations from budget plans are analyzed analytically and intensively. The scale comprises two dimensions: intensity of analysis and analytic analysis.

Origin

Künkele and Schäffer (2007) developed this scale based on the measures for intensity of planning and analytic planning of Willauer (2003). As there existed very high correlations between the indicators of both scales, the two measures were combined by taking the first three respectively two indicators of each scale and relating them to budgetary control.

Samples

Survey data were collected by questionnaire, administered to business unit leaders and the responsible controllers of these business units of 1,120 German companies from 500 to 5,000 employees. The companies were from services and industrial sectors. A total of 140 usable pairs of questionnaires (12.5%) were returned.

Scale Indicators and Reliability / Validity Parameters

Scale: from 1 (definitely false) to 5 (definitely true)

Information on individual indicators regarding "Intensity of Monitoring [Kontrollintensität]"			
Description of indicators	*Item to Total-Correlation*	*Indicator-Reliability*	*t statistic*
1. Im Rahmen der Budgetkontrolle untersuchen wir Abweichungen systematisch.	0.54	0.37	10.20
2. Im Rahmen der Budgetkontrolle besorgen wir uns alle Informationen, die wir bekommen können.	0.68	0.61	14.04
3. Im Rahmen der Budgetkontrolle durchdringen wir die zugrunde liegenden Leistungsprozesse analytisch.	0.61	0.50	12.41
4. Im Rahmen der Budgetkontrolle gehen wir in die Tiefe.	0.61	0.45	11.61
5. Im Rahmen der Budgetkontrolle werden verschiedene Alternativen/Abweichungsursachen genau beleuchtet.	0.58	0.42	11.03

Information on scale "Intensity of Monitoring [Kontrollintensität]"			
Descriptive Statistics		*Result of Exploratory Factor Analysis*	
Cronbach's alpha:	0.81	Total variance explained:	0.57
Results of Confirmatory Factor Analysis			
χ^2-Value (Degrees of Freedom):	9.96 (5)	χ^2-Value/Degrees of Freedom:	1.99
p Value:	0.08	RMSEA:	0.06
NFI:	0.98	NNFI:	0.98
SRMR:	0.03	CFI:	0.99
GFI:	0.99	AGFI:	0.96
Factor reliability:	0.81	Average variance explained:	0.47

References

***Künkele, J./Schäffer, U.* (2007): Zur erfolgreichen Gestaltung der Budgetkontrolle, in: Die Betriebswirtschaft, Vol. 67, pp. 75-92.**

Weber, J /Schäffer, U./Willauer, B. (2003): Skalenübersicht, in: Weber, J./Kunz, J. (Ed.): Empirische Controllingforschung: Begründung, Beispiele, Ergebnisse, Wiesbaden 2003.

98. Intensity of Strategic Monitoring – Analysis [Tiefe der strategischen Kontrolle – Analyse]

Scale Description

The scale measures the amount of efforts in the process of strategic control. The scale is operationalized by the extent to which different causes for potential deviations and alternatives are analyzed in detail by the central controlling department.

Origin

Developed by Schäffer and Willauer (2002), modified by Eckey and Schäffer (2006).

Samples

Eckey and Schäffer (2006) collected data using a survey questionnaire sent to a total of 51 group controlling departments of management holdings listed in the German Prime Standard. The sample of companies represented a variety of industries. 37 usable responses were received, yielding a response rate of 72.5%.

Comments

The original scale developed by Schäffer and Willauer (2002) refers to the amount of effort in the process of planning and has been modified in the context of strategic control. Schäffer and Willauer (2002) reported a coefficient alpha of 0.92. Eckey and Schäffer (2006) reported a mean of 5.04 and standard deviation of 1.24 on a theoretical range of 1-7.

Scale Indicators and Reliability / Validity Parameters

Scale: from 1 (strongly disagree) to 7 (strongly agree)

Information on individual indicators regarding "Intensity of Strategic Monitoring – Analysis [Tiefe der strategischen Kontrolle - Analyse]"			
Description of indicators	*Item to Total-Correlation*	*Indicator-Reliability*	*t statistic*
1. Im Rahmen der strategischen Kontrolle werden verschiedene Abweichungsursachen/Alternativen gründlich untersucht.	0.78	0.66	5.72
2. Im Rahmen der strategischen Kontrolle gehen wir in die Tiefe.	0.73	0.74	5.90
3. Die an der strategischen Kontrolle Beteiligten setzen sich intensiv mit den relevanten Sachverhalten auseinander.	0.79	0.92	7.15
4. Die strategische Kontrolle ist bei uns ein intensiver und aufwendiger Prozess.	0.77	0.59	5.37

Information on scale "Intensity of Strategic Monitoring – Analysis [Tiefe der strategischen Kontrolle – Analyse]"			
Descriptive Statistics		*Result of Exploratory Factor Analysis*	
Cronbach's alpha:	0.90	Total variance explained:	0.76
Results of Confirmatory Factor Analysis			
χ^2-Value (Degrees of Freedom):	0.31 (1)	χ^2-Value/Degrees of Freedom:	0.31
p-value:	0.58	RMSEA:	0.00
NFI:	1.00	NNFI:	1.04
SRMR:	0.01	CFI:	1.00
GFI:	1.00	AGFI:	0.96
Factor reliability:	0.91	Average variance explained:	0.73

References

***Eckey, M./Schäffer, U.* (2006): Kontrolle von Mehrheitsbeteiligungen in börsennotierten Management-Holdings, in: Zeitschrift für Planung & Unternehmenssteuerung, Vol. 17, pp. 251-280.**

Schäffer, U./Willauer, B. (2002): Kontrolle, Effektivität der Planung und Erfolg von Geschäftseinheiten - Ergebnisse einer empirischen Erhebung, in: Zeitschrift für Planung, Vol. 13, pp. 73-97.

99. Intensity of Strategic Monitoring – Corrective Action [Tiefe der strategischen Kontrolle – Maßnahme]

Scale Description

The scale measures the amount of efforts taken in the process of strategic control. The scale is operationalized by the intensity of corrective measures executed in detail by the central controlling department.

Origin

Developed by Schäffer and Willauer (2002), modified by Eckey and Schäffer (2006).

Samples

Eckey and Schäffer (2006) collected data using a survey questionnaire sent to a total of 51 group controlling departments of management holdings listed in the German Prime Standard. The sample of companies represented a variety of industries. 37 usable responses were received, yielding a response rate of 72.5%.

Comments

The original scale developed by Schäffer and Willauer (2002) refers to the amount of effort in the process of planning and has been modified in the context of strategic control. Schäffer and Willauer (2002) reported a coefficient alpha of 0.92. Eckey and Schäffer (2006) reported a mean of 4.70 and standard deviation of 1.27 on a theoretical range of 1-7.

Scale Indicators and Reliability / Validity Parameters

Scale: from 1 (strongly disagree) to 7 (strongly agree)

Information on individual indicators regarding "Intensity of Strategic Monitoring – Corrective Action [Tiefe der strategischen Kontrolle - Maßnahme]"			
Description of indicators	*Item to Total-Correlation*	*Indicator-Reliability*	*t statistic*
1. Das Erarbeiten von Korrekturvorschlägen bei hohen Abweichungen im Rahmen der strategischen Kontrolle ist bei uns ein sehr intensiver und aufwendiger Prozess.	0.64	0.38	3.80
2. Korrekturmaßnahmen werden von uns detailliert ausgearbeitet.	0.86	0.74	5.33
3. Bei hohen Abweichungen im Rahmen der strategischen Kontrolle investiert das zentrale Controlling viel Zeit, um Gegensteuermaßnahmen zu erarbeiten.	0.74	0.64	4.96

Information on scale "Intensity of Strategic Monitoring – Corrective Action [Tiefe der strategischen Kon-trolle - Maßnahme]"			
Descriptive Statistics		*Result of Exploratory Factor Analysis*	
Cronbach's alpha:	0.86	Total variance explained:	0.79
Results of Confirmatory Factor Analysis			
Factor reliability:	0.81	Average variance explained:	0.59

References

***Eckey, M./Schäffer, U.* (2006): Kontrolle von Mehrheitsbeteiligungen in börsennotierten Management-Holdings, in: Zeitschrift für Planung & Unternehmenssteuerung, Vol. 17, pp. 251-280.**

Schäffer, U./Willauer, B. (2002): Kontrolle, Effektivität der Planung und Erfolg von Geschäftseinheiten - Ergebnisse einer empirischen Erhebung, in: Zeitschrift für Planung, Vol. 13, pp. 73-97.

100. Interaction

Scale Description

The scale measures the extent of products managers' interaction with members of areas outside of product management (e.g. personnel in sales, research and development, operations).

Origin

Developed by Andrews and Smith (1996).

Samples

Data were gathered using questionnaires mailed to consumer goods product managers. Product managers were asked to focus on a single product for which they had been highly involved in developing the most recent marketing program. Names and addresses were obtained from the American Marketing Association's membership directory (192) and a purchasing mailing list (459). After removing names of people who were no longer with the company or whose addresses were incorrect, the sampling frame included 578 names. Andrews/Smith received 193 completed questionnaires, yielding a 33.4% response rate.

Comments

Andrews and Smith (1996) reported a scale mean of 4.31 and a standard deviation of 0.87.

Scale Indicators and Reliability / Validity Parameters

Scale: from 1 (strongly disagree) to 7 (strongly agree)

Information on individual indicators regarding "Interaction"
Description of indicators
To what extent did you interact with members of each of the following areas when generating ideas for your product's most recent marketing programs?
1. Research and development
2. Production
3. Finance
4. Market research
5. Channel members
6. Sales force/sales managers
7. Consultants
8. Advertising agency personnel
9. Customers

Information on scale "Interaction"			
Descriptive Statistics		*Result of Exploratory Factor Analysis*	
Cronbach's alpha:	–*	Total variance explained:	–*

*Not available

References

***Andrews, J./Smith, D. C.* (1996): In Search of the Marketing Imagination: Factors Affecting the Creativity of Marketing Programs for Mature Products, in: Journal of Marketing Research, Vol. 33, pp. 174-187.**

101. Interactive Use of Metrics [Interaktive Nutzung von Kennzahlen]

Scale Description

The scale measures the extent to which managers use some metrics continuously in the process of discussing important business issues with colleagues and subordinates.

Origin

The scale was newly developed by Sandt (2004) based on a theory by Simons (1995).

Samples

The questionnaire was sent to 2,386 German upper level managers. 254 responses could be integrated into the analysis, yielding a response rate of 11.1%.

Scale Indicators and Reliability / Validity Parameters

Scale: from 1 (definitely false) to 5 (definitely true)

Information on individual indicators regarding "Diagnostic Use of Metrics [Diagnostische Nutzung von Kennzahlen]"			
Description of indicators	*Item to Total-Correlation*	*Indicator-Reliability*	*t statistic*
1. Einigen Kennzahlen schenke ich erhöhte Aufmerksamkeit, weil sie für den Geschäftsbereich entscheidende Aspekte betreffen.	0.71	0.62	18.57
2. Einige Kennzahlen diskutiere ich häufig mit Kollegen und Mitarbeitern.	0.75	0.70	19.14
3. Einige Kennzahlen veranlassen mich und meine Mitarbeiter, uns mit grundlegenden Annahmen unseres Geschäfts und Maßnahmen zu beschäftigen.	0.61	0.52	17.52
4. Einige Kennzahlen sind mir ständig präsent.	0.74	0.67	18.92
5. Auf einige Kennzahlen fokussiere ich sehr oft und regelmäßig meine Aufmerksamkeit.	0.74	0.70	18.95

Information on scale "Diagnostic Use of Metrics [Diagnostische Nutzung von Kennzahlen]"			
Descriptive Statistics		*Result of Exploratory Factor Analysis*	
Cronbach's alpha:	0.88	Total variance explained:	0.68
Results of Confirmatory Factor Analysis			
χ^2-Value (Degrees of Freedom):	9.86 (5)	χ^2-Value/Degrees of Freedom:	1.97
p Value:	0.08	RMSEA:	0.06
SRMR:	–*	CFI:	1.00
GFI:	0.99	AGFI:	0.98
Factor reliability:	0.90	Average variance explained:	0.64

*Not available

References

***Sandt, J.* (2004): Management mit Kennzahlen und Kennzahlensystemen. Bestandsaufnahme, Determinanten und Erfolgswirkungen, Wiesbaden 2004, pp. 167-170.**

Simons, R. (1995): Levers of Control, Boston 1995.

102. Intercorporate Interaction (in MNCs)

Scale Description

The scale measures the frequency of subsidiary managers' intercorporate interaction.

Origin

The measures used by Barner-Rasmussen (2003) are similar to those used by Gupta et al. (1999), although less elaborate due to the constraints set by the length of his questionnaire.

Samples

Barner-Rasmussen (2003) collected data through structured face-to-face interviews with 89 top managers of Finnish subsidiaries of foreign MNCs. The participating firms were picked from a list of the 150 largest foreign-owned subsidiaries in Finland, resulting in a sample of 30 US-owned, 32 Scandinavian-owned, and 27 European-owned units. Their parent companies' annual turnover ranged from US$ 34 million to 183,000 million and operated in between three and 190 countries.

Comments

The study of Barner-Rasmussen (2003) shows a relative low alpha of 0.57 is explained by the fact that e.g. trips and visits on the one hand, and participation in training on the other, occur at quite different frequencies (although both may be classified as intercorporate interaction).

Scale Indicators and Reliability / Validity Parameters

Scale: from 1 (less than yearly) to 7 (weekly)

Information on individual indicators regarding "Intercorporate Interaction (in MNCs)"			
Description of indicators			
Please indicate the frequency with which you:			
1. make trips and visits to other units of the MNC.			
2. participate in corporate interunit committees, teams, and task forces.			
3. participate in training involving participants from several units.			
4. participate in other corporate activities such as meetings and conferences.			
Information on scale "Intercorporate Interaction (in MNCs)"			
Descriptive Statistics		*Result of Exploratory Factor Analysis*	
Cronbach's alpha:	0.57	Total variance explained:	–*

*Not available

References

Barner-Rasmussen, W. **(2003): Determinants of the Feedback-Seeking Behaviour of Subsidiary Top Managers in Multinational Corporations, in: International Business Review, Vol. 12, pp. 41-60.**

Gupta, A. K./Govindarajan, V./Malhotra, A. (1999): Feedback-Seeking Behavior within Multinational Corporations, in: Strategic Management Journal, Vol. 20, pp. 205-222.

103. Interest Clarity [Interessenklarheit]

Scale Description

The scale measures the extent to which management teams perceive themselves as being free of conflicting interests, e.g. concerning the company's goals.

Origin

The scale was newly developed by Spieker (2004).

Samples

Survey data were collected by questionnaire, administered via internet to 353 managers of German start-up companies. A total of 145 usable questionnaires (41.1%) were returned.

Scale Indicators and Reliability / Validity Parameters

Scale: from 1 (definitely false) to 7 (definitely true)

Information on individual indicators regarding "Interest Clarity [Interessenklarheit]"			
Description of indicators	*Item to Total-Correlation*	*Indicator-Reliability*	*t statistic*
1. Wir sind uns über die langfristig zu verfolgende Exit-Strategie (IPO, Trade-Sell, dauerhafte Privatgesellschaft, etc.) einig.	0.71	0.83	16.89
2. Wir reden sehr offen über die langfristigen Ziele, die jeder Einzelne mit dem Engagement am Start-up verfolgt.	0.67	0.83	16.85
3. Teammitglieder stellen eigene Interessen vor die Interessen des Teams. (R)	0.48	0.62	15.73
4. Entscheidungsprozesse sind durch persönliche Interessen beeinflusst. (R)	0.51	0.60	15.36
5. Wir reden sehr offen über unsere persönlichen Interessen und Ziele.	0.53	0.74	16.34

Information on scale "Interest Clarity [Interessenklarheit]"			
Descriptive Statistics		*Result of Exploratory Factor Analysis*	
Cronbach's alpha:	0.79	Total variance explained:	0.55
Results of Confirmatory Factor Analysis			
χ^2-Value (Degrees of Freedom):	1.09 (5)	χ^2-Value/Degrees of Freedom:	0.22
p Value:	0.43	RMSEA:	0.00
SRMR:	–*	CFI:	1.00
GFI:	1.00	AGFI:	1.00
Factor reliability:	0.93	Average variance explained:	0.73

*Not available

References

Spieker, M. **(2004): Entscheidungen in Gründerteams. Determinanten – Parameter – Erfolgsauswirkungen, Wiesbaden 2004, pp. 245-246.**

104. Internal Complexity [Interne Komplexität]

Scale Description

The scale measures the level of internal complexity of a company's processes, e.g. the diversity of products offered.

Origin

The scale is based on empirical approach Aust (1999).

Samples

Survey data were collected by questionnaire, administered to logistics managers of 1,394 German companies in the manufacturing industry. A total of 316 usable questionnaires (23%) were returned.

Scale Indicators and Reliability / Validity Parameters

Scale: from 1 (definitely false) to 7 (definitely true)

Information on individual indicators regarding "Internal Complexity [Interne Komplexität]"			
Description of indicators	*Item to Total-Correlation*	*Indicator-Reliability*	*t statistic*
1. Die Produkte/Varianten unterscheiden sich sehr stark voneinander.	0.48	0.30	11.83
2. Die Produkte werden aus einer Vielzahl von Einzelteilen hergestellt.	0.59	0.55	13.93
3. Die Zahl der Produktionsstufen ist sehr hoch.	0.62	0.56	13.87
4. Die Einzelteile der Produkte unterscheiden sich bei ihrer Herstellung, ihrem Einbau und ihrer Weiterverarbeitung stark voneinander.	0.63	0.59	13.80

Information on scale "Internal Complexity [Interne Komplexität]"			
Descriptive Statistics		*Result of Exploratory Factor Analysis*	
Cronbach's alpha:	0.77	Total variance explained:	0.60
Results of Confirmatory Factor Analysis			
χ^2-Value (Degrees of Freedom):	3.17 (2)	χ^2-Value/Degrees of Freedom:	1.58
p Value:	0.20	RMSEA:	0.04
SRMR:	–*	CFI:	1.00
GFI:	1.00	AGFI:	0.99
Factor reliability:	0.80	Average variance explained:	0.50

*Not available

References

***Blum, H. S.* (2006): Logistik-Controlling. Kontext, Ausgestaltung und Erfolgswirkungen, Wiesbaden 2006, pp. 104-105.**

Aust, R. (1999): Kostenrechnung als unternehmensinterne Dienstleistung, Wiesbaden 1999.

105. Internal Customer Orientation of the Controlling Department (Direct Measurement) [Direkte Messung der internen Kundenorientierung des Controllerbereichs]

Scale Description

The scale measures the extent to which the controlling department places high emphasis on internal customer orientation.

Origin

The scale was newly developed by Spillecke (2006).

Samples

Survey data were collected by questionnaire, administered via e-mail to 3,312 German managers of companies with at least 200 employees. The companies were from different industrial sectors. A total of 415 usable questionnaires (12.5%) were returned.

Scale Indicators and Reliability / Validity Parameters

Scale: from 1 (definitely false) to 5 (definitely true)

Information on individual indicators regarding "Internal Customer Orientation of the Controlling Department (Direct Measurement) [Direkte Messung der internen Kundenorientierung des Controllerbereichs]"			
Description of indicators	*Item to Total-Correlation*	*Indicator-Reliability*	*t statistic*
1. Unser Controlling richtet sich sehr stark nach seinem internen Kunden, dem Management, aus.	0.90	–*	–*
2. Die interne Kundenorientierung (Ausrichtung am Management) des Controllings ist sehr hoch.	0.90	–*	–*

Information on scale "Internal Customer Orientation of the Controlling Department (Direct Measurement) [Direkte Messung der internen Kundenorientierung des Controllerbereichs]"			
Descriptive Statistics		*Result of Exploratory Factor Analysis*	
Cronbach's alpha:	0.95	Total variance explained:	0.90

*Not feasible

References

Spillecke, D. **(2006): Interne Kundenorientierung des Controllerbereichs. Messung – Erfolgsauswirkungen – Determinanten, Wiesbaden 2006, pp. 122-126.**

106. Internal Dynamics [Interne Dynamik]

Scale Description

The scale measures the level of internal dynamics of a company's processes, e.g. regular changes of products offered.

Origin

The scale is based on empirical approaches of Maltz/Kohli (1996) and Aust (1999).

Samples

Survey data were collected by questionnaire, administered to logistics managers of 1,394 German companies in the manufacturing industry. A total of 316 usable questionnaires (23%) were returned.

Scale Indicators and Reliability / Validity Parameters

Scale: from 1 (definitely false) to 7 (definitely true)

Information on individual indicators regarding "Internal Dynamics [Interne Dynamik]"			
Description of indicators	*Item to Total-Correlation*	*Indicator-Reliability*	*t statistic*
1. Unser Vertrieb ändert häufig seine Strategie.	0.50	0.40	13.01
2. Die von uns angebotenen Produkte/Varianten ändern sich häufig.	0.52	0.36	12.58
3. Unsere Wertschöpfungstiefe ist häufigen Veränderungen ausgesetzt.	0.56	0.55	14.21
4. Unsere Fertigungsabläufe/-prozesse unterliegen häufigen Veränderungen.	0.57	0.53	14.11
5. Unsere Organisationsstruktur wird häufig geändert.	0.37	0.22	10.51

Information on scale "Internal Dynamics [Interne Dynamik]"			
Descriptive Statistics		*Result of Exploratory Factor Analysis*	
Cronbach's alpha:	0.74	Total variance explained:	0.50
Results of Confirmatory Factor Analysis			
χ^2-Value (Degrees of Freedom):	13.56 (5)	χ^2-Value/Degrees of Freedom:	2.71
p Value:	0.02	RMSEA:	0.07
SRMR:	–*	CFI:	0.98
GFI:	0.99	AGFI:	0.97
Factor reliability:	0.77	Average variance explained:	0.41

*Not available

References

***Blum, H. S.* (2006): Logistik-Controlling. Kontext, Ausgestaltung und Erfolgswirkungen, Wiesbaden 2006, pp. 105-106.**

Aust, R. (1999): Kostenrechnung als unternehmensinterne Dienstleistung, Wiesbaden 1999.

Maltz, E./Kohli, A. K. (1996): Market Intelligence Dissemination across Functional Boundaries, in: Journal of Marketing Research, Vol. 33, pp. 47-61.

107. Internal Significance of Logistics [Interne Bedeutung Logistik]

Scale Description

The scale measures other functional unit's and management attention to logistics.

Origin

The scale was newly developed by Blum (2006).

Samples

Survey data were collected by questionnaire, administered to logistics managers of 1,394 German companies in the manufacturing industry. A total of 316 usable questionnaires (23%) were returned.

Scale Indicators and Reliability / Validity Parameters

Scale: from 1 (definitely false) to 7 (definitely true)

Information on individual indicators regarding "Internal Significance of Logistics [Interne Bedeutung Logistik]"			
Description of indicators	*Item to Total-Correlation*	*Indicator-Reliability*	*t statistic*
1. Logistik findet bei unserer Geschäftsleitung hohe Beachtung.	0.66	0.75	12.78
2. Logistik findet bei unserem Marketing/Vertrieb hohe Beachtung.	0.56	0.48	11.95
3. Logistik findet bei unserer Produktion hohe Beachtung.	0.43	0.27	10.95
4. Für Logistik haben wir klare strategische Richtlinien und Ziele.	0.50	0.36	11.58

Information on scale "Internal Significance of Logistics [Interne Bedeutung Logistik]"			
Descriptive Statistics		*Result of Exploratory Factor Analysis*	
Cronbach's alpha:	0.74	Total variance explained:	0.57
Results of Confirmatory Factor Analysis			
χ^2-Value (Degrees of Freedom):	3.43 (2)	χ^2-Value/Degrees of Freedom:	1.72
p Value:	0.02	RMSEA:	0.07
SRMR:	–*	CFI:	1.00
GFI:	1.00	AGFI:	0.98
Factor reliability:	0.77	Average variance explained:	0.46

*Not available

References

***Blum, H. S.* (2006): Logistik-Controlling. Kontext, Ausgestaltung und Erfolgswirkungen, Wiesbaden 2006, pp. 108-109.**

108. Intrinsic Motivation to Plan

Scale Description

The scale measures the extent to which respondents engage in marketing planning and ideation for intrinsically rewarding reasons.

Origin

Andrews and Smith (1996) developed the scale by modifying scales from Lawler III and Hall (1970) and Spiro and Weitz (1990).

Samples

Data were gathered using questionnaires mailed to consumer goods product managers. Product managers were asked to focus on a single product for which they had been highly involved in developing the most recent marketing program. Names and addresses were obtained from the American Marketing Association's membership directory (192) and a purchased mailing list (459). After removing invalid addresses, the sampling frame included 578 names. Andrews/Smith received 193 completed questionnaires, yielding a 33.4% response rate.

Scale Indicators and Reliability / Validity Parameters

Scale: from 1 (strongly disagree) to 7 (strongly agree)

Information on individual indicators regarding "Intrinsic Motivation to Plan"			
Description of indicators			
1. I feel a real sense of accomplishment when I come up with a good marketing program.			
2. Creating marketing strategies for this product is challenging.			
3. I don't especially enjoy coming up with marketing strategies for this product. (R)			
4. Developing marketing programs is one of my least favorite tasks. (R)			
5. Developing marketing programs is one of my most favorite tasks.			
Information on scale "Intrinsic Motivation to Plan"			
Descriptive Statistics		*Result of Exploratory Factor Analysis*	
Cronbach's alpha:	0.60	Total variance explained:	–*

*Not available

References

***Andrews, J./Smith, D. C.* (1996): In Search of the Marketing Imagination: Factors Affecting the Creativity of Marketing Programs for Mature Products, in: Journal of Marketing Research, Vol. 33, pp. 174-187.**

Lawler III, E. E./Hall, D. T. (1970): Relationship of Job Characteristics to Job Involvement, Satisfaction, and Intrinsic Motivation, in: Journal of Applied Psychology, Vol. 54, pp. 305-312.

Spiro, R. L./Weitz, B. A. (1990): Adaptive Selling: Conceptualization, Measurement, and Nomological Validity, in: Journal of Marketing Research, Vol. 27, pp. 61-69.

109. Intuition [Intuition]

Scale Description

The scale measures the extent to which the process of decision-making in management teams is influenced by gut feelings and intuition.

Origin

The scale was newly developed by Spieker (2004).

Samples

Survey data were collected by questionnaire, administered via internet to 353 managers of German start-up companies. A total of 145 usable questionnaires (41.1%) were returned.

Scale Indicators and Reliability / Validity Parameters

Scale: from 1 (definitely false) to 7 (definitely true)

Information on individual indicators regarding "Intuition [Intuition]"			
Description of indicators	*Item to Total-Correlation*	*Indicator-Reliability*	*t statistic*
1. Wir treffen Entscheidungen häufig aus dem Bauch heraus.	0.75	0.37	8.75
2. Viele Probleme sind analytisch nicht zu durchdringen, deswegen müssen wir Entscheidungen häufig aus unternehmerischer Erfahrung heraus treffen.	0.75	0.71	9.58
3. Unternehmerisches Gespür spielt bei Teamentscheidungen eine große Rolle.	0.85	0.51	9.19
4. Wir versuchen auf das „Bauchgefühl" einzelner Teammitglieder einzugehen.	0.71	0.43	8.86

Information on scale "Intuition [Intuition]"			
Descriptive Statistics		*Result of Exploratory Factor Analysis*	
Cronbach's alpha:	0.91	Total variance explained:	0.71
Results of Confirmatory Factor Analysis			
χ^2-Value (Degrees of Freedom):	0.33 (2)	χ^2-Value/Degrees of Freedom:	0.17
p Value:	0.17	RMSEA:	0.00
SRMR:	–*	CFI:	1.00
GFI:	1.00	AGFI:	1.00
Factor reliability:	0.80	Average variance explained:	0.50

*Not available

References

Spieker, M. (2004): Entscheidungen in Gründerteams. Determinanten – Parameter – Erfolgsauswirkungen, Wiesbaden 2004, pp. 237-238.

110. Involvement of a Strategy

Scale Description

The scale measures the extent to which a strategy involves a wide range of managers and functions within the organization.

Origin

Developed by Noble and Mokwa (1999).

Samples

The survey-based study conducted by Noble and Mokwa (1999) involved sampling from two firms: One firm was a large, multi state, financial services organization. Subjects were managers with extensive responsibilities for the implementation of marketing strategies. The other firm was a market share leader in the packaged goods industry. In this company, participants were regional sales managers with full responsibility for a geographic area, including discretionary budgets for promotions and responsibility for implementing corporate promotional strategies. The sample consisted of 254 managers in the financial services company and 534 managers in the packaged goods industry. Usable responses were 161 from the financial service company (63% response rate) and 325 from the other company (61% response rate). The total of 486 usable responses represents an overall 62% response rate.

Scale Indicators and Reliability / Validity Parameters

Scale: from 1 (strongly agree) to 5 (strongly disagree)

Information on individual indicators regarding "Involvement of a strategy"			
Description of indicators	*Item to Total-Correlation*	*Indicator-Reliability*	*t statistic*
1. The strategy was a real company-wide effort.	–*	0.508	5.27
2. People from all over the organization were involved in this strategy.	–*	0.855	7.09
3. A wide range of departments or functions in the company got involved in this strategy.	–*	0.538	5.49

Information on scale "Involvement of a strategy"			
Descriptive Statistics		*Result of Exploratory Factor Analysis*	
Cronbach's alpha:	0.66	Total variance explained:	–*

*Not available

References

Noble, C. H./Mokwa, M. P. **(1999): Implementing Marketing Strategies: Developing and Testing a Managerial Theory, in: Journal of Marketing, Vol. 63, pp. 57-73.**

111. Involvement of External Persons (Argumentation) [Einbeziehung Externer – Argumentation]

Scale Description

The scale measures the extent to which management teams use the services of non-company people or groups to obtain alternative opinions and constructive criticism in the decision-making process.

Origin

The scale was newly developed by Spieker (2004).

Samples

Survey data were collected by questionnaire, administered via internet to 353 managers of German start-up companies. A total of 145 usable questionnaires (41.1%) were returned.

Scale Indicators and Reliability / Validity Parameters

Scale: from 1 (not at all) to 7 (very much)

Information on individual indicators regarding "Involvement of External Persons (Argumentation) [Einbeziehung Externer – Argumentation]"			
Description of indicators	*Item to Total-Correlation*	*Indicator-Reliability*	*t statistic*
Wie sind externe Personen (-gruppen) an wichtigen Entscheidungsprozessen beteiligt?			
1. ...Beteiligung an der Generierung und Bewertung von Entscheidungsalternativen.	0.82	0.75	15.16
2. ...Kritisches Hinterfragen von Entscheidungsannahmen und Szenarien.	0.92	0.92	15.77
3. ...Konstruktive Kritik.	0.93	0.97	15.87
4. ...Konträre Meinungen.	0.82	0.74	15.03

Information on scale "Involvement of External Persons (Argumentation) [Einbeziehung Externer – Argumentation]"			
Descriptive Statistics		*Result of Exploratory Factor Analysis*	
Cronbach's alpha:	0.95	Total variance explained:	0.86
Results of Confirmatory Factor Analysis			
χ^2-Value (Degrees of Freedom):	0.24 (2)	χ^2-Value/Degrees of Freedom:	0.12
p Value:	0.00	RMSEA:	0.00
SRMR:	–*	CFI:	1.00
GFI:	1.00	AGFI:	1.00
Factor reliability:	0.96	Average variance explained:	0.84

*Not available

References

Spieker, M. **(2004): Entscheidungen in Gründerteams. Determinanten – Parameter – Erfolgsauswirkungen, Wiesbaden 2004, pp. 241-242.**

112. Involvement of External Persons (Attitude) [Einbeziehung Externer – Einstellung]

Scale Description

The scale measures management teams' general attitude towards using the services of non-company people or groups in the decision-making process.

Origin

The scale was newly developed by Spieker (2004).

Samples

Survey data were collected by questionnaire, administered via internet to 353 managers of German start-up companies. A total of 145 usable questionnaires (41.1%) were returned.

Scale Indicators and Reliability / Validity Parameters

Scale: from 1 (definitely false) to 7 (definitely true)

Information on individual indicators regarding "Involvement of External Persons (Attitude) [Einbeziehung Externer – Einstellung]"			
Description of indicators	*Item to Total-Correlation*	*Indicator-Reliability*	*t statistic*
1. Wir legen sehr viel Wert auf die Einbindung Externer in unseren Entscheidungsprozess.	0.84	0.87	12.57
2. Externe sind bei jeder wichtigen Entscheidung beteiligt.	0.60	0.39	10.57
3. Unser Team hat die Einbindung externer Personen (-Gruppen) bei wichtigen Entscheidungen als Erfolgsfaktor erkannt.	0.82	0.82	12.40
4. Externe Personen (-Gruppen) konnten in der Vergangenheit nur wenig zu einer effizienten Entscheidungsfindung beitragen. (R)	0.71	0.61	12.06

Information on scale "Involvement of External Persons (Attitude) [Einbeziehung Externer – Einstellung]"			
Descriptive Statistics		*Result of Exploratory Factor Analysis*	
Cronbach's alpha:	0.88	Total variance explained:	0.72
Results of Confirmatory Factor Analysis			
χ^2-Value (Degrees of Freedom):	4.25 (2)	χ^2-Value/Degrees of Freedom:	2.12
p Value:	0.00	RMSEA:	0.09
SRMR:	–*	CFI:	0.99
GFI:	0.99	AGFI:	0.97
Factor reliability:	0.89	Average variance explained:	0.67

*Not available

References

Spieker, M. **(2004): Entscheidungen in Gründerteams. Determinanten – Parameter – Erfolgsauswirkungen, Wiesbaden 2004, pp. 243.**

113. Involvement of External Persons (Establishment of Problem Awareness) [Einbeziehung Externer – Problemanregung]

Scale Description

The scale measures the extent to which management teams use the services of non-company people or groups to establish awareness for deficits and weak-spots in the decision-making process.

Origin

The scale was newly developed by Spieker (2004).

Samples

Survey data were collected by questionnaire, administered via internet to 353 managers of German start-up companies. A total of 145 usable questionnaires (41.1%) were returned.

Scale Indicators and Reliability / Validity Parameters

Scale: from 1 (not at all) to 7 (very much)

Information on individual indicators regarding "Involvement of External Persons (Establishment of Problem Awareness) [Einbeziehung Externer – Problemanregung]"			
Description of indicators	*Item to Total-Correlation*	*Indicator-Reliability*	*t statistic*
Wie sind externe Personen (-gruppen) an wichtigen Entscheidungsprozessen beteiligt?			
1. ...Anregung zu wichtigen Entscheidungen.	0.81	0.78	9.39
2. ...Schaffung eines Problembewusstseins.	0.85	0.97	9.39
3. ...Aufzeigen von Leistungsdefiziten.	0.62	0.45	9.39

Information on scale "Involvement of External Persons (Establishment of Problem Awareness) [Einbeziehung Externer – Problemanregung]"			
Descriptive Statistics		*Result of Exploratory Factor Analysis*	
Cronbach's alpha:	0.87	Total variance explained:	0.79
Results of Confirmatory Factor Analysis			
Factor reliability:	0.89	Average variance explained:	0.73

References

***Spieker, M.* (2004): Entscheidungen in Gründerteams. Determinanten – Parameter – Erfolgsauswirkungen, Wiesbaden 2004, pp. 241-242.**

114. Job Performance

Scale Description

The scale measures the degree of job performance of design engineers using subjective performance ratings on three items.

Origin

Developed by Shields et al. (2000).

Samples

480 questionnaires were distributed to automobile design engineers. Of 480 questionnaires distributed, 413 (86%) were returned. However, only 358 (75%) were usable because 46 respondents' self-reported job titles were not design engineers and 11 had missing data. These 358 usable subjects had a mean of 11.2 (SD=7.3, range=1-33) years of employment with the company and a mean of 7.8 (SD=6.1, range=0-32) years of experience in their current job assignment.

Comments

Shields et al. (2000) reported a scale mean of 11.95 and a standard deviation of 3.05 on actual (theoretical) range of 3-19 (3-21).

Scale Indicators and Reliability / Validity Parameters

Scale: from 1 (extremely low) to 7 (extremely high)

Information on individual indicators regarding "Job Performance"			
Description of indicators			
1. The level of my measured performance relative to my performance standards.			
2. The level of my measured performance relative to other design engineers' measured performance.			
3. The level of my measured performance.			
Information on scale "Job Performance"			
Descriptive Statistics		*Result of Exploratory Factor Analysis*	
Cronbach's alpha:	0.83	Total variance explained:	–*

*Not available

References

Shields, M. D./Deng, F. J./Kato, Y. **(2000): The Design and Effects of Control Systems: Tests of Direct-and Indirect-Effects Models, in: Accounting, Organizations and Society, Vol. 25, pp. 185-202.**

115. Job Satisfaction

Scale Description

The scale measures the degree of both intrinsic and extrinsic job satisfaction. Respondents were asked to indicate how satisfied or dissatisfied they were with various dimensions of their job experience.

Origin

Developed by Weiss et al. (1967).

Samples

Chong and Bateman (2000) chose eighty large manufacturing firms located in Perth, Western Australia, randomly from the Kompass Australia (1996) business directory. From these companies, the names of 150 middle-level managers were gathered; 120 agreed to participate. Finally, a total of 84 questionnaires were returned, yielding a response rate of 70%. Of these, 5 were not fully completed. This leaves the study with 79 usable responses, a usable response rate of 65.83% for data analysis.

Comments

The scale has been extensively used by prior accounting studies (see Harrison (1993); Choo and Tan (1997)). Chong and Bateman (2000) reported a scale mean of 3.75 and a standard deviation of 0.54 on a theoretical range of 1-7.

Scale Indicators and Reliability / Validity Parameters

Scale: from 1 (very dissatisfied) to 7 (very satisfied)

Information on individual indicators regarding "Job Satisfaction"
Description of indicators
1. Being able to keep busy all the time.
2. The chance to work alone on the job.
3. The chance to do different things from time to time.
4. The chance to be „somebody" in the community.
5. The way my boss handles employees.
6. The competence of my superior in making decisions.
7. Being able to do things that do not go against my conscience.
8. The way my job provides for steady employment.
9. The chance to do things for other people.
10. The chance to tell people what to do.
11. The chance to do something that makes use of my abilities.
12. The way company policies are put into practice.
13. My pay and the amount of work I do.
14. The chance for advancement on this job.
15. The freedom to use my own judgment.
16. The chance to try my own methods of doing my job.
17. The working conditions.

18. The way my co-workers get along with each other.			
19. The praise I get for doing a good job.			
20. The feeling of accomplishment I get from the job.			
Information on scale "Job Satisfaction"			
Descriptive Statistics		*Result of Exploratory Factor Analysis*	
Cronbach's alpha:	0.89	Total variance explained:	–*

*Not available

References

***Chong, V. K./Bateman, D.* (2000): The Effects of Role Stress on Budgetary Participation and Job Satisfaction-Performance Linkages: A Test of Two Different Models, in: Advances in Accounting Behavioral Research, Vol. 3, pp. 91-118.**

Choo, F./Tan, K. B. (1997): A Study of the Relations among Disagreement in Budgetary Performance Evaluation Style, Job-Related Tension, Job Satisfaction and Performance, in: Behavioral Research in Accounting, Vol. 9, pp. 199-218.

Harrison, G. L. (1993): Reliance on Accounting Performance Measures in Superior Evaluative Style - the Influence of National Culture and Personality, in: Accounting, Organizations and Society, Vol. 18, pp. 319-339.

Weiss, D. J./Dawis, R. V./England, G. W./Lofquist, L. H. (1967): Manual from the Minnesota Satisfaction Questionnaire, Minneapolis 1967.

116. Job-related Information

Scale Description

The scale assesses the extent to which managers perceived information availability for effective job-related decisions and to evaluate important decision alternatives.

Origin

The scale was obtained from Kren (1992) who used a three-item, seven-point Likert scale.

Samples

Chong and Chong (2002) drew a total of 80 manufacturing companies randomly from the Kompass Australia (1996/1997) business directory. From the 80 companies, the names of 120 middle-level managers were included in the sample. 84 questionnaires were returned, which yielded a response rate of 70 percent.

Comments

Chong and Chong (2002) reported a scale mean of 5.254 and a standard deviation of 1.002 on an actual (theoretical) range of 2.00-7.00 (1.00-7.00).

Scale Indicators and Reliability / Validity Parameters

Scale: from 1 (strongly disagree) to 7 (strongly agree)

Information on individual indicators regarding "Job related Information"			
Description of indicators	*Item to Total-Correlation*	*Indicator-Reliability*	*t statistic*
1. I am always clear about what is necessary to perform well on my job.	–*	0.61	–*
2. I have adequate information to make optimal decisions to accomplish my performance objectives.	–*	0.77	–*
3. I am able to obtain the strategic information necessary to evaluate important decision alternatives.	–*	0.38	–*

Information on scale "Job related Information"			
Descriptive Statistics		*Result of Exploratory Factor Analysis*	
Cronbach's alpha:	–*	Total variance explained:	–*
Results of Confirmatory Factor Analysis			
Factor reliability:	0.81	Average variance explained:	0.58

*Not available

References

***Chong, V. K./Chong, K. M.* (2002): Budget Goal Commitment and Informational Effects of Budget Participation on Performance: A Structural Equation Modeling Approach, in: Behavioral Research in Accounting, Vol. 14, pp. 65-86.**

Kren, L. (1992): Budgetary Participation and Managerial Performance: The Impact of Information and Environmental Volatility, in: The Accounting Review, Vol. 67, pp. 511-526.

117. Job-related Stress

Scale Description

The scale measures the degree of job-related stress.

Origin

Developed by Kahn (1964). The instrument used by Shields et al. (2000) was modified to fit the context of the present research, including six items which were not applicable.

Samples

480 questionnaires were distributed to automobile design engineers. Of 480 questionnaires distributed, 415 (86%) were returned. However, only 358 (74%) were usable because 46 respondents' self-reported job titles were not design engineers and 11 had missing data. These 358 usable subjects had a mean of 11.2 (SD=7.3, range=1-33) years of employment with the company and a mean of 7.8 (SD=6.1, range=0-32) years of experience in their current job assignment.

Scale Indicators and Reliability / Validity Parameters

Scale: 1 (never), 2 (rarely), 3 (sometimes), 4 (often), 5 (almost always)

Information on individual indicators regarding "Job-related Stress"			
Description of indicators			
For each statement, please circle the number which almost closely represents your true beliefs about your work assignments.			
1. Feeling that you have too little authority to carry out the responsibilities assigned to you.			
2. Being unclear on just what the scope and responsibilities of your job are.			
3. Feeling that you have too heavy a work load.			
4. Thinking that you'll not be able to satisfy the conflicting demands of various people over you.			
5. Not knowing what your superior thinks of you, how he evaluates your performance.			
6. The fact that you can't get information needed to carry out your job.			
7. Feeling unable to influence your immediate supervisor's decisions and actions that affect you.			
8. Not knowing just what the people you work with expect of you.			
9. Thinking that the *amount* of work you have to do may interfere with how *well* it gets done.			
Information on scale "Job-related Stress"			
Descriptive Statistics		*Result of Exploratory Factor Analysis*	
Cronbach's alpha:	0.70	Total variance explained:	–*

*Not available

References

***Shields, M. D./Deng, F. J./Kato, Y.* (2000): The Design and Effects of Control Systems: Tests of Direct-and Indirect-Effects Models, in: Accounting, Organizations and Society, Vol. 25, pp. 185-202.**

Kahn, R. L. (1964): Organizational Stress: Studies in Role Conflict and Ambiguity, New York.

118. Learning Tool (Cost Accounting) [Kostenrechnung als Lernapparat]

Scale Description

The scale measures the extent to which the primary clients of accounting information use these data as means of learning about their respective business.

Origin

The scale was newly developed by Aust (1999).

Samples

The scale stems from a questionnaire sent to 1,163 German industrial companies, of which 143 participated, yielding a return rate of 12.3%. The study used a triadic design approach, where the general manager, the marketing or sales director and an accountant of the same company were questioned. Altogether, 105 usable triads were returned.

Scale Indicators and Reliability / Validity Parameters

Scale: from 1 (definitely false) to 5 (definitely true)

Information on individual indicators regarding "Learning Tool (Cost Accounting) [Kostenrechnung als Lernapparat]"			
Description of indicators	*Item to Total-Correlation*	*Indicator-Reliability*	*t statistic*
1. Die Kostenrechnungsinformationen erweitern meine Kenntnisse über das Geschäft, in dem ich tätig bin.	0.67	0.68	14.37
2. Die Kostenrechnungsinformationen tragen mir zum allgemeinen Verständnis der Situation meiner Geschäftseinheit bei.	0.75	0.85	16.85
3. Kostenrechnungsinformationen ermöglichen mir einen Überblick über die Zusammenhänge in meinem Geschäftsbereich.	0.63	0.57	12.89

Information on scale "Learning Tool (Cost Accounting) [Kostenrechnung als Lernapparat]"			
Descriptive Statistics		*Result of Exploratory Factor Analysis*	
Cronbach's alpha:	0.83	Total variance explained:	0.75
Results of Confirmatory Factor Analysis			
Factor reliability:	0.87	Average variance explained:	0.70

References

***Aust, R.* (1999): Kostenrechnung als unternehmensinterne Dienstleistung, Wiesbaden 1999, pp. 103-104.**

119. Logistics Controlling Basis [Logistik-Controlling-Basis]

Scale Description

The scale measures in detail which tasks are performed by a company's logistics department in order to plan and control those logistical activities.

Origin

The scale was newly developed by Blum (2006).

Samples

Survey data were collected by questionnaire, administered to logistics managers of 1,394 German companies in the manufacturing industry. A total of 316 usable questionnaires (23%) were returned.

Scale Indicators and Reliability / Validity Parameters

Scale: from 1 (definitely false) to 7 (definitely true)

Information on individual indicators regarding "Logistics Controlling Basis [Logistik-Controlling-Basis]"			
Description of indicators	*Item to Total-Correlation*	*Indicator-Reliability*	*t statistic*
1. Logistischen Leistungen werden von uns detailliert erfasst.	0.73	0.59	36.42
2. Für die Logistik werden keine detaillierten Kennzahlen ermittelt. (R)	0.57	0.40	30.30
3. Wir führen regelmäßig Benchmarking im Bereich Logistik durch.	0.58	0.45	32.10
4. Es existiert ein ausführliches Berichtswesen für die Logistik.	0.73	0.61	36.79
5. Zur Entscheidungsunterstützung in der Logistik werden regelmäßig Sonderanalysen (z.B. Investitionsrechnung, Wertanalysen, Simulationen) durchgeführt.	0.66	0.51	33.89
6. Es erfolgt eine detaillierte Planung von gesonderten Logistikkosten.	0.71	0.60	36.46
7. Für Logistikkosten werden explizit genaue Zielvorgaben festgelegt (Target Costing bei Produkten).	0.70	0.59	36.13
8. Für logistische Leistungen werden feste Ziele/Planwerte festgelegt.	0.72	0.59	36.39
9. Für Kennzahlen in der Logistik existieren klare Ziele/Planwerte.	0.78	0.68	38.44
10. Es erfolgt eine ausführliche Budgetplanung für die Logistik.	0.76	0.67	38.20
11. Es werden umfassende Soll-/Ist-Vergleiche durchgeführt.	0.76	0.66	37.98
12. Für logistische Leistungen werden regelmäßig Abweichungsanalysen durchgeführt.	0.76	0.65	37.81
13. Für Kennzahlen der Logistik werden durchgängig Soll-/Ist-Vergleiche durchgeführt.	0.75	0.66	37.79
14. Es werden intensive Abweichungsanalysen für Logistikbudgets durchgeführt.	0.72	0.60	36.52

Information on scale "Logistics Controlling Basis [Logistik-Controlling-Basis]"			
Descriptive Statistics		*Result of Exploratory Factor Analysis*	
Cronbach's alpha:	0.94	Total variance explained:	0.57
Results of Confirmatory Factor Analysis			
χ^2-Value (Degrees of Freedom):	78.71 (77)	χ^2-Value/Degrees of Freedom:	1.72
p Value:	0.42	RMSEA:	0.01
SRMR:	–*	CFI:	1.00
GFI:	0.99	AGFI:	0.99
Factor reliability:	0.95	Average variance explained:	0.59

*Not available

References

Blum, H. S. **(2006): Logistik-Controlling. Kontext, Ausgestaltung und Erfolgswirkungen, Wiesbaden 2006, pp. 115-119.**

120. Logistics Controlling Cost Details [Logistik-Controlling-Kostendetails]

Scale Description

The scale measures to which extent costs of a company's logistics department are accounted for in calculations, e.g. as fixed element of profit and loss accounts for products or customers.

Origin

The scale was newly developed by Blum (2006).

Samples

Survey data were collected by questionnaire, administered to logistics managers of 1,394 German companies in the manufacturing industry. A total of 316 usable questionnaires (23%) were returned.

Scale Indicators and Reliability / Validity Parameters

Scale: from 1 (definitely false) to 7 (definitely true)

Information on individual indicators regarding "Logistics Controlling Cost Details [Logistik-Controlling-Kostendetails]"			
Description of indicators	*Item to Total-Correlation*	*Indicator-Reliability*	*t statistic*
1. Logistikkosten werden explizit aus der Kostenrechnung detailliert ermittelt (z.B. auf Vollkostenbasis).	0.53	0.41	12.43
2. Für eine detaillierte Ermittlung gesonderter Logistik-kosten existiert eine Prozeßkostenrechnung bzw. Activity Based Costing.	0.46	0.40	12.43
3. Alle Logistikkosten sind explizit fester Bestandteil der Produktkalkulation.	0.48	0.36	12.43
4. Logistikkosten werden vollständig und separat in unserer Kundenerfolgsrechnung berücksichtigt.	0.54	0.51	12.43
5. Logistikkosten sind kein gesonderter Bestandteil unserer Vertriebserfolgsrechnung. (R)	0.39	0.27	12.43

Information on scale "Logistics Controlling Cost Details [Logistik-Controlling-Kostendetails]"			
Descriptive Statistics		*Result of Exploratory Factor Analysis*	
Cronbach's alpha:	0.72	Total variance explained:	0.48
Results of Confirmatory Factor Analysis			
χ^2-Value (Degrees of Freedom):	11.44 (5)	χ^2-Value/Degrees of Freedom:	2.29
p Value:	0.04	RMSEA:	0.07
SRMR:	–*	CFI:	0.99
GFI:	0.99	AGFI:	0.97
Factor reliability:	0.76	Average variance explained:	0.39

*Not available

References

Blum, H. S. **(2006): Logistik-Controlling. Kontext, Ausgestaltung und Erfolgswirkungen, Wiesbaden 2006, pp. 115-121.**

121. Logistics Performance over Time [Logistikerfolg über Zeit]

Scale Description

The scale measures manager´s assessment of the logistic department's performance over time.

Origin

The scale was newly developed by Blum (2006).

Samples

Survey data were collected by questionnaire, administered to logistics managers of 1,394 German companies in the manufacturing industry. A total of 316 usable questionnaires (23%) were returned.

Scale Indicators and Reliability / Validity Parameters

Scale: from 1 (definitely false) to 7 (definitely true)

Information on individual indicators regarding "Logistics Performance over Time [Logistikerfolg über Zeit]"			
Description of indicators	*Item to Total-Correlation*	*Indicator-Reliability*	*t statistic*
1. Es ist uns gelungen, unsere Logistikkosten in Relation zum Umsatz stetig zu senken.	0.58	0.39	21.11
2. Unsere Liefertreue hat sich konstant verbessert.	0.78	0.75	26.99
3. Es ist uns gelungen, unsere Lieferzeiten kontinuierlich zu verringern.	0.76	0.72	26.66
4. Wir haben unsere Durchlaufzeiten stetig verkürzt.	0.71	0.60	24.86
5. Wir konnten unsere Bestände kontinuierlich senken.	0.56	0.36	20.53
6. Bezüglich unserer Lieferflexibilität haben wir uns stetig verbessert.	0.75	0.69	26.00
7. Wir haben unsere Lieferfähigkeit/-bereitschaft kontinuierlich erhöht.	0.81	0.79	27.22

Information on scale "Logistics Performance over Time [Logistikerfolg über Zeit]"			
Descriptive Statistics		*Result of Exploratory Factor Analysis*	
Cronbach's alpha:	0.90	Total variance explained:	0.64
Results of Confirmatory Factor Analysis			
χ^2-Value (Degrees of Freedom):	20.89 (14)	χ^2-Value/Degrees of Freedom:	1.49
p Value:	0.10	RMSEA:	0.04
SRMR:	–*	CFI:	1.00
GFI:	0.99	AGFI:	0.99
Factor reliability:	0.92	Average variance explained:	0.61

*Not available

References

Blum, H. S. (2006): Logistik-Controlling. Kontext, Ausgestaltung und Erfolgswirkungen, Wiesbaden 2006, pp. 121-124.

122. Management Attention on Cost Accounting [Aufmerksamkeit des Managements für die Kostenrechnung]

Scale Description

The scale measures the extent, to which top management is interested in the processes and output of the accounting department, e.g. by actively being involved in the adaptation of processes.

Origin

The scale was newly developed by Frank (2000) based on research of Franz/Robey (1986).

Samples

The questionnaire was sent to a random sample of small- and medium-sized German companies from the industrial sector. 493 responses could be integrated into the analysis, yielding a response rate of close to 17%.

Scale Indicators and Reliability / Validity Parameters

Scale: from 1 (definitely false) to 5 (definitely true)

Information on individual indicators regarding "Management Attention on Cost Accounting [Aufmerksamkeit des Managements für die Kostenrechnung]"			
Description of indicators	*Item to Total-Correlation*	*Indicator-Reliability*	*t statistic*
1. Die Geschäftsleitung interessiert sich sehr für die Gestaltung der Kostenrechnung.	0.75	0.57	21.12
2. Die Geschäftsleitung bringt häufig ihre Vorstellung bei der Veränderung der Kostenrechnung ein.	0.71	0.53	19.91
3. Die Geschäftsleitung fördert die Verwendung von Informationen der Kostenrechnung im Unternehmen.	0.70	0.51	19.25
4. Die Veränderung/Anpassung der Kostenrechnung wird von der Geschäftsleitung mit großer Aufmerksamkeit betrieben.	0.80	0.64	22.02

Information on scale "Management Attention on Cost Accounting [Aufmerksamkeit des Managements für die Kostenrechnung]"			
Descriptive Statistics		*Result of Exploratory Factor Analysis*	
Cronbach's alpha:	0.88	Total variance explained:	0.74
Results of Confirmatory Factor Analysis			
χ^2-Value (Degrees of Freedom):	3.98 (2)	χ^2-Value/Degrees of Freedom:	1.99
RMSEA:	0.08	CFI:	0.99
GFI:	0.99	AGFI:	0.96
Factor reliability:	0.88	Average variance explained:	0.56

References

***Frank, S.* (2000): Erfolgreiche Gestaltung der Kostenrechnung: Determinanten und Wirkungen am Beispiel mittelständischer Unternehmen, Wiesbaden 2000, 129-130.**

Franz, C. R./Robey, D. (1986): Organizational Contexts, User Involvement, and the Usefulness of Informations Systems, in: Decision Sciences, Vol. 17, pp. 329-356.

123. Management Involvement

Scale Description

The scale measures the level of management involvement in selecting improvement projects and approving the formation of improvement teams.

Origin

A major international management consulting firm developed the construct in 1991.

Samples

Ittner and Larcker (1997) examined the use and performance consequences of strategic control systems using survey data collected by a major international management consulting firm during 1991. The survey covered the automobile and computer industries in Canada, Germany, Japan, and the United States. All automobile assemblers and a random sample of their suppliers were invited to participate. A total of 249 organizations agreed to participate, representing an 85% response rate.

Comments

The scale emerged from a principal component analysis used to reduce the dimensionality of 36 questions from a survey assessing the extent to which organizations employ strategic control practices discussed in the quality literature.

Scale Indicators and Reliability / Validity Parameters

Scale: 1 (never), 2 (seldom), 3 (occasionally), 4 (usually), 5 (always or almost always)

Information on individual indicators regarding "Management Involvement"			
Description of indicators			
1. To what extent does management approve the formation of teams?			
2. To what extent does management approve the projects worked on by teams?			
Information on scale "Management Involvement"			
Descriptive Statistics		*Result of Exploratory Factor Analysis*	
Cronbach's alpha:	0.81	Total variance explained:	–*

*Not available

References

Ittner, C. D./Larcker, D. F. **(1997): Quality Strategy, Strategic Control Systems, and Organizational Performance, in: Accounting, Organizations and Society, Vol. 22, pp. 293-314.**

124. Managerial Performance

Scale Description

The scale measures the degree of managerial performance by a self-rating scale. The nine-dimensional seven-point Likert-type scale instrument includes eight items that attempt to capture the multi-dimensional nature of performance and an overall performance dimension.

Origin

Developed by Mahoney et al. (1963, 1965).

Samples

Chong and Bateman (2000) chose eighty large manufacturing firms located in Perth, Western Australia, randomly from the Kompass Australia (1996) business directory. From these companies, the names of 150 middle-level managers were gathered; 120 agreed to participate. Finally, a total of 84 questionnaires were returned, yielding a response rate of 70%. Of these, 5 were not fully completed. This leaves the study with 79 usable responses, a usable response rate of 65.83% for data analysis.

Comments

The scale has been previously used extensively in management accounting and control research (e.g. Brownell and Dunk (1991); Lau et al. (1997); Chong (1998)). Chong and Bateman (2000) reported a scale mean of 5.50 and a standard deviation of 1.24 on an actual range of 2-7.

Scale Indicators and Reliability / Validity Parameters

Scale: from 1 (very low) to 7 (very high)

Information on individual indicators regarding "Managerial Performance"			
Description of indicators			
1. Planning			
2. Investigating			
3. Coordinating			
4. Evaluating			
5. Supervising			
6. Staffing			
7. Negotiating			
8. Representing			
9. Overall performance			
Information on scale "Managerial Performance"			
Descriptive Statistics		*Result of Exploratory Factor Analysis*	
Cronbach's alpha:	–*	Total variance explained:	–*

*Not available

References

***Chong, V. K./Bateman, D.* (2000): The Effects of Role Stress on Budgetary Participation and Job Satisfaction-Performance Linkages: A Test of Two Different Models, in: Advances in Accounting Behavioral Research, Vol. 3, pp. 91-118.**

Brownell, P./Dunk, A. S. (1991): Task Uncertainty and Its Interaction with Budgetary Participation and Budget Emphasis: Some Methodological Issues and Empirical Investigation, in: Accounting, Organizations and Society, Vol. 16, pp. 693-703.

Chong, V. K. (1998): Testing the Contingency „Fit“ between Management Accounting Systems and Managerial Performance: A Research Note on the Moderating Role of Tolerance for Ambiguity, in: The British Accounting Review, Vol. 30, pp. 331-342.

Lau, C. M./Low, L. C./Eggleton, I. R. C. (1997): The Interactive Effect of Budget Emphasis, Participation and Task Difficulty on Managerial Performance: A Cross-Cultural Study, in: Accounting, Auditing & Accountability Journal, Vol. 10, pp. 175-197.

Mahoney, T. A./Jerdee, T. H./Carroll, S. J. (1963): Development of Managerial Performance: A Research Approach, Cincinnati 1963.

Mahoney, T. A./Jerdee, T. H./Carroll, S. J. (1965): The Job(s) of Management, in: Industrial Relations, Vol. 4, pp. 97-110.

125. Manipulation of Performance Measures

Scale Description

The scale measures the extent to which managers manipulate budgetary data.

Origin

The scale was developed by Merchant (1990).

Samples

Field interviews were conducted in two Fortune 300 U.S. divisionalized manufacturing corporations. Both people from staff and line positions were interviewed. The most intensive interviewing was done with profit center managers. Survey data were collected by questionnaire, administered to 62 profit center managers of a Fortune 300 U.S. divisionalized manufacturing corporation. A total of 59 usable questionnaires (95%) were returned.

Comments

The questions about the manipulation of performance measures were not asked in the questionnaire but only in the interview phase of the study to avoid negative reactions to the questionnaire.

Scale Indicators and Reliability / Validity Parameters

Scale: from 1 (never) to 4 (frequently)

Information on individual indicators regarding "Manipulation of Performance Measures"
Description of indicators
1. I pulled profits from future periods into the current period by: a) deferring a needed expenditure; b) accelerating a sale.
2. I shifted funds between accounts to avoid budget overruns.
3. I bought equipment from outside so that the design portion of the expenditure could be capitalized, even though the job could have been done as well within.

Information on scale "Manipulation of Performance Measures"			
Descriptive Statistics		*Result of Exploratory Factor Analysis*	
Cronbach's alpha:	–*	Total variance explained:	–*

*Not available

References

Merchant, K. A. **(1990): The Effects of Financial Controls on Data Manipulation and Management Myopia, in: Accounting, Organizations and Society, Vol. 15, pp. 297-313.**

126. Market-based Performance [Marktbezogener Erfolg]

Scale Description

The scale measures manager's assessment of the company's success in terms of market-based indicators.

Origin

The scale was newly developed by Spillecke (2006) based on items by Schäffer/Willauer (2002) and Sandt (2004). Willauer (2005) used a similar approach.

Samples

Survey data were collected by questionnaire, administered via e-mail to 3,312 German managers of companies with at least 200 employees. The companies were from different industrial sectors. A total of 415 usable questionnaires (12.5%) were returned.

Scale Indicators and Reliability / Validity Parameters

Scale: from 1 (very bad) to 5 (very good)

Information on individual indicators regarding "Market-based Performance [Marktbezogener Erfolg]"			
Description of indicators	*Item to Total-Correlation*	*Indicator-Reliability*	*t statistic*
1. Erreichung des angestrebten Wachstums	0.72	–*	–*
2. Erreichung des angestrebten Marktanteils	0.72	–*	–*

Information on scale "Market-based Performance [Marktbezogener Erfolg]"			
Descriptive Statistics		*Result of Exploratory Factor Analysis*	
Cronbach's alpha:	0.83	Total variance explained:	0.86

*Not feasible

References

***Spillecke, D.* (2006): Interne Kundenorientierung des Controllerbereichs. Messung – Erfolgsauswirkungen – Determinanten, Wiesbaden 2006, pp. 167-168.**

Sandt, J. (2004): Management mit Kennzahlen und Kennzahlensystemen. Bestandsaufnahme, Determinanten und Erfolgswirkungen, Wiesbaden 2004.

Schäffer, U./Willauer, B. (2002): Kontrolle, Effektivität der Planung und Erfolg von Geschäftseinheiten - Ergebnisse einer empirischen Erhebung, in: Zeitschrift für Planung, Vol. 13, pp. 73-97.

Willauer, B. (2005): Consensus as a Key Success Factor in Strategy-Making, Wiesbaden 2005.

127. Market Dynamics [Marktdynamik]

Scale Description

The scale measures manager´s assessment of the market dynamics the company has to face, e.g. fast-changing customer demands.

Origin

The scale is based on items by Farrell (2000).

Samples

Survey data were collected by questionnaire, administered to business unit leaders of 3,500 German companies with 100 to 2,000 employees from the industrial sector. A total of 449 usable questionnaires (12.8%) were returned.

Comments

Three of five items had to be eliminated due to a lack of Item-to-Total Correlation.

Scale Indicators and Reliability / Validity Parameters

Scale: from 1 (definitely false) to 5 (definitely true)

Information on individual indicators regarding "Market Dynamics [Marktdynamik]"			
Description of indicators	*Item to Total-Correlation*	*Indicator-Reliability*	*t statistic*
1. In unserem Geschäft ändern sich die Kundenanforderungen ziemlich stark über die Zeit.	0.49	_*	_*
2. Unsere Kunden suchen ständig nach neuen Produkten.	0.49	_*	_*

Information on scale "Market Dynamics [Marktdynamik]"			
Descriptive Statistics		*Result of Exploratory Factor Analysis*	
Cronbach's alpha:	0.66	Total variance explained:	0.75

*Not feasible

References

***Schäffer, U./Steiners, D.* (2004): Zur Nutzung von Controllinginformationen, in: Zeitschrift für Planung und Unternehmenssteuerung, Vol. 15, pp. 377-404.**

Farrell, M. A. (2000): Developing a Market-Oriented Learning Organisation, in: Australian Journal of Management, Vol. 25, pp. 201-223.

128. Market Orientation

Scale Description

The scale measures the extent to which functional managers in a business unit direct their efforts towards the needs of the market.

Origin

Willauer (2005) created the scale drawing on approaches of Ruekert (1992), Greenley (1995) and Deshpandé/Farley (1998).

Samples

Survey data were collected by questionnaire, administered to managers of planning departments of 4,186 German companies from the industrial sector. A total of 298 usable questionnaires (7.1%) were returned.

Scale Indicators and Reliability / Validity Parameters

Scale: from 1 (definitely false) to 7 (definitely true)

Information on individual indicators regarding "Market Orientation"			
Description of indicators	*Item to Total-Correlation*	*Indicator-Reliability*	*t statistic*
1. In this business unit, the functional managers frequently con-tact their customers and suppliers to find out which products and services they will demand and supply in the future.	0.51	0.34	12.37
2. Our functional managers lead conferences or workshops at least once per term to discuss trend and developments in the relevant markets.	0.65	0.62	14.16
3. Our functional managers frequently meet to discuss re-actions on changes in our business unit.	0.75	0.91	14.61
4. When something relevant happens concerning an impor-tant customer or market , nearly the whole business unit is informed about it within a very short time.	0.47	0.30	11.89

Information on scale "Market Orientation"			
Descriptive Statistics		*Result of Exploratory Factor Analysis*	
Cronbach's alpha:	0.78	Total variance explained:	0.61
Results of Confirmatory Factor Analysis			
χ^2-Value (Degrees of Freedom):	2.09 (2)	χ^2-Value/Degrees of Freedom:	1.05
p Value:	0.35	RMSEA:	0.01
SRMR:	–*	CFI:	1.00
GFI:	1.00	AGFI:	0.99
Factor reliability:	0.82	Average variance explained:	0.54

*Not available

References

***Willauer, B.* (2005): Consensus as a Key Success Factor in Strategy-Making, Wiesbaden 2005, pp. 201-204.**

Deshpandé, R./Farley, J. U. (1998) : The Market Orientation Construct: Correlations, Culture, and Comprehensiveness, in: Journal of Market Focused Management, Vol. 2, pp. 237-239.

Greenley, G. E. (1995): Market Orientation and Company Performance: Empirical Evidence From UK Companies, in: British Journal of Management, Vol. 6, pp. 1-13.

Ruekert, R. W. (1992): Developing a market orientation: An organizational strategy perspective, in: International Journal of Research in Marketing, Vol. 9, pp. 225-245.

129. Market Research

Scale Description

The scale measures the frequency or importance of customer surveys, market research studies, and competitor comparison measurement in monitoring the organization's competitive position and strategy implementation process.

Origin

A major international management consulting firm developed the construct in 1991.

Samples

Ittner and Larcker (1997) examined the use and performance consequences of strategic control systems using survey data collected by a major international management consulting firm during 1991. The survey covered the automobile and computer industries in Canada, Germany, Japan, and the United States. All automobile assemblers and a random sample of their suppliers were invited to participate. A total of 249 organizations agreed to participate, representing an 85% response rate.

Comments

The scale emerged from a principal component analysis used to reduce the dimensionality of 36 questions from a survey assessing the extent to which organizations employ strategic control practices discussed in the quality literature.

Scale Indicators and Reliability / Validity Parameters

Scale:

Item no. 1: 1 (never), 2 (rarely), 3 (frequently), 4 (regularly)

Item no. 2: 1 (not at all), 2 (irregularly), 3 (yearly), 4 (several times a year), 5 (quarterly), 6 (monthly), 7 (weekly or more often)

Item no. 3: 1 (slight or not at all), 2 (secondary), 3 (major), 4 (primary)

Information on individual indicators regarding "Market Research"			
Description of indicators			
1. How often are market surveys used to monitor the position of your operations?			
2. How often are market research studies used to evaluate the implementation of your organization's total quality performance?			
3. How often are competitor comparison measurements in your organization's strategic planning process?			
Information on scale "Market Research"			
Descriptive Statistics		*Result of Exploratory Factor Analysis*	
Cronbach's alpha:	0.62	Total variance explained:	–*

*Not available

References

***Ittner, C. D./Larcker, D. F.* (1997): Quality Strategy, Strategic Control Systems, and Organizational Performance, in: Accounting, Organizations and Society, Vol. 22, pp. 293-314.**

130. Meeting Participation (for Quality Discussion)

Scale Description

The scale measures the percentage of senior managers, middle managers, and non-management personnel participating in meetings whose primary purpose is discussing quality.

Origin

A major international management consulting firm developed the construct in 1991.

Samples

Ittner and Larcker (1997) examined the use and performance consequences of strategic control systems using survey data collected by a major international management consulting firm during 1991. The survey covered the automobile and computer industries in Canada, Germany, Japan, and the United States. All automobile assemblers and a random sample of their suppliers were invited to participate. A total of 249 organizations agreed to participate, representing an 85% response rate.

Comments

The scale emerged from a principal component analysis used to reduce the dimensionality of 36 questions from a survey assessing the extent to which organizations employ strategic control practices discussed in the quality literature.

Scale Indicators and Reliability / Validity Parameters

Scale: 1 (never), 2 (seldom), 3 (occasionally), 4 (usually), 5 (always or almost always)

Information on individual indicators regarding "Meeting Participation (for Quality Discussion)"
Description of indicators
1. What percentage of senior management participates in meetings whose primary purpose is to discuss quality?
2. What percentage of middle management participates in meetings whose primary purpose is to discuss quality?
3. What percentage of first-line supervisors participates in meetings whose primary purpose is to discuss quality?

Information on scale "Meeting Participation (for Quality Discussion)"			
Descriptive Statistics		*Result of Exploratory Factor Analysis*	
Cronbach's alpha:	0.87	Total variance explained:	–*

*Not available

References

***Ittner, C. D./Larcker, D. F.* (1997): Quality Strategy, Strategic Control Systems, and Organizational Performance, in: Accounting, Organizations and Society, Vol. 22, pp. 293-314.**

131. Mentoring

Scale Description

The scale measures two career mentoring functions (career-related mentoring, and protection and assistance) and two psychological support functions (social support and role modeling).

Origin

Adapted from scales used in previous mentoring research (Chao and Walz (1992); Dreher and Ash (1990); Noe (1988)).

Samples

Viator (2001) collected data through a mail survey of 3,000 CPAs in large public accounting firms. A mailing list was obtained from the American Institute of CPAs, with support provided by the institute's academic relations division. A total of 903 surveys were returned, representing a 30% response rate. 13 responses were deleted for coding errors or incomplete surveys. Of the remaining 890 responses, other participants excluded from this study were 25 who had left public accounting, 27 who were employed by either regional of local public firms, and 44 who were partners/directors in large firms. The remaining 794 participants were included in the study.

Comments

The scale consists of four „sub-constructs": Items 1-3: career-related mentoring, items 4-6: protection and assistance, items 7-12: social support, items 13-16 role modeling. Confirmatory factor analysis indicated that all items, expect two social support items, had significant factor loadings greater than 0.50. After dropping the two social support items, the remaining 14 items loaded on four separate factors.

Scale Indicators and Reliability / Validity Parameters

Scale: from 1 (strongly disagree) to 5 (strongly agree)

Information on individual indicators regarding "Mentoring"
Description of indicators
1. My mentor has recommended me (or supported me) in obtaining assignments which increased my contact with important clients.
2. My mentor has recommended me (or supported me) in obtaining assignments which increased my personal contact with important (key) managers or partners in the firm.
3. My mentor has recommended me (or supported me) in obtaining assignments which offered opportunities to learn new skills, or develop expertise in a specific area.
4. My mentor has alerted me to potential conflicts with managers (or partner) before I knew about their likes/dislikes, opinions on controversial topics, or the policies in the firm.
5. My mentor has helped me finish assignments or meet deadlines that otherwise would have been difficult to complete.
6. My mentor has kept me informed about what is going on at higher levels, or how external conditions are influencing the firm.
7. My mentor has discussed concerns I have regarding feeling of competence, relationship with peers and supervisors, and/or work/family conflicts.

8.	My mentor has encouraged me to talk openly about anxiety and fears that detract from my work.
9.	My mentor has conveyed empathy for the concerns and feelings I have discussed.
10.	My mentor has conveyed feelings of respect for me as an individual. (item dropped due to load factor loadings and significant cross-loadings)
11.	My mentor has shared personal experiences as an alternative perspective to my problems.
12.	My mentor has discussed my concerns about advancement opportunities with the firm. (item dropped due to load factor loadings and significant cross-loadings)
13.	I tried to model my behavior after my mentor.
14.	I admire my mentor's ability to motivate others.
15.	I respect my mentor's knowledge of the accounting profession.
16.	I respect my mentor's ability to teach and instruct others.

Information on scale "Mentoring"			
Descriptive Statistics		*Result of Exploratory Factor Analysis*	
Cronbach's alpha:	0.89 to 0.96, depending on sub-constructs	Total variance explained:	–*

*Not available

References

Viator, R. E. (2001): The Association of Formal and Informal Public Accounting Mentoring with Role Stress and Related Job Outcomes, in: Accounting, Organizations and Society, Vol. 26, pp. 73-93.

Chao, G. T./Walz, P. M. (1992): Formal and Informal Mentorships: A Comparison on Mentoring Functions and Contrast with Nonmentored Counterparts, in: Personnel Psychology, Vol. 45, pp. 619-636.

Dreher, G. F./Ash, R. (1990): A Comparative Study of Mentoring among Men and Women in Managerial, Professional, and Technical Positions, in: Journal of Applied Psychology, Vol. 75, pp. 539-546.

Noe, R. A. (1988): An Investigation of the Determinants of Successful Assigned, in: Personnel Psychology, Vol. 41, pp. 457-479.

132. Meta-Communication [Metakommunikation]

Scale Description

The scale measures the extent to which the process of interaction between team members is discussed in management teams on a meta-level.

Origin

The scale was newly developed by Spieker (2004) following Martin's approach (1998).

Samples

Survey data were collected by questionnaire, administered via internet to 353 managers of German start-up companies. A total of 145 usable questionnaires (41.1%) were returned.

Scale Indicators and Reliability / Validity Parameters

Scale: from 1 (definitely false) to 7 (definitely true)

Information on individual indicators regarding "Meta-Communication [Metakommunikation]"			
Description of indicators	*Item to Total-Correlation*	*Indicator-Reliability*	*t statistic*
1. Während oder nach einer Diskussion im Team thematisieren wir die Art und Weise, wie wir miteinander diskutieren.	0.77	0.73	11.58
2. Diese Art des Feedbacks ist konkret und von konstruktiven Vorschlägen begleitet.	0.72	0.66	11.48
3. Wir haben versucht, Spielregeln aufzustellen, wie wir angemessen miteinander diskutieren.	0.71	0.52	10.88
4. Wir machen uns viele Gedanken über die Art der Interaktion in unserem Team.	0.57	0.34	7.95

Information on scale "Meta-Communication [Metakommunikation]"			
Descriptive Statistics		*Result of Exploratory Factor Analysis*	
Cronbach's alpha:	0.84	Total variance explained:	0.70
Results of Confirmatory Factor Analysis			
χ^2-Value (Degrees of Freedom):	2.08 (2)	χ^2-Value/Degrees of Freedom:	1.04
p Value:	0.02	RMSEA:	0.02
SRMR:	–*	CFI:	1.00
GFI:	0.99	AGFI:	0.98
Factor reliability:	0.83	Average variance explained:	0.56

*Not available

References

Spieker, M. **(2004): Entscheidungen in Gründerteams. Determinanten – Parameter – Erfolgsauswirkungen, Wiesbaden 2004, pp. 235-236.**

Martin, A. (1998): Affekt, Kommunikation und Rationalität in Entscheidungsprozessen: Ergebnisse einer Studie über den Einfluß von Gruppenstrukturen auf das Problemlösungsverhalten, München 1998.

133. Model Affirmation [Modellbestätigung]

Scale Description

The scale measures the extent to which managers use MAS information to confirm their own attitudes and beliefs.

Origin

The scale is based on indicators developed by Vandenbosch (1993).

Samples

Survey data were collected by questionnaire, administered to business unit leaders of 3,500 German companies with 100 to 2,000 employees from the industrial sector. A total of 449 usable questionnaires (12.8%) were returned.

Comments

Scale Indicators and Reliability / Validity Parameters

Scale: from 1 (definitely false) to 5 (definitely true)

Information on individual indicators regarding "[Modellbestätigung]"			
Description of indicators	*Item to Total-Correlation*	*Indicator-Reliability*	*t statistic*
1. Die Informationen des Controllingsystems helfen mir, meine bestehenden Annahmen zu bestätigen.	0.64	0.52	15.83
2. Die Informationen des Controllingsystems helfen mir, meine Perspektiven zu untermauern.	0.76	0.90	21.42
3. Die Informationen des Controllingsystems helfen mir, meine Handlungen zu unterstützen.	0.60	0.44	14.44

Information on scale "[Modellbestätigung]"			
Descriptive Statistics		*Result of Exploratory Factor Analysis*	
Cronbach's alpha:	0.81	Total variance explained:	0.73
Results of Confirmatory Factor Analysis			
Factor reliability:	0.83	Average variance explained:	0.62

References

***Schäffer, U./Steiners, D.* (2004): Zur Nutzung von Controllinginformationen, in: Zeitschrift für Planung und Unternehmenssteuerung, Vol. 15, pp. 377-404.**

Vandenbosch, B. (1993): Executive Support System Impact Viewed from a Learning Perspective, Ontario 1993.

134. Model Change [Modelländerung]

Scale Description

The scale measures the extent to which managers use MAS information to adjust their own attitudes and beliefs.

Origin

The scale is based on items developed by Vandenbosch (1993).

Samples

Survey data were collected by questionnaire, administered to business unit leaders of 3,500 German companies with 100 to 2,000 employees from the industrial sector. A total of 449 usable questionnaires (12.8%) were returned.

Comments

Scale Indicators and Reliability / Validity Parameters

Scale: from 1 (definitely false) to 5 (definitely true)

Information on individual indicators regarding "Model Change [Modelländerung]"			
Description of indicators	*Item to Total-Correlation*	*Indicator-Reliability*	*t statistic*
1. Die Informationen des Controllingsystems helfen mir, meine Kreativität zu fördern.	0.68	0.54	17.33
2. Die Informationen des Controllingsystems helfen mir, mein Denken neu auszurichten.	0.82	0.81	23.27
3. Die Informationen des Controllingsystems helfen mir, meinen Blickwinkel zu erweitern.	0.77	0.70	20.84
4. Die Informationen des Controllingsystems helfen mir, meine bisherigen Ansichten zu überdenken.	0.69	0.56	17.95

Information on scale "Model Change [Modelländerung]"			
Descriptive Statistics		*Result of Exploratory Factor Analysis*	
Cronbach's alpha:	0.88	Total variance explained:	0.73
Results of Confirmatory Factor Analysis			
χ^2-Value (Degrees of Freedom):	6.21(2)	χ^2-Value/Degrees of Freedom:	3.11
p Value:	0.05	RMSEA:	0.07
NFI:	0.99	NNFI:	0.99
SRMR:	0.01	CFI:	1.0
GFI:	0.99	AGFI:	0.97
Factor reliability:	0.88	Average variance explained:	0.65

References

***Schäffer, U./Steiners, D.* (2004): Zur Nutzung von Controllinginformationen, in: Zeitschrift für Planung und Unternehmenssteuerung, Vol. 15, pp. 377-404.**

Vandenbosch, B. (1993): Executive Support System Impact Viewed from a Learning Perspective, Ontario 1993.

135. Monitoring [Kontrolle]

Scale Description

The scale indicates manager´s perception of the controlling staff's involvement and scope of activities in the process of analyzing deviations and developing recommendations for future decisions.

Origin

The scale was newly developed by Bauer (2002).

Samples

Survey data were collected by questionnaire, administered via mail to 2,527 German companies. A total of 347 companies sent usable answers, yielding a 14.8% return rate.

Comments

The study used a dyadic design approach, where a manager and a controller of the same company were questioned. The data for this scale sole stem from the answers of the managers.

Scale Indicators and Reliability / Validity Parameters

Scale: from 1 (definitely false) to 7 (definitely true)

Information on individual indicators regarding "Monitoring [Kontrolle]"			
Description of indicators	*Item to Total-Correlation*	*Indicator-Reliability*	*t statistic*
1. Unser Controller analysiert Plan-Ist-Abweichungen nach deren Ursachen.	0.70	0.59	27.2
2. Unser Controller erarbeitet konkrete Maßnahmen bzw. Lösungsansätze.	0.80	0.76	28.6
3. Aus den Ergebnissen der Kontrolle heraus entwickelt unser Controller Vorschläge zur besseren Umsetzung von zukünftigen Entscheidungen.	0.82	0.81	29.1
4. Unser Controller interpretiert die Kontrollergebnisse kritisch, um die Prämissen von zukünftigen Entscheidungen zu verbessern.	0.79	0.73	28.5

Information on scale "Monitoring [Kontrolle]"			
Descriptive Statistics		*Result of Exploratory Factor Analysis*	
Cronbach's alpha:	0.90	Total variance explained:	0.77
Results of Confirmatory Factor Analysis			
χ^2-Value (Degrees of Freedom):	4.48 (2)	χ^2-Value/Degrees of Freedom:	2.24
p Value:	0.11	RMSEA:	0.04
NFI:	1.00	NNFI:	–*
GFI:	1.00	AGFI:	0.99
Factor reliability:	0.91	Average variance explained:	0.72

*Not available

References

Bauer, M. **(2002): Controllership in Deutschland. Zur erfolgreichen Zusammenarbeit von Controllern und Managern, Wiesbaden 2002, pp. 199-201.**

136. Monitoring Ability

Scale Description

The scale measures the extent to which an organization can monitor a division manager's decision making and behavior. It comprises five dimensions: specific action controls, results control, personnel control, detail in control reports and frequency of reporting

Origin

The scale was developed by Kren (1993). He developed an overall monitoring measure based on the characterization of control system techniques developed by Merchant (1982, 1985). As Merchant did not explicitly include the organization's information system in his control system typology, although he suggested that information for control should be precise and timely, Kren (1993) added two questions in his questionnaire to measure the detail in control reports and the frequency of reporting.

Samples

Survey data were collected using a questionnaire survey sent to 192 executive level profit center managers from 96 Fortune-500 manufacturing firms. 154 potential respondents remained after excluding managers that had retired, left the company, or had changed to new positions. A total of 80 usable questionnaires (51.9%) were returned. In addition, ten profit center managers contacted through a university executive program participated in the study so that finally 90 questionnaires were used for analysis.

Scale Indicators and Reliability / Validity Parameters

Scale: Item no. 1-8: from 1 (very little) to 7 (a great deal); Item no. 9: from 1 (aggregated, summaries only) to 7 (highly detailed, breakdown by unit and task); Item no. 10: daily, weekly, biweekly, monthly, quarterly, longer

Information on individual indicators regarding "Monitoring Ability"
Description of indicators
1. Decision making is affected by: approval limits for capital expenditures
2. Decision making is affected by: approval levels for headcount
3. Decision making is affected by: pre-action reviews for specific projects
4. Decision making is affected by: pre-action reviews for day-to-day activities
5. Decision making is affected by: policies and procedures manuals
6. Decision making is affected by: formal meetings to review your decisions
7. Decision making is affected by: required explanations for variance from plan
8. Decision making is affected by: informal contracts with your superiors
9. How much detail is included in control reports to managers at your superior's level, such as reports showing budget and actual data?
10. What is the reporting frequency of control reports to managers at your superior's level, such as reports showing budget and actual data?

Information on scale "Monitoring Ability"			
Descriptive Statistics		*Result of Exploratory Factor Analysis*	
Cronbach's alpha:	0.77	Total variance explained:	–*

*Not available

References

***Kren, L.* (1993): Control System Effects on Budget Slack, in: Advances in Management Accounting, Vol. 2, pp. 109-118.**

Merchant, K. A. (1982): The Control Function of Management, in: Sloan Management Review, Vol. 23, pp. 43-55.

Merchant, K. A. (1985): Control in Business Organizations, Boston 1985.

137. Monitoring (Ex Post Learning) [Kontrolle – Lernen ex post]

Scale Description

The scale measures the extent to which managers use MAS information for the monitoring of specific relations of means and ends.

Origin

The first indicator stems from Karlshaus´ (2000) scale of instrumental use of information. The last three items were newly developed by Schäffer/Steiners (2004).

Samples

Survey data were collected by questionnaire, administered to business unit leaders of 3,500 German companies with 100 to 2,000 employees from the industrial sector. A total of 449 usable questionnaires (12.8%) were returned.

Scale Indicators and Reliability / Validity Parameters

Scale: from 1 (definitely false) to 5 (definitely true)

Information on individual indicators regarding "Monitoring (Ex Post Learning) [Kontrolle – Lernen ex post]"			
Description of indicators	*Item to Total-Correlation*	*Indicator-Reliability*	*t statistic*
1. Die Informationen helfen mir bei der Überwachung der Aktivität in meinem Verantwortungsbereich.	0.62	0.52	15.83
2. Die Informationen helfen mir dabei, Abweichungen vom angestrebten Ziel zu Erkennen.	0.67	0.63	17.81
3. Ich nutze die Informationen zur Kontrolle wichtiger Erfolgsgrößen (z.B. Kosten, Deckungsbeiträge).	0.61	0.49	15.39
4. Die Informationen helfen mir, die Umsetzung meiner Entscheidungen zu überwachen (z.B. durch Soll/Ist-Werte).	0.55	0.37	12.94

Information on scale "Monitoring (Ex Post Learning) [Kontrolle – Lernen ex post]"			
Descriptive Statistics		*Result of Exploratory Factor Analysis*	
Cronbach's alpha:	0.79	Total variance explained:	0.63
Results of Confirmatory Factor Analysis			
χ^2-Value (Degrees of Freedom):	1.98 (2)	χ^2-Value/Degrees of Freedom:	0.99
p Value:	0.38	RMSEA:	0.00
NFI:	1.00	NNFI:	1.00
SRMR:	0.01	CFI:	1.00
GFI:	1.00	AGFI:	0.99
Factor reliability:	0.79	Average variance explained:	0.49

References

***Schäffer, U./Steiners, D.* (2004): Zur Nutzung von Controllinginformationen, in: Zeitschrift für Planung und Unternehmenssteuerung, Vol. 15, pp. 377-404.**

Karlshaus, J. T. (2000): Die Nutzung von Kostenrechnungsinformationen im Marketing, Wiesbaden 2000.

138. Monitoring Intensity – Analysis [Intensität der Kontrolle – Analyse]

Scale Description

Control intensity measures the amount of effort in the process of control. The scale is operationalized by the intensity different causes for potential deviations and alternatives are analyzed in detail.

Origin

Developed by Schäffer and Willauer (2002).

Samples

Schäffer and Willauer (2002) used a survey questionnaire sent to a total of 4,186 business units of German companies. The survey led to an effective sample of 298 questionnaires, which corresponds to a response rate of 7.1%.

Scale Indicators and Reliability / Validity Parameters

Scale: from 1 (strongly disagree) to 7 (strongly agree)

Information on individual indicators regarding "Monitoring Intensity – Analysis [Intensität der Kontrolle – Analyse]"			
Description of indicators	*Item to Total-Correlation*	*Indicator-Reliability*	*t statistic*
1. Die Soll-Ist Abweichungen werden gründlichst analysiert.	–*	0.70	–*
2. Im Rahmen der Abweichungsanalyse gehen wir in die Tiefe.	–*	0.84	–*
3. Im Rahmen der Abweichungsanalyse werden verschiedene Abweichungsursachen genau beleuchtet.	–*	0.88	–*
4. Die an der Abweichungsanalyse Beteiligten setzen sich intensiv mit den zu kontrollierenden Leistungsprozessen auseinander.	–*	0.79	–*
5. Die an der Abweichungsanalyse Beteiligten geben sich sehr viel Mühe.	–*	0.63	–*

Information on scale "Monitoring Intensity – Analysis [Intensität der Kontrolle – Analyse]"			
Descriptive Statistics		*Result of Exploratory Factor Analysis*	
Cronbach's alpha:	0.92	Total variance explained:	–*
Results of Confirmatory Factor Analysis			
Factor reliability:	0.94	Average variance explained:	0.50

*Not available

References

Schäffer, U./Willauer, B. **(2002): Kontrolle, Effektivität der Planung und Erfolg von Geschäftseinheiten - Ergebnisse einer empirischen Erhebung, in: Zeitschrift für Planung, Vol. 13, pp. 73-97.**

139. Monitoring of Assumptions [Prämissenkontrolle]

Scale Description

The scale measures the degree to which premises of subsidiaries set during the planning and implementation process are monitored by the central controlling department.

Origin

Developed by Eckey and Schäffer (2006) based on Schreyögg/Steinmann (1987).

Samples

Eckey and Schäffer (2006) collected data using a survey questionnaire sent to a total of 51 group controlling departments of management holdings listed in the German Prime Standard. The sample of companies represented a variety of industries. 37 usable responses were received, yielding a response rate of 72.5%.

Comments

Eckey and Schäffer (2006) reported a mean of 5.70 and standard deviation of 1.04 on a theoretical range of 1-7.

Scale Indicators and Reliability / Validity Parameters

Scale: from 1 (strongly disagree) to 7 (strongly agree)

Information on individual indicators regarding "Monitoring of Assumptions [Prämissenkontrolle]"			
Description of indicators	*Item to Total-Correlation*	*Indicator-Reliability*	*t statistic*
1. Wir überprüfen, ob die formulierte Strategie der Tochtergesellschaft vor dem Hintergrund interner und externer Veränderungen weiterhin begründet ist.	0.60	0.40	4.07
2. Wir kontrollieren die im Rahmen der strategischen Planung gesetzten Prämissen auf ihre Gültigkeit bei der derzeitigen und der zu erwartenden internen Ressourcensituation.	0.81	0.88	6.70
3. Wir kontrollieren die im Rahmen der strategischen Planung gesetzten Prämissen auf ihre Gültigkeit in Bezug auf externe Chancen und Risiken.	0.79	0.79	6.23

Information on scale "Monitoring of Assumptions [Prämissenkontrolle]"			
Descriptive Statistics		*Result of Exploratory Factor Analysis*	
Cronbach's alpha:	0.85	Total variance explained:	0.78
Results of Confirmatory Factor Analysis			
Factor reliability:	0.87	Average variance explained:	0.69

References

***Eckey, M./Schäffer, U.* (2006): Kontrolle von Mehrheitsbeteiligungen in börsennotierten Management-Holdings, in: Zeitschrift für Planung & Unternehmenssteuerung, Vol. 17, pp. 251-280.**

Schreyögg, G./Steinmann, H. (1987): Strategic Control: A new Perspective, in: Academy of Management Review, Vol. 12, pp. 91-103.

140. Neglect of Non-Monitored Areas [Vernachlässigung nichtkontrollierter Bereiche]

Scale Description

The scale measures the extent to which managers solely concentrate on aspects that are monitored in the process of budgetary control while neglecting areas that are not monitored.

Origin

The first two indicators of the 6-item dysfunctional behavior scale of Jaworski and MacInnis (1989) were used because they reflect the neglect of non-controlled areas. Three additional indicators were added to the scale.

Samples

Survey data were collected by questionnaire, administered to business unit leaders and the responsible controllers of these business units of 1,120 German companies from 500 to 5,000 employees. The companies were from services and industrial sectors. A total of 140 usable pairs of questionnaires (12.5%) were returned.

Comments

The dysfunctional behavior measure of Jaworski and MacInnis (1989) has been used by Ramaswami (1996), who found good reliability coefficients (Cronbach's alpha = 0.78). Ramaswami (1996) reported a mean of 2.45 and a standard deviation of 0.75.

Scale Indicators and Reliability / Validity Parameters

Scale: from 1 (definitely false) to 5 (definitely true)

Information on individual indicators regarding "Neglect of Non-Monitored Areas [Vernachlässigung nicht-kontrollierter Bereiche]"			
Description of indicators	*Item to Total-Correlation*	*Indicator-Reliability*	*t statistic*
1. Manager tendieren dazu, gewisse Aufgaben zu ignorieren, weil sie ohnehin nicht kontrolliert werden.	0.63	0.71	13.01
2. Manager arbeiten an unwichtigen Dingen, nur weil sie von ihren Vorgesetzten kontrolliert werden.	0.62	0.55	11.68
3. In Bereichen, die die Vorgesetzten nicht kontrollieren, geben sich die Manager weniger Mühe.	0.46	0.32	9.04

Information on scale "Neglect of Non-Monitored Areas [Vernachlässigung nicht-kontrollierter Bereiche]"			
Descriptive Statistics		*Result of Exploratory Factor Analysis*	
Cronbach's alpha:	0.74	Total variance explained:	0.66
Results of Confirmatory Factor Analysis			
Factor reliability:	0.76	Average variance explained:	0.76

References

Künkele, J./Schäffer, U. **(2007): Zur erfolgreichen Gestaltung der Budgetkontrolle, in: Die Betriebswirtschaft, Vol. 67, pp. 75-92.**

Jaworski, B. J./MacInnis, D. J. (1989): Marketing Jobs and Management Controls: Toward a Framework, in: Journal of Marketing Research, Vol. 26, pp. 406-419.

Ramaswami, S. N. (1996): Marketing Controls and Dysfunctional Employee Behaviors: A Test of Traditional and Contingency Theory Postulates, in: Journal of Marketing, Vol. 60, pp. 105-120.

141. Openness to Innovation [Innovationskultur]

Scale Description

The scale measures the extent a firm is open to innovation and reacts promptly to change.

Origin

The scale is based on items developed by Menon et al. (1999).

Samples

Survey data were collected by questionnaire, administered to business unit leaders of 3,500 German companies with 100 to 2,000 employees from the industrial sector. A total of 449 usable questionnaires (12.8%) were returned.

Comments

Scale Indicators and Reliability / Validity Parameters

Scale: from 1 (definitely false) to 5 (definitely true)

Information on individual indicators regarding "Openness to Innovation [Innovationskultur]"			
Description of indicators	*Item to Total-Correlation*	*Indicator-Reliability*	*t statistic*
1. Unser Unternehmen ist dynamisch und unternehmerfreudig.	0.62	0.50	15.55
2. Wichtige Informationen werden bei uns sofort offen kommuniziert.	0.66	0.57	16.90
3. Unser Unternehmen fördert Innovationen und Veränderung.	0.54	0.42	12.60
4. Die Zusammenarbeit im Management ist von gegenseitigem Vertrauen geprägt.	0.58	0.44	14.23

Information on scale "Openness to Innovation [Innovationskultur]"			
Descriptive Statistics		*Result of Exploratory Factor Analysis*	
Cronbach's alpha:	0.81	Total variance explained:	0.64
Results of Confirmatory Factor Analysis			
χ^2-Value (Degrees of Freedom):	3.29 (2)	χ^2-Value/Degrees of Freedom:	1.65
p Value:	0.19	RMSEA:	0.04
NFI:	1.0	NNFI:	0.99
SRMR:	0.01	CFI:	1.0
GFI:	1.0	AGFI:	0.98
Factor reliability:	0.81	Average variance explained:	0.52

References

***Schäffer, U./Steiners, D.* (2004): Zur Nutzung von Controllinginformationen, in: Zeitschrift für Planung und Unternehmenssteuerung, Vol. 15, pp. 377-404.**

Menon, A./Bharadwaj, S./Adidam, P. T./Edison, S. W. (1999): Antecedents and Consequences of Marketing Strategy Making: A Model and a Test, in: Journal of Marketing, Vol. 63, pp. 18-40.

142. Organizational Buy-in

Scale Description

The scale measures the degree of organizational buy-in, or an organization wide commitment and positive affect toward a marketing strategy.

Origin

Developed by Noble and Mokwa (1999).

Samples

The survey-based study conducted by Noble and Mokwa (1999) involved sampling from two firms: One firm was a large, multi state, financial services organization. Subjects were managers with extensive responsibilities for the implementation of marketing strategies. The other firm was a market share leader in the packaged goods industry. In this company, participants were regional sales managers with full responsibility for a geographic area, including discretionary budgets for promotions and responsibility for implementing corporate promotional strategies. The sample consisted of 254 managers in the financial services company and 534 managers in the packaged goods industry. Usable responses were 161 from the financial service company (63% response rate) and 325 from the other company (61% response rate). The total of 486 usable responses represents an overall 62% response rate.

Scale Indicators and Reliability / Validity Parameters

Scale: from 1 (strongly agree) to 5 (strongly disagree)

Information on individual indicators regarding "Organizational Buy-in"			
Description of indicators	*Item to Total-Correlation*	*Indicator-Reliability*	*t statistic*
1. Across the organization, there was a high level of „buy-in" for this strategy.	–*	0.597	7.36
2. Our work group felt like we were on our own in trying to make the strategy a success. (R)	–*	0.756	9.78
3. There was a general lack of support for this strategy across the organization. (R)	–*	0.739	9.52
4. There was a tremendous ground swell of support in the organization for this strategy.	–*	0.690	8.77

Information on scale "Organizational Buy-in"			
Descriptive Statistics		*Result of Exploratory Factor Analysis*	
Cronbach's alpha:	0.79	Total variance explained:	–*

*Not available

References

Noble, C. H./Mokwa, M. P. **(1999): Implementing Marketing Strategies: Developing and Testing a Managerial Theory, in: Journal of Marketing, Vol. 63, pp. 57-73.**

143. Organizational Commitment

Scale Description

The scale measures the extent to which a person identifies with and works toward organization-related goals and values.

Origin

Developed by Mowday et al. (1979).

Samples

The survey-based study conducted by Noble and Mokwa (1999) involved sampling from two firms: One firm was a large, multi state, financial services organization. Subjects were managers with extensive responsibilities for the implementation of marketing strategies. The other firm was a market share leader in the packaged goods industry. In this company, participants were regional sales managers with full responsibility for a geographic area, including discretionary budgets for promotions and responsibility for implementing corporate promotional strategies. The sample consisted of 254 managers in the financial services company and 534 managers in the packaged goods industry. Usable responses were 161 from the financial service company (63% response rate) and 325 from the other company (61% response rate). The total of 486 usable responses represents an overall 62% response rate.

Scale Indicators and Reliability / Validity Parameters

Scale: from 1 (strongly agree) to 5 (strongly disagree)

Information on individual indicators regarding "Organizational Commitment"			
Description of indicators	*Item to Total-Correlation*	*Indicator-Reliability*	*t statistic*
1. I really care about the fate of this company.	–*	0.612	8.11
2. I talk up this company to my friends as a great one to work for.	–*	0.811	11.87
3. I am extremely glad I chose this company to work for over others I was considering at the time I joined.	–*	0.748	10.55
4. I am proud to tell others that I am part of this company.	–*	0.868	13.18
5. This company really inspires the very best in me in the way of job performance.	–*	0.557	7.22
6. For me, this is the best of all possible companies for which to work.	–*	0.671	9.12
7. I would accept almost any type of job assignment in order to keep working for this company.	–*	0.367	4.51
8. I find that my values and the company's values are very similar.	–*	0.550	7.12
9. I am willing to put in a great deal of effort beyond that normally expected in order to help this company be successful.	–*	0.488	6.18

Information on scale "Organizational Commitment"			
Descriptive Statistics		*Result of Exploratory Factor Analysis*	
Cronbach's alpha:	0.86	Total variance explained:	–*

*Not available

References

Noble, C. H./Mokwa, M. P. **(1999): Implementing Marketing Strategies: Developing and Testing a Managerial Theory, in: Journal of Marketing, Vol. 63, pp. 57-73.**

Mowday, R. T./Steers, R. M./Porter, L. W. (1979): The Measurement of Organizational Commitment, in: Journal of Vocational Behavior, Vol. 14, pp. 224-247.

144. Organizational Performance (of Subsidiaries)

Scale Description

The scale measures the divisional headquarters' assessment of the subsidiary's influence on decisions concerning investments in new product lines and influence on where to place production units in the division.

Origin

Developed by Andersson et al. (2001).

Samples

Andersson et al. (2001) collected data from 98 subsidiaries belonging to 20 international divisions within 15 Swedish MNCs. The division headquarters were all located in Sweden. The majority of the subsidiaries were located in Europe and a few (five) in North America. The sample was chosen to represent a wide spectrum of Swedish industry and involves large and well-known companies in industries such as pulp and paper, telecommunications equipment, petrochemicals, power distribution, hard metal tools, saws and chains, gas applications, transportation, software, management training and industrial equipment.

Scale Indicators and Reliability / Validity Parameters

Scale: from 1 (very low) to 5 (very high)

Information on individual indicators regarding "Organizational Performance (of Subsidiaries)"			
Description of indicators	*Item to Total-Correlation*	*Indicator-Reliability*	*t statistic*
1. The subsidiary generally has a considerable influence on decisions concerning investments in new product lines.	–*	0.87	5.38
2. The subsidiary highly affects where to place production units within the global division in the next coming years.	–*	0.72	5.50

Information on scale "Organizational Performance (of Subsidiaries)"			
Descriptive Statistics		*Result of Exploratory Factor Analysis*	
Cronbach's alpha:	–*	Total variance explained:	–*

*Not available

References

Andersson, U./Forsgren, M./Pedersen, T. **(2001): Subsidiary Performance in Multinational Corporations: The Importance of Technology Embeddedness, in: International Business Review, Vol. 10, pp. 3-23.**

145. Output Quality [Ergebnisqualität]

Scale Description

The scale measures the quality of the controlling department's results from the viewpoint of the internal client.

Origin

The scale was newly developed by Spillecke (2006) based on Homburg (2000). Schäffer/Steiners used a similar operationalization in 2004.

Samples

Survey data were collected by questionnaire, administered via e-mail to 3,312 German managers of companies with at least 200 employees. The companies were from different industrial sectors. A total of 415 usable questionnaires (12.5%) were returned.

Scale Indicators and Reliability / Validity Parameters

Scale: from 1 (definitely false) to 5 (definitely true)

Information on individual indicators regarding "Output Quality [Ergebnisqualität]"			
Description of indicators	*Item to Total-Correlation*	*Indicator-Reliability*	*t statistic*
1. Die Arbeitsergebnisse des Controllings haben meine Qualitätsanforderungen immer voll erfüllt.	0.75	0.82	–
2. Ich konnte mich bisher nie über eine mangelnde Qualität der Arbeitsergebnisse des Controllings beklagen.	0.80	0.91	18.69
3. Die Arbeitsergebnisse des Controllings sind fehlerfrei.	0.71	0.76	16.78

Information on scale "Output Quality [Ergebnisqualität]"			
Descriptive Statistics		*Result of Exploratory Factor Analysis*	
Cronbach's alpha:	0.87	Total variance explained:	0.69
Results of Confirmatory Factor Analysis			
Factor reliability:	0.87	Average variance explained:	0.70

*Not feasible

References

Spillecke, D. (2006): Interne Kundenorientierung des Controllerbereichs. Messung – Erfolgsauswirkungen – Determinanten, Wiesbaden 2006, pp. 140-144.

Homburg, C. (2000): Kundennähe von Industriegüterunternehmen: Konzeptionen – Erfolgsauswirkungen – Determinanten, 3rd ed., Wiesbaden 2000.

Schäffer, U./Steiners, D. (2004): Zur Nutzung von Controllinginformationen, in: Zeitschrift für Planung und Unternehmenssteuerung, Vol. 15, pp. 377-404.

146. Output Quality (of Cost Accounting) [Ergebnisqualität der Kostenrechnung]

Scale Description

The scale measures the primary clients' assessment of the accounting department's output quality, e.g. scope, timeliness, accuracy.

Origin

The scale was developed by Aust (1999). A similar approach was used by Hunold (2003).

Samples

The scale stems from a questionnaire sent to 1,163 German industrial companies, of which 143 participated, yielding a return rate of 12.3%. The study used a triadic design approach, where the general manager, the marketing or sales director and an accountant of the same company were questioned. Altogether, 105 usable triads were returned.

Scale Indicators and Reliability / Validity Parameters

Scale: from 1 (definitely false) to 5 (definitely true)

Information on individual indicators regarding "Output Quality (of Cost Accounting) [Ergebnisqualität der Kostenrechnung]"			
Description of indicators	*Item to Total-Correlation*	*Indicator-Reliability*	*t statistic*
1. Die Breite des Informationsangebots der Kostenrechnung (Anzahl der Berichte und Analysen) entspricht meinen Vorstellungen.	0.70	0.69	15.15
2. Umfang und Detaillierungsgrad der einzelnen Berichte und Analysen der Kostenrechnung erfüllen meine Informationsbedürfnisse.	0.75	0.76	16.4
3. Die Informationen der Kostenrechnung bilden die tatsächlichen Verhältnisse wirklichkeitsgetreu ab.	0.76	0.65	14.49
4. Die Informationen der Kostenrechnung zeichnen sich durch eine große Genauigkeit aus.	0.67	0.52	12.38
5. Die Informationen der Kostenrechnung widersprechen einander teilweise. (R)	0.52	0.31	8.90
6. Die Informationen der Kostenrechnung basieren auf plausiblen Annahmen.	0.44	0.25	7.89
7. Die Informationen der Kostenrechnung sind frei von subjektiven Meinungen und Einflüssen.	0.42	0.18	6.44
8. Die Informationen der Kostenrechnung sind aktuell.	0.69	0.53	12.57
9. Die Informationen der Kostenrechnung sind fehlerfrei.	0.66	0.44	10.99
10. Die Kostenrechnung liefert mir häufig neue Informationen.	0.48	0.28	8.42
11. Die zur Erstellung der Kostenrechnungsinformationen verwendeten Methoden sind für mich leicht nachvoll-ziehbar.	0.54	0.35	9.64
12. Die Informationen der Kostenrechnung sind übersichtlich dargestellt.	0.64	0.56	13.01
13. Die von der Kostenrechnung bereitgestellten Informationen sind übersichtlich dargestellt.	0.62	0.50	12.12

Information on scale „Output Quality (of Cost Accounting) [Ergebnisqualität der Kosten-rechnung]"			
Descriptive Statistics		*Result of Exploratory Factor Analysis*	
Cronbach's alpha:	0.90	Total variance explained:	0.46
Results of Confirmatory Factor Analysis			
Factor reliability:	0.92	Average variance explained:	0.46

References

***Aust, R.* (1999): Kostenrechnung als unternehmensinterne Dienstleistung, Wiesbaden 1999, pp. 108-110.**

Hunold, C. (2003): Kommunale Kostenrechnung. Gestaltung, Nutzung und Erfolgsfaktoren, Wiesbaden 2003.

147. Output Quality (of the Controlling Department) [Ergebnisqualität der Controlling-Abteilung]

Scale Description

The scale measures the quality of the controlling department's output quality, e.g. scope, timeliness, accuracy.

Origin

The scale was newly developed by Bauer (2002) adapting items from Aust (1999).

Samples

Survey data were collected by questionnaire, administered via mail to 2,527 German companies. A total of 347 companies sent usable answers, yielding a 14.8% return rate.

Comments

The study used a dyadic design approach, where a manager and a controller of the same company were questioned. The data for this scale solely stem from the answers of the managers.

Scale Indicators and Reliability / Validity Parameters

Scale: from 1 (definitely false) to 7 (definitely true)

Information on individual indicators regarding "Output Quality [Ergebnisqualität der Controlling-Abteilung]"			
Description of indicators	*Item to Total-Correlation*	*Indicator-Reliability*	*t statistic*
1. Inhaltlich decken die Berichte alle für mich wichtigen Bereiche des Geschäfts ab.	0.70	0.58	23.4
2. Das Controlling bildet mit seinem Informationssystem die tatsächlichen Verhältnisse umfassend und wirklichkeitsgetreu ab.	0.78	0.72	25.4
3. Die Informationen aus unserem Controlling sind sehr genau.	0.79	0.77	26.3
4. Die Informationen aus unserem Controlling sind für mich aktuell genug.	0.71	0.59	23.9
5. Unser Controlling verwendet nachvollziehbare Methoden und Techniken.	0.67	0.56	23.4
6. Die Informationen aus unserem Controlling sind fehlerfrei.	0.64	0.50	22.3
7. Unser Controller liefert mir häufig neue Informationen.	0.64	0.43	21.0
8. Die aus unserem Controlling bereitgestellten Reports sind leicht verständlich.	0.70	0.60	24.0

Information on scale "Output Quality [Ergebnisqualität der Controlling-Abteilung]"			
Descriptive Statistics		*Result of Exploratory Factor Analysis*	
Cronbach's alpha:	0.91	Total variance explained:	0.61
Results of Confirmatory Factor Analysis			
χ^2-Value (Degrees of Freedom):	15.6 (20)	χ^2-Value/Degrees of Freedom:	0,78
p Value:	0.74	RMSEA:	0.00
NFI:	0.99	NNFI:	–*
SRMR:	–*	CFI:	1.00
GFI:	1.00	AGFI:	0.99
Factor reliability:	0.92	Average variance explained:	0.59

*Not available

References

***Bauer, M.* (2002): Controllership in Deutschland. Zur erfolgreichen Zusammenarbeit von Controllern und Managern, Wiesbaden 2002, pp. 216-218.**

Aust, R. (1999): Kostenrechnung als unternehmensinterne Dienstleistung, Wiesbaden 1999.

148. Participation [Partizipation]

Scale Description

The scale measures the extent to which all hierarchy levels and functional areas participate in the strategic planning process within a firm.

Origin

The scale was newly developed by Willauer as part of a doctoral research project. Results were published in Weber/Schäffer/Willauer (2003).

Samples

Data were collected by questionnaire, administered to planning department managers of 4,186 German industrial companies. A total of 298 usable questionnaires (7.1%) were returned.

Scale Indicators and Reliability / Validity Parameters

Scale: from 1 (definitely false) to 7 (definitely true)

Information on individual indicators regarding "Participation [Partizipation]"			
Description of indicators	*Item to Total-Correlation*	*Indicator-Reliability*	*t statistic*
1. Bei uns werden Ideen und Anregungen über Hierarchiestufen hinweg in den Prozess der strategischen/langfristigen Planung eingebracht.	0.55	0.44	12.57
2. Das planungsrelevante Wissen der dezentralen Einheiten wird im Rahmen der strategischen/langfristigen Planung von der Zentrale genutzt.	0.70	0.81	13.19
3. Im Prozess der strategischen/langfristigen Planung werden Informationen über Hierarchiestufen hinweg offen und frei ausgetauscht.	0.55	0.42	11.60
4. Dezentrale Einheiten bringen ihr Wissen in die strategische/langfristige Planung ein.	0.47	0.31	10.87

Information on scale "Participation [Partizipation]"			
Descriptive Statistics		*Result of Exploratory Factor Analysis*	
Cronbach's alpha:	0.77	Total variance explained:	0.59
Results of Confirmatory Factor Analysis			
χ^2-Value (Degrees of Freedom):	25.93 (2)	χ^2-Value/Degrees of Freedom:	12.96
p Value:	0.00	RMSEA:	0.02
SRMR:	–*	CFI:	1.00
GFI:	0.97	AGFI:	0.87
Factor reliability:	0.79	Average variance explained:	0.50

*Not available

References

***Weber, J /Schäffer, U./Willauer, B.* (2003): Skalenübersicht, in: Weber, J./Kunz, J. (Ed.): Empirische Controllingforschung: Begründung, Beispiele, Ergebnisse, Wiesbaden 2003, pp. 385-467.**

149. Participative Standard Setting

Scale Description

The scale measures the degree of subordinate participation in setting performance goals or standards.

Origin

Adapted from Shields and Young (1993).

Samples

480 questionnaires were distributed to automobile design engineers. Of 480 questionnaires distributed, 415 (86%) were returned. However, only 358 (74%) were usable because 46 respondents' self-reported job titles were not design engineers and 11 had missing data. These 358 usable subjects had a mean of 11.2 (SD=7.3, range=1-33) years of employment with the company and a mean of 7.8 (SD=6.1, range=0-32) years of experience in their current job assignment.

Comments

Shields et al. (2000) reported a scale mean of 31.49 and a standard deviation of 7.51 on an actual (theoretical) range of 8-49 (8-56).

Scale Indicators and Reliability / Validity Parameters

Scale: from 1 (extremely low) to 7 (extremely high)

Information on individual indicators regarding "Participative Standard Setting"
Description of indicators
1. The extent to which your superiors sought your input into the setting of your performance standards.
2. The extent to which your superiors sought your input in determining the amount of resources needed for your design assignments.
3. The importance that your superiors placed on including changes you had suggested in your performance standards.
4. The importance that your superiors placed on including changes you had suggested into the determination of the amount of resources to be provided for your design assignments.
5. The importance that your superiors placed on not finalizing your performance standards until you were satisfied with them.
6. The importance that your superiors placed on not finalizing the amount of resourced to be provided for your design assignments until you were satisfied with them.
7. Overall, the influence that you had in setting your performance standards.
8. Overall, the influence that you had in determining the amount of resources to be provided for your design assignments.

Information on scale "Participative Standard Setting"			
Descriptive Statistics		*Result of Exploratory Factor Analysis*	
Cronbach's alpha:	0.85	Total variance explained:	–*

*Not available

References

***Shields, M. D./Deng, F. J./Kato, Y.* (2000): The Design and Effects of Control Systems: Tests of Direct-and Indirect-Effects Models, in: Accounting, Organizations and Society, Vol. 25, pp. 185-202.**

Shields, M. D./Young, S. M. (1993): Antecedents and Consequences of Participative Budgeting: Evidence on the Effects of Asymmetrical Information, in: Journal of Management Accounting Research, Vol. 5, pp. 265-280.

150. Pay Equity

Scale Description

The scale measures the degree of perceived pay equity.

Origin

Developed by Quirin et al. (2001).

Samples

Data was collected using a survey questionnaire sent to a total of 240 managers from a cross-section of 15 large U.S. companies. The sample of companies represented a variety of industries. Of the 240 surveys distributed, respondents returned a total 105 usable surveys for a response rate of 44%.

Comments

Quirin et al. (2001) reported a scale mean of 24.18 and a standard deviation of 5.87 on a range of 11-35.

Scale Indicators and Reliability / Validity Parameters

Scale: from 1 (strongly disagree) to 7 (strongly agree)

Information on individual indicators regarding "Pay Equity"			
Description of indicators			
I feel my pay is equitable when compared to			
1. Others in this company at my job level.			
2. What other employers are paying for the type of work I am asked to do.			
3. What others below me in the company are being paid.			
4. What my superior is paid.			
5. What the company told me I would be paid.			
Information on scale "Pay Equity"			
Descriptive Statistics		*Result of Exploratory Factor Analysis*	
Cronbach's alpha:	0.89	Total variance explained:	–*

*Not available

References

Quirin, J. J./Donnelly, D. P./O'Bryan, D. **(2001): Antecedents of Organizational Commitment: The Role of Perception of Equity, in: Advances in Accounting Behavioral Research, Vol. 4, pp. 261-280.**

151. Perceived Effectiveness

Scale Description

The scale measures the degree to which marketers and engineers perceived that interactions with personnel from other functional areas (especially from product planning) were worthwhile, productive, and satisfying.

Origin

Adapted from Ruekert and Walker Jr. (1987).

Samples

Ayers et al. (1997) collected data on 19 new product development projects undertaken by a major U.S. computer manufacturer. Seven project members from each team were selected to participate in the study, five of whom were R&D and the remaining two from marketing. Of the 132 questionnaire booklets distributed, 115 usable surveys were returned.

Scale Indicators and Reliability / Validity Parameters

Scale: from 1 (strongly disagree) to 7 (strongly agree)

Information on individual indicators regarding "Perceived Effectiveness"
Description of indicators
1. To what extent did you have an effective working relationship with product planners?
2. To what did product planners carry out responsibilities and commitments to you?
3. To what extent did you carry out responsibilities and commitments to the product planners?
4. To what extent did you feel that the relationship between yourself and product planners was productive?
5. To what extent was the time and effort spent in developing and maintaining the relationship with product planners worthwhile?
6. Overall, to what extent were you satisfied with the relationship between yourself and the product planners?

Information on scale "Perceived Effectiveness"			
Descriptive Statistics		*Result of Exploratory Factor Analysis*	
Cronbach's alpha:	0.93	Total variance explained:	–*

*Not available

References

***Ayers, D./Dahlstrom, R./Skinner, S. J.* (1997): An Exploratory Investigation of Organizational Antecedents to New Product Success, in: Journal of Marketing Research, Vol. 34, pp. 107-116.**

Ruekert, R. W./Walker Jr., O. C. (1987): Marketing's Interaction with Other Functional Units: A Conceptual Framework and Empirical Evidence, in: Journal of Marketing, Vol. 51, pp. 1-19.

152. Perceived Environmental Uncertainty (PEU)

Scale Description

The scale measures the degree of environmental uncertainty public accounting employees are likely to experience from their work environment.

Origin

Based on scale items adopted from Rebele and Michaels (1990) and Otley and Pierce (1995).

Samples

Viator (2001) collected data through a mail survey of 3,000 CPAs in large public accounting firms. A mailing list was obtained from the American Institute of CPAs, with support provided by the institute's academic relations division.

A total of 903 surveys were returned, representing a 30% response rate. 13 responses were deleted for coding errors or incomplete surveys. Of the remaining 890 responses, other participants excluded from this study were 25 who had left public accounting, 27 who were employed by either regional of local public firms, and 44 who were partners/directors in large firms. The remaining 794 participants were included in the study.

Comments

Cronbach's alpha is slightly less than the 0.73 and 0.71 coefficients obtained by Rebele and Michaels (1990) and Ferris (1977), respectively.

Scale Indicators and Reliability / Validity Parameters

Scale: from 1 (strongly disagree) to 5 (strongly agree)

Information on individual indicators regarding "Perceived Environmental Uncertainty"			
Description of indicators			
1. I am almost always sure about what approaches would be best for dealing with job-related problems that arise on an engagement (client work). (R)			
2. I am almost always certain about how to deal with changes in social, economic, political, or technical conditions outside of the firm. (R)			
3. It is very often difficult for me to determine if a job-related decision is a correct one.			
4. I seldom know how to obtain information necessary for job-related decision-making.			
Information on scale "Perceived Environmental Uncertainty"			
Descriptive Statistics		*Result of Exploratory Factor Analysis*	
Cronbach's alpha:	0.69	Total variance explained:	–*

*Not available

References

***Viator, R. E.* (2001): The Association of Formal and Informal Public Accounting Mentoring with Role Stress and Related Job Outcomes, in: Accounting, Organizations and Society, Vol. 26, pp. 73-93.**

Ferris, K. R. (1977): Perceived Uncertainty and Job Satisfaction in the Accounting Environment, in: Accounting, Organizations and Society, Vol. 2, pp. 23-28.

Otley, D. T./Pierce, B. J. (1995): The Control Problem in Public Accounting Firms: An Empirical Study of the Impact of Leadership Style, in: Accounting, Organizations and Society, Vol. 20, pp. 405-420.

Rebele, J. E./Michaels, R. E. (1990): Independent Auditors' Role Stress: Antecedent, Outcome, and Moderating Variables, in: Behavioral Research in Accounting, Vol. 2, pp. 124-153.

153. Performance Compared to Competitors [Leistungsfähigkeit im Wettbewerbsvergleich]

Scale Description

The scale measures the management teams' assessment of the company's performance compared to competitors in different sectors, e.g. customer satisfaction, productivity and growth.

Origin

The scale was developed by Spieker (2004) following Burke (1984) and Kotabe (1990).

Samples

Survey data were collected by questionnaire, administered via internet to 353 managers of German start-up companies. A total of 145 usable questionnaires (41.1%) were returned.

Scale Indicators and Reliability / Validity Parameters

Scale: from 1 (very bad) to 7 (very good)

Information on individual indicators regarding "Performance Compared to Competitors [Leistungsfähigkeit im Wettbewerbsvergleich]"			
Description of indicators	*Item to Total-Correlation*	*Indicator-Reliability*	*t statistic*
Wie hat Ihr Unternehmen im Vergleich zu Ihren Konkurrenten in folgenden Bereichen abgeschnitten?			
1. …Erreichen von Kundenzufriedenheit.	0.49	0.25	10.83
2. …Erhaltung und Erweiterung des Kundenstamms.	0.61	0.48	14.35
3. …Anpassung von Produkten und Prozesse an neue Kundenbedürfnisse.	0.64	0.49	14.54
4. …Anpassung an Veränderungen in den Marktstrategien der Konkurrenten.	0.72	0.63	16.00
5. …Produktivität der Leistungserstellung.	0.60	0.33	12.52
6. …Effizienz des Managements.	0.80	0.71	16.64
7. …Wachstum.	0.62	0.49	14.57
8. …Umsatzrendite.	0.67	0.47	14.31

Information on scale "Performance Compared to Competitors [Leistungsfähigkeit im Wettbewerbsvergleich]"			
Descriptive Statistics		*Result of Exploratory Factor Analysis*	
Cronbach's alpha:	0.88	Total variance explained:	0.54
Results of Confirmatory Factor Analysis			
χ^2-Value (Degrees of Freedom):	33.41 (20)	χ^2-Value/Degrees of Freedom:	1.67
p Value:	0.20	RMSEA:	0.00
SRMR:	–*	CFI:	0.99
GFI:	0.98	AGFI:	0.96
Factor reliability:	0.88	Average variance explained:	0.48

*Not available

References

Spieker, M. **(2004): Entscheidungen in Gründerteams. Determinanten – Parameter – Erfolgsauswirkungen, Wiesbaden 2004, pp. 254-255.**

Burke, M. C. (1984): Strategic Choice and Marketing Managers: An Examination of Business-Level Marketing Objectives, in: Journal of Marketing Research, Vol. 21, pp. 345-359.

Kotabe, M. (1990): Corporate Product Policy and Innovative Behavior of European and Japanese Multinationals: An Empirical Investigation, in: Journal of Marketing, Vol. 54, pp. 19-33.

154. Performance (Concerning Customers) [Kundenbezogener Erfolg]

Scale Description

The scale measures manager's assessment of the company's success in terms of customer relationship management.

Origin

The scale was newly developed by Spillecke (2006) based on items by Schäffer/Willauer (2002) and Sandt (2004).

Samples

Survey data were collected by questionnaire, administered via e-mail to 3,312 German managers of companies with at least 200 employees. The companies were from different industrial sectors. A total of 415 usable questionnaires (12.5%) were returned.

Scale Indicators and Reliability / Validity Parameters

Scale: from 1 (very bad) to 5 (very good)

Information on individual indicators regarding "Performance (Concerning Customers) [Kundenbezogener Erfolg]"				
Description of indicators		*Item to Total-Correlation*	*Indicator-Reliability*	*t statistic*
1. Erzielung von hoher (Markt-) Kundenzufriedenheit		0.61	_*	_*
2. Erzielung eines hohen Nutzens für die (Markt-) Kunden		0.61	_*	_*
Information on scale "Performance (Concerning Customers) [Kundenbezogener Erfolg]"				
Descriptive Statistics		*Result of Exploratory Factor Analysis*		
Cronbach's alpha:	0.76	Total variance explained:		0.80

*Not feasible

References

***Spillecke, D.* (2006): Interne Kundenorientierung des Controllerbereichs. Messung – Erfolgsauswirkungen – Determinanten, Wiesbaden 2006, pp. 167-168.**

Sandt, J. (2004): Management mit Kennzahlen und Kennzahlensystemen. Bestandsaufnahme, Determinanten und Erfolgswirkungen 2004, Wiesbaden.

Schäffer, U./Willauer, B. (2002): Kontrolle, Effektivität der Planung und Erfolg von Geschäftseinheiten - Ergebnisse einer empirischen Erhebung, in: Zeitschrift für Planung, Vol. 13, pp. 73-97.

155. Personnel Control (in R&D Organizations)

Scale Description

The scale measures the extent to which reliance is placed on personnel control. The length of professional training and socialization processes to which they are exposed can represent an individual's level of professionalism. It is these processes which lead professionals to behave according to the collegial model of control noted by Perrow (1970).

Origin

Abernethy and Brownell (1997) used the measure of formal training from Hage and Aiken (1967).

Samples

Data were collected by both questionnaire and interview, administered to 150 senior research officers in the research and development (R&D) divisions of a large Australian industrial company and a major US scientific organization. A total of 138 questionnaires (92%) were returned, eleven of which were incomplete, resulting in a useable sample set of 127.

Comments

Abernethy and Brownell (1997) reported a mean of 5.30 and standard deviation of 0.96 on a theoretical range of 1-6.

Scale Indicators

Scale: from 1 (low) to 6 (high)

Information on individual indicators regarding "Personnel Control (in R&D Organizations)"
What level of formal education did you complete (Check one)
1. High school graduate (or less) with no professional training.
2. High school graduate (or less) with some professional training.
3. College degree, or some college education, but no professional training.
4. College degree, or some college education and some professional training.
5. Post-graduate degree, but no professional training.
6. Post-graduate degree and some professional training.

Information on scale "Personnel Control (in R&D Organizations)"			
Descriptive Statistics		*Result of Exploratory Factor Analysis*	
Cronbach's alpha:	–*	Total variance explained:	–*

*Not available

References

Abernethy, M. A./Brownell, P. **(1997): Management Control Systems in Research and Development Organizations: The Role of Accounting, Behavior, and Personnel Controls, in: Accounting, Organizations and Society, Vol. 22, pp. 233-248.**

Hage, J./Aiken, M. (1967): Relationship of Centralization to Other Structural Properties, in: Administrative Science Quarterly, Vol. 12, pp. 72-92.

Perrow, C. (1970): Organizational Analysis: A Sociologic View, London 1970.

156. Planning Intensity [Planungsintensität]

Scale Description

The scale measures how much time and energy is devoted to the strategic planning process.

Origin

The scale was newly developed by Willauer (2003).

Samples

Survey data were collected using a questionnaire survey sent to 4,186 business units of German companies from manufacturing and service industries. Controllers were asked to answer the questionnaire. A total of 298 usable questionnaires (7.1%) were returned.

Scale Indicators and Reliability / Validity Parameters

Scale: from 1 (definitely false) to 5 (definitely true)

Information on individual indicators regarding "Planning Intensity [Planungsintensität]"			
Description of indicators	*Item to Total-Correlation*	*Indicator-Reliability*	*t statistic*
1. Die zu planenden Sachverhalte werden im Rahmen der strategischen/langfristigen Planung gründlich untersucht.	0.74	0.66	24.31
2. Im Rahmen der strategischen/langfristigen Planung gehen wir in die Tiefe.	0.77	0.71	25.08
3. Im Rahmen der strategischen/langfristigen Planung werden die verschiedenen Alternativen genau beleuchtet.	0.74	0.65	24.38
4. Die an der strategischen/langfristigen Planung Beteiligten setzen sich intensiv mit den zu planenden Projekten/ Bereichen auseinander.	0.79	0.74	25.35
5. Die strategische/langfristige Planung ist bei uns ein sehr intensiver und aufwendiger Prozess.	0.78	0.71	24.93
6. Die an der strategischen/langfristigen Planung Beteiligten geben sich sehr viel Mühe.	0.76	0.68	24.93

Information on scale "Planning Intensity [Planungsintensität]"			
Descriptive Statistics		*Result of Exploratory Factor Analysis*	
Cronbach's alpha:	0.92	Total variance explained:	0.71
Results of Confirmatory Factor Analysis			
χ^2-Value (Degrees of Freedom):	6.89 (9)	χ^2-Value/Degrees of Freedom:	0.77
p Value:	0.65	RMSEA:	0.00
SRMR:	–*	CFI:	1.00
GFI:	1.00	AGFI:	0.99
Factor reliability:	0.93	Average variance explained:	0.69

*Not available

References

Willauer, B. **(2003): Gestaltung der Planung, in: Weber, J./Kunz, J. (Ed.): Empirische Controllingforschung: Begründung, Beispiele, Ergebnisse, Wiesbaden 2003, pp. 386-394.**

157. Planning Process Formalization

Scale Description
The scale measures the degree of emphasis organizations place on rules and procedures when developing marketing plans.

Origin
Derived from the work of John and Martin (1984) on organizational structure and marketing planning.

Samples
Data was gathered using questionnaires mailed to consumer goods product managers. Product managers were asked to focus on a single product for which they had been highly involved in developing the most recent marketing program. Names and addresses were obtained from the American Marketing Association's membership directory (192) and a purchasing mailing list (459). After removing names of people who were no longer with the company or whose addresses were incorrect, the sampling frame included 578 names. Andrews/Smith received 193 completed questionnaires, yielding a 33.4% response rate.

Comments
Andrews and Smith (1996) reported a mean of 3.37 and a standard deviation of 1.53.

Scale Indicators and Reliability / Validity Parameters
Scale: from 1 (strongly disagree) to 7 (strongly agree)

Information on individual indicators regarding "Planning Process Formalization"			
Description of indicators			
1. In my company, marketing plans have a specific format that is used by everyone.			
2. We have clearly defined procedures for completing each section of the marketing program.			
3. We are told exactly which information sources must be used to develop the marketing plan.			
4. We have a precise timetable for completing marketing plans.			
Information on scale "Planning Process Formalization"			
Descriptive Statistics		*Result of Exploratory Factor Analysis*	
Cronbach's alpha:	0.78	Total variance explained:	–*

*Not available

References

***Andrews, J./Smith, D. C.* (1996): In Search of the Marketing Imagination: Factors Affecting the Creativity of Marketing Programs for Mature Products, in: Journal of Marketing Research, Vol. 33, pp. 174-187.**

John, G./Martin, J. (1984): Effects of Organizational Structure of Marketing Planning on Credibility and Utilization of Plan Output, in: Journal of Marketing Research, Vol. 21, pp. 170-183.

158. Political Behavior

Scale Description

The scale measures the extent to which managers believe that a company's planning process is dominated by personal interests of the participants in contrast to objective decision-making.

Origin

The scale was newly developed by Willauer (2005) based on Dean/Sharfman (1996).

Samples

Survey data were collected by questionnaire, administered to managers of planning departments of 4,186 German companies from the industrial sector. A total of 298 usable questionnaires (7.1%) were returned.

Scale Indicators and Reliability / Validity Parameters

Scale: from 1 (definitely false) to 7 (definitely true)

Information on individual indicators regarding "Political Behavior"			
Description of indicators	*Item to Total-Correlation*	*Indicator-Reliability*	*t statistic*
1. Planning at our business unit is characterized by objective and technical reasons. (R)	0.48	0.31	12.79
2. The strategic/long-term planning process is characterized by a high degree of personal interests and power.	0.75	0.85	15.84
3. Within the strategic/long-term planning process, individual interests and their achievement dominate.	0.62	0.56	15.21
4. The strategic/long-term planning process is to a large extent a political process.	0.64	0.58	14.90

Information on scale "Political Behavior"			
Descriptive Statistics		*Result of Exploratory Factor Analysis*	
Cronbach's alpha:	0.81	Total variance explained:	0.64
Results of Confirmatory Factor Analysis			
χ^2-Value (Degrees of Freedom):	1.57 (2)	χ^2-Value/Degrees of Freedom:	0.78
p Value:	0.46	RMSEA:	0.00
SRMR:	–*	CFI:	1.00
GFI:	1.00	AGFI:	0.99
Factor reliability:	0.84	Average variance explained:	0.58

*Not available

References

***Willauer, B.* (2005): Consensus as a Key Success Factor in Strategy-Making, Wiesbaden 2005, pp. 204-206.**

Dean, J. W./Sharfman, M. P. (1996): Does Decision Process Matter? A Study of Strategic Decision Making Effectiveness, Academy of Management Journal, Vol. 39, pp. 369-396.

159. Potential Quality of Cost Accounting [Potenzialqualität der Kostenrechnung]

Scale Description

The scale measures the quality of the accounting department's potential and resources to fulfil its management support tasks, e.g. the quality of the IT equipment or the staff's business expertise.

Origin

The scale was newly developed by Aust (1999). He based the development of his indicators on the success factors of service provisions of Kleinaltenkamp (1998). A similar approach was used by Hunold (2003).

Samples

Survey data were collected by questionnaire administered to general managers as well as managers of accounting and marketing units from 1,163 German companies from the manufacturing industry which had more than 50 employees. A total of 105 usable triads of questionnaires (9%) were returned.

Scale Indicators and Reliability / Validity Parameters

Scale: from 1 (definitely false) to 5 (definitely true)

Information on individual indicators regarding "Potential Quality of Cost Accounting [Potenzial-qualität der Kostenrechnung]"			
Description of indicators	*Item to Total-Correlation*	*Indicator-Reliability*	*t statistic*
1. Die technische Ausstattung der Kostenrechung ermöglicht den Kostenrechnern eine problemlose Erfüllung ihrer Aufgaben.	0.47	0.40	7.49
2. Die personelle Ausstattung der Kostenrechnung ist ausreichend.	0.55	0.74	8.90
3. Die fachliche Kompetenz der Kostenrechnung erscheint mir sehr hoch.	0.36	0.20	5.87

Information on scale "Potential Quality of Cost Accounting [Potenzialqualität der Kostenrechnung]"			
Descriptive Statistics		*Result of Exploratory Factor Analysis*	
Cronbach's alpha:	0.64	Total variance explained:	0.58
Results of Confirmatory Factor Analysis			
Factor reliability:	0.69	Average variance explained:	0.44

*Not available

References

***Aust, R.* (1999): Kostenrechnung als unternehmensinterne Dienstleistung, Wiesbaden 1999, pp. 105-106.**

Hunold, C. (2003): Kommunale Kostenrechnung. Gestaltung, Nutzung und Erfolgsfaktoren, Wiesbaden 2003.

Kleinaltenkamp, M. (1998): Angebotsbearbeitung - Schnittstelle zwischen Kunden und Lieferanten: Kundenorientierte Angebotsbearbeitung für Investitionsgüter und industrielle Dienstleistungen, Berlin 1998.

160. Potential Quality of Controlling Department [Potenzialqualität der Controlling-Abteilung]

Scale Description

The scale measures the quality of the controlling department's potential and resources to fulfil its tasks in support of the management, e.g. the business expertise of the staff.

Origin

The scale was newly developed by Bauer (2002) adapting items from Aust (1999).

Samples

Survey data were collected by questionnaire, administered via mail to 2,527 German companies. A total of 347 companies sent usable answers, yielding a 14.8% return rate.

Comments

The study used a dyadic design approach, where a manager and a controller of the same company were questioned. The data for this scale solely stem from the answers of the managers. Three items were eliminated to increase reliability.

Scale Indicators and Reliability / Validity Parameters

Scale: from 1 (definitely false) to 7 (definitely true)

Information on individual indicators regarding "Potential Quality of Controlling Department [Potenzialqualität der Controlling-Abteilung]"			
Description of indicators	*Item to Total-Correlation*	*Indicator-Reliability*	*t statistic*
1. Die fachliche Kompetenz unserer Controller ist völlig ausreichend.	0.57	0.52	9.9
2. Unser Controller-Bereich kennt die wichtigsten Besonderheiten meines/unseres eigentlichen Geschäfts sehr gut.	0.53	0.56	9.9
3. Unser Controlling hat im Rahmen unserer Zusammenarbeit ausreichend Gelegenheit, seine Vorschläge und sein Wissen nutzbringend einzusetzen.	0.57	0.55	9.9

Information on scale "Potential Quality of Controlling Department [Potenzialqualität der Controlling-Abteilung]"			
Descriptive Statistics		*Result of Exploratory Factor Analysis*	
Cronbach's alpha:	0.73	Total variance explained:	0.54
Results of Confirmatory Factor Analysis			
Factor reliability:	0.78	Average variance explained:	0.65

References

Bauer, M. (2002): Controllership in Deutschland. Zur erfolgreichen Zusammenarbeit von Controllern und Managern, Wiesbaden 2002, pp. 212-214.

Aust, R. (1999): Kostenrechnung als unternehmensinterne Dienstleistung, Wiesbaden 1999.

161. Preparation of Decision Enforcement [Vorbereitung der Umsetzung der Entscheidung]

Scale Description

The scale measures the extent to which controllers are involved in the process of preparing the enforcement of organizational decisions, e.g. questioning budget data.

Origin

The scale was newly developed by Bauer (2002).

Samples

Survey data were collected by questionnaire, administered via mail to 2,527 German companies. A total of 347 companies returned usable answers, yielding a 14.8% return rate.

Comments

The study used a dyadic design approach, where a manager and a controller of the same company were questioned. The data for this scale stem from the answers of the managers and controllers.

Scale Indicators and Reliability / Validity Parameters

Scale: from 1 (definitely false) to 7 (definitely true)

Information on individual indicators regarding "Preparation of Decision Enforcement of [Vorbereitung der Umsetzung einer Maßnahme]"			
Description of indicators	*Item to Total-Correlation*	*Indicator-Reliability*	*t statistic*
1. Bei der Festlegung der konkreten Zielvorgaben, die sich aus der Entscheidung ergeben, unterstützt mich unser Controller maßgeblich.	0.59	0.63	23.2
2. Unser Controller sorgt dafür, dass die operativen Vorgaben der Umsetzung zur Zielerreichung geeignet sind.	0.69	0.64	23.1
3. Unser Controller weist auf widersprüchliche und unrealistische Zielsetzungen hin.	0.64	0.58	22.7
4. Die Vergabe von Ressourcen für die Umsetzung (Budgetierung) erfolgt unter maßgeblicher Beteiligung des Controllers.	0.69	0.46	21.5

Information on scale "Preparation of Decision Enforcement of [Vorbereitung der Umsetzung einer Maßnahme]"			
Descriptive Statistics		*Result of Exploratory Factor Analysis*	
Cronbach's alpha:	0.83	Total variance explained:	0.66
Results of Confirmatory Factor Analysis			
χ^2-Value (Degrees of Freedom):	2.71 (2)	χ^2-Value/Degrees of Freedom:	1.36
p Value:	0.26	RMSEA:	0.02
SRMR:	–*	CFI:	1.00
GFI:	1.00	AGFI:	0.99
Factor reliability:	0.85	Average variance explained:	0.58

*Not available

References

Bauer, M. **(2002): Controllership in Deutschland. Zur erfolgreichen Zusammenarbeit von Controllern und Managern, Wiesbaden 2002, pp. 197-199.**

162. Process Rationality (Assurance of) [Sicherer der Prozessrationalität]

Scale Description

The scale indicates in how far controllers perceive themselves as being responsible for the assurance of the quality of the management processes, e.g. ensuring efficient and effective planning and control.

Origin

The scale was newly developed by Bauer (2002).

Samples

Survey data were collected by questionnaire, administered via mail to 2,527 German companies. A total of 347 companies sent usable answers, yielding a 14.8% return rate.

Comments

The study used a dyadic design approach, where a manager and a controller of the same company were questioned. The data for this scale solely stem from the answers of the controllers.

Scale Indicators and Reliability / Validity Parameters

Scale: from 1 (definitely false) to 7 (definitely true)

Information on individual indicators regarding "Process Rationality (Assurance of) [Sicherer der Prozessrationalität]"			
Description of indicators	*Item to Total-Correlation*	*Indicator-Reliability*	*t statistic*
1. Wir schaffen generell die Bedingungen für eine effiziente Durchführung der Führungsprozesse in der Geschäftseinheit, wie z.B. bei Planung und Kontrolle.	0.66	0.65	16.5
2. Diese Führungsprozesse werden von uns ständig aktiv vorangetrieben.	0.80	0.79	16.9
3. Wir sichern die Qualität der Führungsprozesse.	0.76	0.66	16.4

Information on scale "Process Rationality (Assurance of) [Sicherer der Prozessrationalität]"			
Descriptive Statistics		*Result of Exploratory Factor Analysis*	
Cronbach's alpha:	0.86	Total variance explained:	0.74
Results of Confirmatory Factor Analysis			
Factor reliability:	0.88	Average variance explained:	0.70

References

***Bauer, M.* (2002): Controllership in Deutschland. Zur erfolgreichen Zusammenarbeit von Controllern und Managern, Wiesbaden 2002, pp. 189-191.**

163. Process Quality of Cost Accounting [Prozessqualität der Kostenrechnung]

Scale Description

The scale measures the extent to which the process of budgeting is supported by controllers. The scale comprises four dimensions: timeliness of supplied information, relevance of supplied information, adaptiveness of supplied information as well as explanations and advice from controllers.

Origin

The scale was newly developed by Aust (1999). He based the development of his indicators on the success factors of service provisions of Kleinaltenkamp (1998). A similar approach was used by Hunold (2003).

Samples

Survey data were collected by questionnaire administered to general managers as well as managers of accounting and marketing units from 1,163 German companies from the manufacturing industry, which had more than 50 employees. A total of 105 usable triads of questionnaires (9%) were returned.

Scale Indicators and Reliability / Validity Parameters

Scale: from 1 (definitely false) to 5 (definitely true)

Information on individual indicators regarding "Process Quality of Cost Accounting [Prozessqualität der Kostenrechnung]"			
Description of indicators	*Item to Total-Correlation*	*Indicator-Reliability*	*t statistic*
1. Zugesagte Termine für Leistungen der Kostenrechnung werden in der Regel eingehalten.	0.66	0.54	12.37
2. Aus meiner Sicht laufen die Prozesse der Erstellung von Standardberichten und Standardanalysen sehr zügig und ohne Verzögerungen ab.	0.64	0.53	12.29
3. Die Kostenrechner gehen sehr spezifisch auf meine individuellen Bedürfnisse ein.	0.71	0.66	14.23
4. Die Kostenrechner passen ihre Berichte und Analysen geschäftsbereichsinternen und -externen Veränderungen an.	0.74	0.69	14.77
5. Die Informationen der Kostenrechnung werden in ausreichendem Maße von Beratungen bzw. Erläuterungen durch die Kostenrechner begleitet.	0.67	0.62	13.69

Information on scale "Process Quality of Cost Accounting [Prozessqualität der Kosten-rechnung]"			
Descriptive Statistics		*Result of Exploratory Factor Analysis*	
Cronbach's alpha:	0.86	Total variance explained:	0.65
Results of Confirmatory Factor Analysis			
Factor reliability:	0.89	Average variance explained:	0.61

*Not available

References

Aust, R. **(1999): Kostenrechnung als unternehmensinterne Dienstleistung, Wiesbaden 1999, pp. 106-107.**

Hunold, C. (2003): Kommunale Kostenrechnung. Gestaltung, Nutzung und Erfolgsfaktoren, Wiesbaden 2003.

Kleinaltenkamp, M. (1998): Angebotsbearbeitung - Schnittstelle zwischen Kunden und Lieferanten: Kundenorientierte Angebotsbearbeitung für Investitionsgüter und industrielle Dienstleistungen, Berlin 1998.

164. Process Quality of Controlling Department [Prozessqualität der Controlling-Abteilung]

Scale Description

The scale measures the quality of the controlling department's processes in management support tasks, e.g. if the controlling staff is willing to answer additional questions and is responsive to the needs of the management.

Origin

The scale was newly developed by Bauer (2002) adapting items from Aust (1999).

Samples

Survey data were collected by questionnaire, administered via mail to 2,527 German companies. A total of 347 companies sent usable answers, yielding a 14.8% return rate.

Comments

The study used a dyadic design approach, where a manager and a controller of the same company were questioned. The data for this scale stem solely from the answers of the managers.

Scale Indicators and Reliability / Validity Parameters

Scale: from 1 (definitely false) to 7 (definitely true)

Information on individual indicators regarding "Process Quality of Controlling Department [Prozessqualität der Controlling-Abteilung]"			
Description of indicators	*Item to Total-Correlation*	*Indicator-Reliability*	*t statistic*
1. Aus meiner Sicht läuft die Erstellung von Standard-Berichten sehr zügig ab.	0.56	0.43	17.4
2. Unser Controller geht sehr spezifisch auf meine (Informations-)Bedürfnisse ein.	0.76	0.72	20.4
3. Der Controller passt seine Berichte und Analysen geschäftsbereichsinternen und -externen Veränderungen selbständig und zügig an.	0.63	0.64	18.6
4. Die Informationen aus unserem Controlling werden in ausreichendem Maße von Beratungen bzw. Erläuterungen durch den Controller begleitet.	0.66	0.54	18.6
5. Unser Controlling ist Rückfragen gegenüber jederzeit offen.	0.67	0.62	13.69
6. Um Entscheidungsunterstützung zu erhalten, frage ich aktiv unseren Controller.	0.61	0.53	18.4

Information on scale "Process Quality of Controlling Department [Prozessqualität der Controlling-Abteilung]"			
Descriptive Statistics		*Result of Exploratory Factor Analysis*	
Cronbach's alpha:	0.86	Total variance explained:	0.59
Results of Confirmatory Factor Analysis			
χ^2-Value (Degrees of Freedom):	9.55 (9)	χ^2-Value/Degrees of Freedom:	1.06
p Value:	0.39	RMSEA:	0.016
NFI:	0.99	NNFI:	–*
SRMR:	–*	CFI:	1.00
GFI:	1.00	AGFI:	0.99
Factor reliability:	0.88	Average variance explained:	0.60

*Not available

References

***Bauer, M.* (2002): Controllership in Deutschland. Zur erfolgreichen Zusammenarbeit von Controllern und Managern, Wiesbaden 2002, pp. 215-216.**

Aust, R. (1999): Kostenrechnung als unternehmensinterne Dienstleistung, Wiesbaden 1999.

165. Process Rationality [Prozedurale Rationalität]

Scale Description

The scale measures how regularly accounting information is asked for and used by managers.

Origin

The scale was newly developed by Hunold (2003) based on an approach of Dean/Sharfman (1996).

Samples

Survey data were collected by questionnaire administered to treasurers and accountants of 1,520 German municipalities as part of a dyadic research design. A total of 201 usable dyads (13.22%) were returned.

Scale Indicators and Reliability / Validity Parameters

Scale: from 1 (definitely false) to 7 (definitely true)

Information on individual indicators regarding "Process Rationality [Prozedurale Rationalität]"			
Description of indicators	*Item to Total-Correlation*	*Indicator-Reliability*	*t statistic*
1. Entscheidungen werden oftmals intuitiv getroffen (R).	0.37	0.19	7.67
2. Es werden zur Entscheidungsfindung möglichst viele verschiedene Informationen herangezogen.	0.58	0.55	10.67
3. Entscheidungen werden nicht „über Köpfe hinweg" getroffen.	0.66	0.66	10.42
4. Das Entscheidungsverhalten hat sich verbessert.	0.54	0.52	10.68

Information on scale "Process Rationality [Prozedurale Rationalität]"			
Descriptive Statistics		*Result of Exploratory Factor Analysis*	
Cronbach's alpha:	0.74	Total variance explained:	0.57
Results of Confirmatory Factor Analysis			
χ^2-Value (Degrees of Freedom):	3.08 (2)	χ^2-Value/Degrees of Freedom:	–*
p Value:	0.21	RMSEA:	0.05
SRMR:	–*	CFI:	1.00
GFI:	1.00	AGFI:	0.98
Factor reliability:	0.78	Average variance explained:	0.48

*Not available

References

Hunold, C. (2003): Kommunale Kostenrechnung. Gestaltung, Nutzung und Erfolgsfaktoren, Wiesbaden 2003, pp. 218-219.

Dean, J. W./Sharfman, M. P. (1996): Does Decision Process Matter? A Study of Strategic Decision Making Effectiveness, in: Academy of Management Journal, Vol. 39, pp. 369-396.

166. Product Complexity and Diversity

Scale Description

The scale measures the type of complexity and diversity of business. According to Cagwin and Bouwman (2002), a company's complexity increases as the breadth of its product line expands, as each product uses more unique components, and as more process options are available to manufacture the product or provide services (Swenson (1998)).

Origin

Developed by Estrin et al. (1994) and used by Krumwiede (1996), (1998).

Samples

A questionnaire was distributed to 1,058 internal auditing professionals. 204 completed usable responses were received. 134 are from the first and 67 from the second mailings, yielding a response rate of 21.2%. 65 responses (31.8%) indicate some use of ABC. The remaining 139 responses serve as a non-user control group.

Comments

Two items were eliminated to increase reliability.

Scale Indicators and Reliability / Validity Parameters

Scale: from 1 (strongly disagree) to 5 (strongly agree)

Information on individual indicators regarding "Product Complexity and Diversity"			
Description of indicators			
1. There are major differences in lot sizes between products.			
2. There are major changes in volumes within products.			
3. Over time, there are major changes in volumes within products.			
4. Costs of support departments are similar for each product.			
5. Product lines are diverse.			
6. Within product lines, products require similar processes to design, manufacture and distribute.			
7. There are frequent changes to your products, services, and processes.			
Information on scale "Product Complexity and Diversity"			
Descriptive Statistics		*Result of Exploratory Factor Analysis*	
Cronbach's alpha:	0.79	Total variance explained:	–*
Results of Confirmatory Factor Analysis			
χ^2-Value (Degrees of Freedom):	1.81 (4)	χ^2-Value/Degrees of Freedom:	0.45
p Value:	0.77	RMSEA:	0.012
NFI:	0.99	NNFI:	–*
SRMR:	–*	CFI:	–*
GFI:	1.00	AGFI:	0.99
Factor reliability:	–*	Average variance explained:	–*

*Not available

References

***Cagwin, D./Bouwman, M. J.* (2002): The Association between Activity-Based Costing and Improvement in Financial Performance, in: Management Accounting Research, Vol. 13, pp. 1-39.**

Estrin, T. L./Kantor, J./Albers, D. C. (1994): Is ABC Suitable for Your Company?, in: Management Accounting. Vol. 75, pp. 40-45.

Krumwiede, K. R. (1996): An Empirical Examination of Factors Affecting the Adoption and Infusion of Activity-Based Costing, Dissertation University of Tennessee 1996.

Krumwiede, K. R. (1998): The Implementation Stages of Activity-Based Costing and the Impact of Contextual and Organizational Factors, in: Journal of Management Accounting Research, Vol. 10, pp. 239-277.

Swenson, D. W. (1998): Managing Costs through Complexity Reduction at Carrier Corporation, in: Management Accounting, Vol. 79, pp. 20-28.

167. Professional Commitment

Scale Description

The scale measures the degree of commitment to an organization.

Origin

Developed by Porter et al. (1974), adapted by Aranya et al. (1981) to measure commitment to an organization.

Samples

Clikeman et al. (2001) surveyed 480 individuals beginning their careers with two Big 5 accounting firms. Sixty-six individuals did not provide demographic data or did not answer all the questions, resulting in 414 useable responses.

Most of the respondents were between the ages of 21 and 25 (86%); a little over half were female (55%); most had completed a 4-year bachelor's program. Another 21% had completed a master's program, while 19 (5%) had earned a second baccalaureate.

Comments

Clikeman et al. (2001) reported a scale mean of 5.36 and a standard deviation of 0.74. Many previous studies have used the instrument from Aranya et al. (1981) to measure accountants' professional commitment (Harrell et al. (1986); McGregor Jr. et al. (1989); Jeffrey and Weatherholt (1996)). Each of the aforementioned studies reported a high level of internal reliability for the instrument from Aranya et al. (1981).

Scale Indicators and Reliability / Validity Parameters

Scale: from 1 (strongly disagree) to 7 (strongly agree)

Information on individual indicators regarding "Professional Commitment"
Description of indicators
1. I am willing to put a great deal of effort beyond that normally expected in order to help make the accounting profession successful.
2. I talk up the accounting profession to my friends as a great profession to be associated with.
3. I feel very little loyalty to the accounting profession. (R)
4. I would accept almost any type of job assignment in order to keep working in areas that are associated with the accounting profession.
5. I find that my values and the accounting profession's values are very similar.
6. I am proud to tell others that I am part of the accounting profession.
7. I could just as well be associated with another profession as long as the type of work was similar. (R)
8. Being a member of the accounting profession really inspires the very best in me in the way of job performance.
9. It would take very little change in my present circumstances to cause me to work in areas that are not associated with the accounting profession. (R)
10. I am extremely glad that I chose the accounting profession to work for over others that I was considering at the time I joined.
11. There is not too much to be gained by sticking with the accounting profession indefinitely. (R)

12. Often, I find it difficult to agree with the accounting profession's policies on important matters relating to its members. (R)			
13. I really care about the fate of the accounting profession.			
14. For me, the accounting profession is the best of all possible professions of which to be a member.			
15. Deciding to be a member of the accounting profession was a definite mistake on my part. (R)			
Information on scale "Professional Commitment"			
Descriptive Statistics		*Result of Exploratory Factor Analysis*	
Cronbach's alpha:	0.85	Total variance explained:	–*

*Not available

References

***Clikeman, P. M./Schwartz, B. N./Lathan, M. H.* (2001): The Effect of the 150-Hour Requirement on New Accountants' Professional Commitment, Ethical Orientation, and Professionalism, in: Critical Perspectives on Accounting, Vol. 12, pp. 627-645.**

Aranya, N./Pollock, J./Amernic, J. (1981): An Examination of Professional Commitment in Public Accounting, in: Accounting, Organizations and Society, Vol. 6, pp. 271-280.

Harrell, A./Chewning, E./Taylor, M. (1986): Organizational-Professional Conflict and the Job Satisfaction and Turnover Intentions of Internal Auditors, in: Auditing, Vol. 5, pp. 109-121.

Jeffrey, C./Weatherholt, N. (1996): Ethical Development, Professional Commitment, and Rule Observance Attitudes: A Study of CPAs and Corporate Accountants, in: Behavioral Research in Accounting, Vol. 8, pp. 8-31.

McGregor Jr., C. C./Killough, L. N./Brown, R. M. (1989): An Investigation of Organizational-Professional Conflict in Management Accounting, in: Journal of Management Accounting Research, Vol. 1, pp. 104-118.

Porter, L. W./Steers, R. M./Mowday, R. T./Boulian, P. V. (1974): Organizational Commitment, Job Satisfaction, and Turnover among Psychiatric Technicians, in: Journal of Applied Psychology, Vol. 59, pp. 603-609.

168. Professionalism

Scale Description

The scale measures the degree of professionalism. Snizek (1972) designed the instrument to contain five statements related to each of the five dimensions of professionalism. Clikeman et al. (2001) measured the use of the professional organization as a referent (PO), belief in public service (PS), belief in self-regulation (SR), sense of calling (SC), and autonomy (AUTO) by the mean of the responses to the five statements corresponding to each dimension of professionalism.

Origin

Developed by Hall (1968) to measure professionalism using a 50-item questionnaire. Snizek (1972) reduced Hall's questionnaire to 25 items.

Samples

Clikeman et al. (2001) surveyed 480 individuals beginning their careers with two Big 5 accounting firms. Sixty-six individuals did not provide demographic data or did not answer all the questions, resulting in 414 useable responses.

Most of the respondents were between the ages of 21 and 25 (86%); a little over half were female (55%); most had completed a 4-year bachelor's program. Another 21% had completed a master's program, while 19 (5%) had earned a second baccalaureate.

Comments

The following table lists mean values and standard deviations of Clikeman et al. (2001) for the five professionalism variables:

Snizek's reduction of the 50-item questionnaire to 25 items only had a minimal effect on scale reliability. Morrow and Goetz Jr. (1988) used Snizek's 25-item instrument to study accounting practitioners' professionalism. Morrow/Goetz reported adequate levels of internal reliability and high correlations between measures of professionalism and professional behaviors. Kalbers and Fogarty (1995) adapted Snizek's instrument to study the professionalism of internal auditors. The alphas measured by Clikeman et al. (2001) were slightly lower than the values reported by Morrow and Goetz Jr. (1988).

Scale Indicators and Reliability / Validity Parameters

Scale: from 1 (very poorly) to 5 (very well)

Information on individual indicators regarding "Professionalism"
Description of indicators
1. I systematically read the professional journals.
2. Other professions are actually more vital to society than mine. (R)
3. I make my own decisions in regard to what is to be done in my work.
4: I regularly attend professional meetings at the local level.
5. I think that my profession, more than any other, is essential for society.
6. My fellow professionals have a pretty good idea about each other's competence.

7. People in this profession have a real „calling" for their work.			
8. The importance of my profession is sometimes overstressed. (R)			
9. The dedication of people in my field is most gratifying.			
10. I don't have much opportunity to exercise my own judgment.			
11. I believe that the professional organizations(s) should be supported.			
12. Some other occupations are actually more important to society than is mine. (R)			
13. A problem in this profession is that no one really knows what her/his colleagues are doing. (R)			
14. It is encouraging to see the high level of idealism which is maintained by people in this field.			
15. This professional organization doesn't really do too much for the average member. (R)			
16. We really have no way of judging each other's competence. (R)			
17. Although I would like to, I really don't read the journals too often. (R)			
18. Most people would stay in the profession even if their incomes were reduced.			
19. My own decisions are subject to review. (R)			
20. There is not much opportunity to judge how another person does his work. (R)			
21. I am my own boss in almost every work-related situation.			
22. If ever an occupation is indispensable, it is this one.			
23. My colleagues pretty well know how well we all do in our work.			
24. There are very few people who don't really believe in their work.			
25. Most of my decisions are reviewed by other people. (R)			
Information on scale "Professionalism"			
Descriptive Statistics		*Result of Exploratory Factor Analysis*	
Cronbach's alpha: Profession as referent (PO) Belief in service (PS) Belief in self-regulation (SR) Sense of calling (SC) Autonomy (AUTO)	 0.59 0.60 0.55 0.49 0.51	Total variance explained:	–*

*Not available

References

***Clikeman, P. M./Schwartz, B. N./Lathan, M. H.* (2001): The Effect of the 150-Hour Requirement on New Accountants' Professional Commitment, Ethical Orientation, and Professionalism, in: Critical Perspectives on Accounting, Vol. 12, pp. 627-645.**

Hall, R. H. (1968): Professionalization and Bureaucratization, in: American Sociological Review, Vol. 33, pp. 92-104.

Kalbers, L. P./Fogarty, T. J. (1995): Professionalism and Its Consequences: A Study of Internal Auditors, in: Auditing, Vol. 14, pp. 64-86.

Morrow, P. C./Goetz Jr., J. F. (1988): Professionalism as a Form of Work Commitment, in: Journal of Vocational Behavior, Vol. 32, pp. 92-111.

Snizek, W. E. (1972): Hall's Professionalism Scale: An Empirical Reassessment, in: American Sociological Review, Vol. 37, pp. 109-114.

169. Propensity to Create Budgetary Slack

Scale Description

The scale indicates a manager's attitude toward slack.

Origin

The 4-item scale was developed by Onsi (1973).

Samples

Survey data were collected by questionnaire, administered to Group A: divisional controllers, budget directors, and cost analysts, Group B: manufacturing managers and Group C: sales managers of seven large-size US-based multinational corporations. 44 managers of each group were selected to fill out the questionnaire. A total of 107 usable questionnaires (81.1%) were returned.

Comments

The measure of the propensity to create budgetary slack from Onsi (1973) has been used by Merchant (1985a), who found good reliability coefficients (Cronbach's alpha = 0.70). Merchant (1985a) reported a theoretical range of 4-20, an actual range of 4-17, a mean of 11.1 and a standard deviation of 2.7.

Scale Indicators and Reliability / Validity Parameters

Scale: from 1 (very little) to 7 (a great deal)

Information on individual indicators regarding "Propensity to Create Budgetary Slack"			
Description of indicators			
1. To protect himself, a manager submits a budget that can safely be attained.			
2. The plant manager sets two levels of standards: one between himself and production (sales) manager, another standard between himself and top management, to be safe.			
3. In good business times, the plant manager accepts a reasonable level of slack in departmental budget.			
4. Slack in the budget is good to do things that cannot be officially approved.			
Information on scale "Propensity to Create Budgetary Slack"			
Descriptive Statistics		*Result of Exploratory Factor Analysis*	
Cronbach's alpha:	–*	Total variance explained:	–*

*Not available

References

***Onsi, M.* (1973): Factor Analysis of Behavioral Variables Affecting Budgetary Slack, in: The Accounting Review, Vol. 48, pp. 535-548.**

Merchant, K. A. (1985): Budgeting and the Propensity to Create Budgetary Slack, in: Accounting, Organizations and Society, Vol. 10, pp. 201-210.

170. Propensity to Create Budgetary Slack [Pufferbildung]

Scale Description

The scale measures the extent to which managers overestimate cost or underestimate revenues when budgets are being planned. The scale comprises only one dimension.

Origin

The scale was developed by Onsi (1973) and has been translated into German by Künkele/Schäffer (2007).

Samples

Survey data were collected by questionnaire, administered to business unit leaders and the responsible controllers of these business units of 1,120 German companies from 500 to 5,000 employees. The companies were from services and industrial sectors. A total of 140 usable pairs of questionnaires (12.5%) were returned.

Comments

The measure of the propensity to create budgetary slack of Onsi (1973) has been used by Merchant (1985a), who found good reliability coefficients (Cronbach's alpha = 0.70). Merchant (1985a) reported a theoretical range of 4-20, an actual range of 4-17, a mean of 11.1 and a standard deviation of 2.7.

Scale Indicators and Reliability / Validity Parameters

Scale: from 1 (definitely false) to 5 (definitely true)

Information on individual indicators regarding "Propensity to Create Budgetary Slack [Pufferbildung]"			
Description of indicators	*Item to Total-Correlation*	*Indicator-Reliability*	*t statistic*
1. Um sich selbst zu schützen, verabschieden Manager Budgets, die sie sicher erreichen können.	0.51	–*	–*
2. Um sich abzusichern, vereinbaren Budgetverantwortliche mit ihren Mitarbeitern anspruchsvollere Budgetziele als mit ihren Vorgesetzten.	0.51	–*	–*

Information on scale "Propensity to Create Budgetary Slack [Pufferbildung]"			
Descriptive Statistics		*Result of Exploratory Factor Analysis*	
Cronbach's alpha:	0.67	Total variance explained:	0.75

*Not feasible

References

***Künkele, J./Schäffer, U.* (2007): Zur erfolgreichen Gestaltung der Budgetkontrolle, in: Die Betriebswirtschaft, Vol. 67, pp. 75-92.**

Merchant, K. A. (1985): Budgeting and the Propensity to Create Budgetary Slack, in: Accounting, Organizations and Society, Vol. 10, pp. 201-210.

Onsi, M. (1973): Factor Analysis of Behavioral Variables Affecting Budgetary Slack, in: The Accounting Review, Vol. 48, pp. 535-548.

171. Quality (of Information) [Informationsqualität]

Scale Description

The scale measures the level of quality of accounting information. The scale comprises four dimensions: breadth, timeliness, reliability and understandability.

Origin

Karlshaus (2000) developed this instrument based on a variety of scales used for measuring quality of information. He identified breadth, timeliness, reliability and understandability to be the most important dimensions of information quality and summed 13 indicators mainly stemming from the scales of Wild (1971), Zmud (1978), O'Reilly III (1982), Gupta and Wilemon (1988), Moenaert and Souder (1990) as well as Maltz and Kohli (1996).

Samples

Survey data were collected by questionnaire, administered to managers of accounting and marketing units from 1,163 German companies from manufacturing industries, which had more than 50 employees. A total of 112 usable pairs of questionnaires (10.2%) were returned.

Comments

The instrument of Karlshaus (2000) has been used recently by Schäffer and Steiners (2004). They concentrated on five indicators and have found good reliability coefficients.

Scale Indicators and Reliability / Validity Parameters

Scale: from 1 (definitely false) to 5 (definitely true)

Information on individual indicators regarding "Quality (of Information) [Informationsqualität]"			
Description of indicators	*Item to Total-Correlation*	*Indicator-Reliability*	*t statistic*
1. Die Breite des Informationsangebotes der Kostenrechnung (Anzahl der Berichte und Analysen) entspricht meinen Vorstellungen.	0.72	0.61	17.49
2. Umfang und Detaillierungsgrad der einzelnen Berichte und Analysen der Kostenrechnung erfüllen meine Informationsbedürfnisse.	0.76	0.68	18.19
3. Die Informationen der Kostenrechnung bilden die tatsächlichen Verhältnisse wirklichkeitsgetreu ab.	0.73	0.61	17.78
4. Die Informationen der Kostenrechnung zeichnen sich durch eine große Genauigkeit aus.	0.61	0.44	15.31
5. Die Informationen der Kostenrechnung widersprechen einander teilweise. (R)	0.43	0.21	11.05
6. Die Informationen der Kostenrechnung basieren auf plausiblen Annahmen.	0.45	0.29	12.84
7. Die Informationen der Kostenrechnung sind frei von subjektiven Meinungen und Einflüssen.	0.50	0.30	13.03
8. Die Informationen der Kostenrechnung sind aktuell.	0.71	0.63	18.00

9. Die bei der Erstellung der Kostenrechnungsinformationen verwendeten Methoden sind für mich leicht nachvollziehbar.	0.51	0.33	13.61
10. Die Informationen der Kostenrechnung sind fehlerfrei.	0.67	0.52	16.48
11. Die Kostenrechnung liefert mir häufig neue Informationen.	0.41	0.22	11.18
12. Die Informationen der Kostenrechnung sind übersichtlich dargestellt.	0.59	0.46	15.73
13. Die von der Kostenrechnung bereitgestellten Informationen sind sprachlich leicht verständlich.	0.58	0.42	14.87

Information on scale "Quality (of Information) [Informationsqualität]"			
Descriptive Statistics		*Result of Exploratory Factor Analysis*	
Cronbach's alpha:	0.89	Total variance explained:	0.66
Results of Confirmatory Factor Analysis			
χ^2-Value (Degrees of Freedom):	110.52 (65)	χ^2-Value/Degrees of Freedom:	1.70
p Value:	0.00	RMSEA:	0.05
SRMR:	–*	CFI:	0.97
GFI:	0.95	AGFI:	0.94
Factor reliability:	0.91	Average variance explained:	0.44

*Not available

References

***Karlshaus, J. T.* (2000): Die Nutzung von Kostenrechnungsinformationen im Marketing: Bestandsaufnahme, Determinanten und Erfolgsauswirkungen, Wiesbaden 2000.**

Gupta, A. K./Wilemon, D. (1988): The Credibility-Cooperation Connection at the R&D-Marketing Interface, in: Journal of Product Innovation Management, Vol. 5, pp. 20-31.

Maltz, E./Kohli, A. K. (1996): Market Intelligence Dissemination across Functional Boundaries, in: Journal of Marketing Research, Vol. 33, pp. 47-61.

Moenaert, R. K./Souder, W. E. (1990): An Analysis of the Use of Extrafunctional Information by R&D and Marketing Personnel: Review and Model, in: Journal of Product Innovation Management, Vol. 7, pp. 213-229.

O'Reilly III, C. A. (1982): Variations in Decision Makers' Use of Information Sources: The Impact of Quality and Accessibility of Information, in: Academy of Management Journal, Vol. 25, pp. 756-771.

Schäffer, U./Steiners, D. (2004): Zur Nutzung von Controllinginformationen, in: Zeitschrift für Planung und Unternehmenssteuerung, Vol. 15, pp. 377-404.

Wild, J. (1971): Zur Problematik der Nutzenbewertung von Informationen, in: Zeitschrift für Betriebswirtschaft, Vol. 41, pp. 315-334.

Zmud, R. W. (1978): An Empirical Investigation of the Dimensionality of the Concept of Information, in: Decision Sciences, Vol. 9, pp. 187-195.

172. Quality of MAS Information [Qualität von Controllinginformationen]

Scale Description

The scale measures to what extent a user believes in quality (e.g. accuracy, relevancy) of the MAS information given.

Origin

The indicators stem from a scale developed by Karlshaus (2000) and were adapted by Schäffer/Steiners (2004).

Samples

Survey data were collected by questionnaire, administered to business unit leaders of 3,500 German companies with 100 to 2,000 employees from the industrial sector. A total of 449 usable questionnaires (12.8%) were returned.

Comments

The original scale consists of 13 indicators.

Scale Indicators and Reliability / Validity Parameters

Scale: from 1 (definitely false) to 5 (definitely true)

Information on individual indicators regarding "Quality of MAS Information [Qualität von Controllinginformationen]"			
Description of indicators	*Item to Total-Correlation*	*Indicator-Reliability*	*t statistic*
1. Die Breite des Informationsangebots (Anzahl Berichte und Analysen) entspricht meinen Vorstellungen.	0.57	0.41	13.68
2. Die Informationen bilden die tatsächlichen Verhältnisse wirklichkeitsgetreu ab.	0.65	0.56	16.76
3. Die Informationen sind aktuell.	0.67	0.59	17.37
4. Die Informationen sind fehlerfrei.	0.63	0.54	16.28

Information on scale "Quality of MAS Information [Qualität von Controllinginformationen]"			
Descriptive Statistics		*Result of Exploratory Factor Analysis*	
Cronbach's alpha:	0.81	Total variance explained:	0.64
Results of Confirmatory Factor Analysis			
χ^2-Value (Degrees of Freedom):	0.31 (2)	χ^2-Value/Degrees of Freedom:	0.16
p Value:	0.86	RMSEA:	0.00
NFI:	1.0	NNFI:	1.0
SRMR:	0.00	CFI:	1.0
GFI:	1.0	AGFI:	1.0
Factor reliability:	0.81	Average variance explained:	0.52

References

***Schäffer, U./Steiners, D.* (2004): Zur Nutzung von Controllinginformationen, in: Zeitschrift für Planung und Unternehmenssteuerung, Vol. 15, pp. 377-404.**

Karlshaus, J. T. (2000): Die Nutzung von Kostenrechnungsinformationen im Marketing, Wiesbaden 2000.

173. Quality of Management Cycle [Qualität des Führungszyklus]

Scale Description

The scale measures manager´s assessment of the company's leadership cycle, comprising the phases of the decision-making process from planning over implementation to control of decisions.

Origin

The scale was newly developed by Spillecke (2006) based on theoretical assumptions by Weber/Schäffer (1999). A similar operationalization was used by Sandt (2004).

Samples

Survey data were collected by questionnaire, administered via e-mail to 3,312 German managers of companies with at least 200 employees. The companies were from different industrial sectors. A total of 415 usable questionnaires (12.5%) were returned.

Scale Indicators and Reliability / Validity Parameters

Scale: from 1 (definitely false) to 5 (definitely true)

Information on individual indicators regarding "Quality of Management Cycle [Qualität des Führungszyklus]"			
Description of indicators	*Item to Total-Correlation*	*Indicator-Reliability*	*t statistic*
1. Mit der Informationsgrundlage bei wichtigen Entscheidungen in unserem Hause bin ich sehr zufrieden.	0.79	0.72	–*
2. Mit dem Prozess der Entscheidungsfindung bin ich sehr zufrieden.	0.80	0.76	21.45
3. Mit den Ergebnissen wichtiger Entscheidungen bin ich sehr zufrieden.	0.78	0.70	20.37
4. Mit der Kontrolle wichtiger Entscheidungen bin ich sehr zufrieden.	0.79	0.80	14.56

Information on scale "Quality of Management Cycle [Qualität des Führungszyklus]"			
Descriptive Statistics		*Result of Exploratory Factor Analysis*	
Cronbach's alpha:	0.90	Total variance explained:	0.69
Results of Confirmatory Factor Analysis			
χ^2-Value (Degrees of Freedom):	1.74 (2)	χ^2-Value/Degrees of Freedom:	0.87
p Value:	0.02	RMSEA:	0.00
SRMR:	–**	CFI:	0.99
GFI:	1.00	AGFI:	0.99
Factor reliability:	0.90	Average variance explained:	0.69

*Not feasible; **not available

References

Spillecke, D. **(2006): Interne Kundenorientierung des Controllerbereichs. Messung – Erfolgsauswirkungen – Determinanten, Wiesbaden, pp. 149-154.**

Sandt, J. (2004): Management mit Kennzahlen und Kennzahlensystemen. Bestandsaufnahme, Determinanten und Erfolgswirkungen, Wiesbaden 2004.

Weber, J./Schäffer, U. (1999): Sicherstellung der Rationalität von Führung als Aufgabe des Controlling?, in: Die Betriebswirtschaft, Vol. 59, pp. 731-747.

174. Rationalization Tool (Cost Accounting) [Kostenrechnung als Begründungsapparat]

Scale Description

The scale measures the extent to which the primary clients of accounting information use these data as rationalization for the enforcement of decisions.

Origin

The scale was newly developed by Aust (1999).

Samples

The scale stems from a questionnaire sent to 1,163 German industrial companies, of which 143 participated, yielding a return rate of 12.3%. The study used a triadic design approach, where the general manager, the marketing or sales director and an accountant of the same company were questioned. Altogether, 105 usable triads were returned.

Scale Indicators and Reliability / Validity Parameters

Scale: from 1 (definitely false) to 5 (definitely true)

Information on individual indicators regarding "Rationalization Tool (Cost Accounting) [Kostenrechnung als Begründungsapparat]"			
Description of indicators	*Item to Total-Correlation*	*Indicator-Reliability*	*t statistic*
1. Kostenrechnungsinformationen helfen mir bei der Durchsetzung von Entscheidungen bei anderen Personen.	0.51	0.37	9.31
2. Die geeignete Interpretation der Kostenrechnungsin-formationen erlaubt es mir, Entscheidungen zu beeinflussen.	0.54	0.42	10.16
3. Kostenrechnungsinformationen helfen mir bei der Begründung bereits getroffener Entscheidungen.	0.67	0.75	14.31
4. Ich setze Kostenrechnungsinformationen ein, um Entscheidungen, die ich bereits getroffen habe, anderen mitzuteilen.	0.55	0.51	11.32

Information on scale "Rationalization Tool (Cost Accounting) [Kostenrechnung als Begründungsapparat]"			
Descriptive Statistics		*Result of Exploratory Factor Analysis*	
Cronbach's alpha:	0.76	Total variance explained:	0.59
Results of Confirmatory Factor Analysis			
Factor reliability:	0.80	Average variance explained:	0.51

References

***Aust, R.* (1999): Kostenrechnung als unternehmensinterne Dienstleistung, Wiesbaden 1999, pp. 102-104.**

175. Reaction of Controlling Department [Reaktion des Controllerbereichs]

Scale Description

The scale measures the extent to which the controlling department reacts adequately and timely to the needs of the managers.

Origin

The indicators are based on a scale created by Jaworski/Kohli (1993).

Samples

Survey data were collected by questionnaire, administered via e-mail to 3,312 German managers of companies with at least 200 employees. The companies were from different industrial sectors. A total of 415 usable questionnaires (12.5%) were returned.

Scale Indicators and Reliability / Validity Parameters

Scale: from 1 (definitely false) to 5 (definitely true)

Information on individual indicators regarding "Reaction of Controlling Department [Reaktion des Controllerbereichs]"			
Description of indicators	*Item to Total-Correlation*	*Indicator-Reliability*	*t statistic*
1. Unsere Controller benötigen sehr lange, um auf Anfragen der Manager zu reagieren. (R)	0.62	0.45	–*
2. Unsere Controller tendieren dazu, Veränderungen im Informationsbedarf der Manager zu ignorieren.	0.72	0.72	14.02
3. Beschwerden des Managements fallen auf „taube Ohren" im Controlling.	0.69	0.64	13.58
4. Unser Controlling kann gute Ideen nicht in angemessener Zeit umsetzen.	0.52	0.31	9.97
5. Unsere Controller unternehmen alles, um den Änderungswünschen der Manager gerecht zu werden.	0.62	0.45	11.75

Information on scale "Reaction of Controlling Department [Reaktion des Controllerbereichs]"			
Descriptive Statistics		*Result of Exploratory Factor Analysis*	
Cronbach's alpha:	0.83	Total variance explained:	0.51
Results of Confirmatory Factor Analysis			
χ^2-Value (Degrees of Freedom):	13.86 (5)	χ^2-Value/Degrees of Freedom:	2.77
p Value:	0.02	RMSEA:	0.07
SRMR:	–**	CFI:	0.99
GFI:	0.99	AGFI:	0.96
Factor reliability:	0.82	Average variance explained:	0.49

*Not feasible; ** not available

References

***Spillecke, D.* (2006): Interne Kundenorientierung des Controllerbereichs. Messung – Erfolgsauswirkungen – Determinanten, Wiesbaden 2006, pp. 118-121.**

Jaworski, B. J./Kohli, A.K. (1993): Market Orientation: Antecedents and Consequences, in: Journal of Marketing, Vol. 57, pp. 53-70.

176. Regulation (in the Context of Business Networks) [Regulation im Kontext von Unternehmensnetzwerken]

Scale Description

The scale measures the degree of detailedness of regulations in business networks.

Origin

The scale was first used by Möller (2006).

Samples

Survey data were collected by questionnaire, administered to business unit leaders or responsible controllers of 5,717 German companies. A total of 102 questionnaires (1.9%) were returned.

Scale Indicators and Reliability / Validity Parameters

Scale: from 1 (definitely false) to 5 (definitely true)

Information on individual indicators regarding "Regulation (in the Context of Business Networks) [Regulation im Kontext von Unternehmensnetzwerken]"			
Description of indicators	*Item to Total-Correlation*	*Indicator-Reliability*	*t statistic*
1. Wie detailliert ist das Konfliktmanagement in Ihrem Netzwerk ausgestaltet?	0.48	0.32	–*
2. Wie detailliert sind die Anzeizsysteme in Ihrem Netzwerk ausgestaltet?	0.45	0.40	3.67
3. Wie detailliert ist die Netzwerkplanung in Ihrem Netzwerk ausgestaltet?	0.48	0.49	3.67
4. Wie detailliert ist die Auftragssteuerung in Ihrem Netzwerk ausgestaltet?	0.31	0.13	2.82

Information on scale "Regulation (in the Context of Business Networks) [Regulation im Kontext von Unternehmensnetzwerken]"			
Descriptive Statistics		*Result of Exploratory Factor Analysis*	
Cronbach's alpha:	0.52	Total variance explained:	0.49
Results of Confirmatory Factor Analysis			
Factor reliability:	0.69	Average variance explained:	0.33

*Not feasible

References

Möller, K. **(2006): Unternehmensnetzwerke und Erfolg – eine empirische Analyse von Einfluss- und Gestaltungsfaktoren, in: Zeitschrift für betriebswirtschaftliche Forschung (zfbf), Vol. 58, pp. 1051-1076.**

177. Relevance of Incentive System [Bedeutung des Anreizsystems]

Scale Description

The scale measures the extent to which a company's compensation and benefits are dependent on a manager's performance.

Origin

The scale was newly developed by Dehler (2001).

Samples

Survey data were collected by questionnaire, administered to logistics managers of 1,394 German companies in the manufacturing industry. A total of 316 usable questionnaires (23%) were returned.

Scale Indicators and Reliability / Validity Parameters

Scale: from 1 (definitely false) to 7 (definitely true)

Information on individual indicators regarding "Relevance of Incentive System [Bedeutung des Anreizsystems]"			
Description of indicators	*Item to Total-Correlation*	*Indicator-Reliability*	*t statistic*
1. Ein hoher Anteil der Führungskräfte unserer Geschäftseinheit wird durch eine variable Gehaltskomponente leistungsabhängig vergütet.	0.73	0.84	15.99
2. Der variable Anteil des Gehalts unserer Führungskräfte ist sehr hoch.	0.75	0.83	15.99
3. Ein hoher Anteil der Mitarbeiter unserer Geschäftseinheit wird durch eine variable Gehaltskomponente leistungsabhängig vergütet.	0.54	0.42	15.99

Information on scale "Relevance of Incentive System [Bedeutung des Anreizsystems]"			
Descriptive Statistics		*Result of Exploratory Factor Analysis*	
Cronbach's alpha:	0.81	Total variance explained:	0.73
Results of Confirmatory Factor Analysis			
Factor reliability:	0.87	Average variance explained:	0.70

References

Dehler, M. (2001): Entwicklungsstand der Logistik. Messung – Determinanten – Erfolgswirkungen, Wiesbaden 2006, pp. 146-148.

178. Reliability of Budgetary Information [Zuverlässigkeit von Budgetierungsinformationen]

Scale Description

The scale measures the extent to which budgetary information can be relied on. The scale comprises four dimensions: replication of real circumstances, accuracy, flawlessness and contrariness.

Origin

Künkele and Schäffer (2007) used indicators of the 13-item scale of Karlshaus (2000) in a modified form to measure reliability of information. The instrument was developed by Karlshaus to measure the quality of accounting information and was initially conceived as having four dimensions: breadth, timeliness, reliability and understandability. In order to test the impact of these dimensions separately, the items relating to the dimension reliability were extracted and related to budgeting.

Samples

Survey data were collected by questionnaire, administered to business unit leaders and the responsible controllers of these business units of 1,120 German companies from 500 to 5,000 employees. The companies were from services and industrial sectors. A total of 140 usable pairs of questionnaires (12.5%) were returned.

Comments

The instrument of Karlshaus (2000) has been used recently by Schäffer and Steiners (2004). They concentrated on five indicators and have found good reliability coefficients (Cronbach's alpha = 0.81).

Scale Indicators and Reliability / Validity Parameters

Scale: from 1 (definitely false) to 5 (definitely true)

Information on individual indicators regarding "Reliability of Budgetary Information [Zuverlässigkeit von Budgetierungsinformationen]"			
Description of indicators	*Item to Total-Correlation*	*Indicator-Reliability*	*t statistic*
1. Die Informationen in der Budgetierung bilden die tatsächlichen Verhältnisse wirklichkeitsgetreu ab.	0.59	0.53	11.57
2. Die Informationen in der Budgetierung zeichnen sich durch eine große Genauigkeit aus.	0.65	0.78	13.83
3. Die Informationen in der Budgetierung sind sehr häufig widersprüchlich. (R)	0.51	0.33	9.27

Information on scale "Reliability of Budgetary Information [Zuverlässigkeit von Budgetierungsinformationen]"			
Descriptive Statistics		*Result of Exploratory Factor Analysis*	
Cronbach's alpha:	0.76	Total variance explained:	0.67
Results of Confirmatory Factor Analysis			
Factor reliability:	0.77	Average variance explained:	0.53

References

***Künkele, J./Schäffer, U.* (2007): Zur erfolgreichen Gestaltung der Budgetkontrolle, in: Die Betriebswirtschaft, Vol. 67, pp. 75-92.**

Karlshaus, J. T. (2000): Die Nutzung von Kostenrechnungsinformationen im Marketing: Bestandsaufnahme, Determinanten und Erfolgsauswirkungen, Wiesbaden 2000.

Schäffer, U./Steiners, D. (2004): Zur Nutzung von Controllinginformationen, in: Zeitschrift für Planung und Unternehmenssteuerung, Vol. 15, pp. 377-404.

179. Reliability of Controlling Information [Zuverlässigkeit von Controlling-Informationen]

Scale Description

The scale measures the degree to which information delivered by the de-central management accounting (controlling) department is considered to be reliable, realistically representing the actual facts.

Origin

Developed by Eckey and Schäffer (2006).

Samples

Eckey and Schäffer (2006) collected data using a survey questionnaire sent to a total of 51 group controlling departments of management holdings listed in the German Prime Standard. The sample of companies represented a variety of industries. 37 usable responses were received, yielding a response rate of 72.5%.

Comments

Eckey and Schäffer (2006) reported a mean of 5.15 and standard deviation of 1.10 on a theoretical range of 1-7.

Scale Indicators and Reliability / Validity Parameters

Scale: from 1 (strongly disagree) to 7 (strongly agree)

Information on individual indicators regarding "Reliability of Controlling Information [Zuverlässigkeit von Controlling-Informationen]"			
Description of indicators	*Item to Total-Correlation*	*Indicator-Reliability*	*t statistic*
1. Das dezentrale Controlling fühlt sich stets an Normen einer ehrlichen Berichterstattung gebunden.	0.75	0.59	5.41
2. Die Informationen sind frei von subjektiven Meinungen und Einflüssen.	0.62	0.35	3.80
3. Bewusst verzerrte Informationsübermittelung der Tochtergesellschaft an die Mutter kommt bei uns nie vor.	0.69	0.55	5.15
4. Ich halte die vom dezentralen Controlling übermittelten Informationen stets für glaubwürdig.	0.84	0.88	7.33
5. Die Informationen bilden die tatsächlichen Verhältnisse wirklichkeitsgetreu ab.	0.84	0.88	7.31

Information on scale "Reliability of Controlling Information [Zuverlässigkeit von Controlling-Informationen]"			
Descriptive Statistics		*Result of Exploratory Factor Analysis*	
Cronbach's alpha:	0.90	Total variance explained:	0.72
Results of Confirmatory Factor Analysis			
χ^2-Value (Degrees of Freedom):	1.13 (4)	χ^2-Value/Degrees of Freedom:	0.28
p-value:	0.89	RMSEA:	0.00
NFI:	0.99	NNFI:	1.05
SRMR:	0.02	CFI:	1.00
GFI:	0.99	AGFI:	0.95
Factor reliability:	0.90	Average variance explained:	0.65

References

***Eckey, M./Schäffer, U.* (2006): Kontrolle von Mehrheitsbeteiligungen in börsennotierten Management-Holdings, in: Zeitschrift für Planung & Unternehmenssteuerung, Vol. 17, pp. 251-280.**

180. Role Ambiguity

Scale Description

The scale measures the extent of role ambiguity.

Origin

Developed by Rizzo et al. (1970).

Samples

Chong and Bateman (2000) chose eighty large manufacturing firms located in Perth, Western Australia, randomly from the Kompass Australia (1996) business directory. From these companies, the names of 150 middle-level managers were gathered; 120 agreed to participate. Finally, a total of 84 questionnaires were returned, yielding a response rate of 70%. Of these, 5 were not fully completed. This leaves the study with 79 usable responses, a usable response rate of 65.83% for data analysis.

Comments

The scale has been extensively used by other accounting researchers (e.g. Chenhall and Brownell (1988); O' Connor (1995)). Chong and Bateman (2000) reported a scale mean of 2.61 and a standard deviation of 1.03 on a theoretical range of 1-7.

Scale Indicators and Reliability / Validity Parameters

Scale: from 1 (strongly disagree) to 7 (strongly agree)

Information on individual indicators regarding "Role Ambiguity"			
Description of indicators			
1. I feel certain about how much authority I have. (R)			
2. I have clear, planned goals and objectives for my jobs. (R)			
3. I know that I have divided my time properly. (R)			
4. I know what my responsibilities are. (R)			
5. I know exactly what is expected of me. (R)			
6. I receive a clear explanation of what has to be done. (R)			
Information on scale "Role Ambiguity"			
Descriptive Statistics		*Result of Exploratory Factor Analysis*	
Cronbach's alpha:	0.87	Total variance explained:	–*

*Not available

References

***Chong, V. K./Bateman, D.* (2000): The Effects of Role Stress on Budgetary Participation and Job Satisfaction-Performance Linkages: A Test of Two Different Models, in: Advances in Accounting Behavioral Research, Vol. 3, pp. 91-118.**

Chenhall, R. H./Brownell, P. (1988): The Effect of Participative Budgeting on Job Satisfaction and Performance: Role Ambiguity as an Intervening Variable, in: Accounting, Organizations and Society, Vol. 13, pp. 225.

O' Connor, N. G. (1995): The Influence of Organizational Culture on the Usefulness of Budget Participation by Singaporean-Chinese Managers, in: Accounting, Organizations and Society, Vol. 20, pp. 383-403.

Rizzo, J. R./House, R. J./Lirtzman, S. I. (1970): Role Conflict and Ambiguity in Complex Organizations, in: Administrative Science Quarterly, Vol. 15, pp. 150-163.

181. Role Autonomy

Scale Description

The scale measures the extent to which a manager has freedom to make meaningful decisions and independently adjust behaviors in performing a role.

Origin

Developed by Aiken and Hage (1965).

Samples

The survey-based study conducted by Noble and Mokwa (1999) involved sampling from two firms: One firm was a large, multi state, financial services organization. Subjects were managers with extensive responsibilities for the implementation of marketing strategies. The other firm was a market share leader in the packaged goods industry. In this company, participants were regional sales managers with full responsibility for a geographic area, including discretionary budgets for promotions and responsibility for implementing corporate promotional strategies. The sample consisted of 254 managers in the financial services company and 534 managers in the packaged goods industry. Usable responses were 161 from the financial service company (63% response rate) and 325 from the other company (61% response rate). The total of 486 usable responses represents an overall 62% response rate.

Scale Indicators and Reliability / Validity Parameters

Scale: from 1 (strongly agree) to 5 (strongly disagree)

Information on individual indicators regarding "Role Autonomy"			
Description of indicators	*Item to Total-Correlation*	*Indicator-Reliability*	*t statistic*
1. In implementing this strategy, managers were allowed to do as they pleased.	–*	0.67	8.68
2. I had a great deal of autonomy during the strategy.	–*	0.70	9.32
3. I felt I was my own boss in implementing the strategy.	–*	0.75	10.02
4. In implementing this strategy, a manager could make his/her own decisions.	–*	0.80	10.88

Information on scale "Role Autonomy"			
Descriptive Statistics		*Result of Exploratory Factor Analysis*	
Cronbach's alpha:	0.82	Total variance explained:	–*

*Not available

References

Noble, C. H./Mokwa, M. P. **(1999): Implementing Marketing Strategies: Developing and Testing a Managerial Theory, in: Journal of Marketing, Vol. 63, pp. 57-73.**

Aiken, M./Hage, J. (1965): Organizational Alienations: A Comparative Analysis, in: American Sociological Review, Vol. 31, pp. 497-507.

182. Role Commitment

Scale Description

The scale measures the extent to which a manager is determined to perform his individual implementation responsibilities well, regardless of her beliefs about the overall strategy.

Origin

Developed by Noble and Mokwa (1999).

Samples

The survey-based study conducted by Noble and Mokwa (1999) involved sampling from two firms: One firm was a large, multi state, financial services organization. Subjects were managers with extensive responsibilities for the implementation of marketing strategies. The other firm was a market share leader in the packaged goods industry. In this company, participants were regional sales managers with full responsibility for a geographic area, including discretionary budgets for promotions and responsibility for implementing corporate promotional strategies. The sample consisted of 254 managers in the financial services company and 534 managers in the packaged goods industry. Usable responses were 161 from the financial service company (63% response rate) and 325 from the other company (61% response rate). The total of 486 usable responses represents an overall 62% response rate.

Scale Indicators and Reliability / Validity Parameters

Scale: from 1 (strongly agree) to 5 (strongly disagree)

Information on individual indicators regarding "Role Commitment"			
Description of indicators	*Item to Total-Correlation*	*Indicator-Reliability*	*t statistic*
1. I took tremendous pride in my responsibilities in this strategy.	–*	0.635	8.32
2. I was committed to my role in implementing this strategy.	–*	0.797	11.28
3. I was determined to meet my personal objectives in this strategy.	–*	0.664	8.82
4. In implementing this strategy, I tried to work as hard as possible.	–*	0.682	9.14
5. I intentionally expended a great deal of effort in carrying out my responsibilities in this strategy.	–*	0.713	9.69
6. I gave tremendous effort in implementing the strategy.	–*	0.740	10.18

Information on scale "Role Commitment"			
Descriptive Statistics		*Result of Exploratory Factor Analysis*	
Cronbach's alpha:	0.85	Total variance explained:	–*

*Not available

References

***Noble, C. H./Mokwa, M. P.* (1999): Implementing Marketing Strategies: Developing and Testing a Managerial Theory, in: Journal of Marketing, Vol. 63, pp. 57-73.**

183. Role Conflict

Scale Description

The scale measures the extent of role conflict.

Origin

Developed by Rizzo et al. (1970).

Samples

Chong and Bateman (2000) chose eighty large manufacturing firms located in Perth, Western Australia, randomly from the Kompass Australia (1996) business directory. From these companies, the names of 150 middle-level managers were gathered; 120 agreed to participate. Finally, a total of 84 questionnaires were returned, yielding a response rate of 70%. Of these, 5 were not fully completed. This leaves the study with 79 usable responses, a usable response rate of 65.83% for data analysis.

Comments

The scale has been tested widely in prior research and found to have high levels of validity and reliability (Schuler et al. (1977)). This instrument has been used extensively by other accounting researchers (e.g. Senatra (1980); Abernethy and Stoelwinder (1995); Comerford and Abernethy (1999)). Chong and Bateman (2000) reported a scale mean of 3.50 and a standard deviation of 1.21 on a theoretical range of 1-7.

Scale Indicators and Reliability / Validity Parameters

Scale: from 1 (strongly disagree) to 7 (strongly agree)

Information on individual indicators regarding "Role Conflict"
Description of indicators
1. I have to do things that should be done differently.
2. I receive assignments without the manpower to complete them.
3. I have to buck a rule or policy in order to carry out an assignment.
4. I receive incompatible requests from two or more people.
5. I do things that are apt to be accepted by one person and not accepted by others.
6. I receive assignments without adequate resources and materials to execute them.
7. I work on unnecessary things.
8. I work with two or more groups who operate quite differently.

Information on scale "Role Conflict"			
Descriptive Statistics		*Result of Exploratory Factor Analysis*	
Cronbach's alpha:	0.85	Total variance explained:	–*

*Not available

References

***Chong, V. K./Bateman, D.* (2000): The Effects of Role Stress on Budgetary Participation and Job Satisfaction-Performance Linkages: A Test of Two Different Models, in: Advances in Accounting Behavioral Research, Vol. 3, pp. 91-118.**

Abernethy, M. A./Stoelwinder, J. U. (1995): The Role of Professional Control in the Management of Complex Organizations, in: Accounting, Organizations and Society, Vol. 20, pp. 1-17.

Comerford, S. E./Abernethy, M. A. (1999): Budgeting and the Management of Role Conflict in Hospitals, in: Behavioral Research in Accounting, Vol. 11, pp. 93-110.

Rizzo, J. R./House, R. J./Lirtzman, S. I. (1970): Role Conflict and Ambiguity in Complex Organizations, in: Administrative Science Quarterly, Vol. 15, pp. 150-163.

Schuler, R. S./Aldag, R. J./Brief, A. P. (1977): Role Conflict and Ambiguity: A Scale Analysis, in: Organizational Behavior & Human Performance, Vol. 20, pp. 111-128.

Senatra, P. T. (1980): Role Conflict, Role Ambiguity, and Organizational Climate in a Public Accounting Firm, in: The Accounting Review, Vol. 55, pp. 594-603.

184. Role Conflict (in MNCs)

Scale Description

The scale measures the degree of incompatibility between the different expectations associated with a work role in the MNC context.

Origin

Adapted from Rizzo et al. (1970).

Samples

Gupta et al. (1999) mailed questionnaires to the heads of 987 foreign subsidiaries of major MNCs headquartered in the United States, Japan, and Europe. A total of 374 subsidiaries (38%) of 74 MNCs participated in the study.

Comments

Gupta et al. (1999) reported a scale mean of 3.48 and a standard deviation of 1.13.

Scale Indicators and Reliability / Validity Parameters

Scale: from 1 (strongly disagree) to 7 (strongly agree)

Information on individual indicators regarding "Role Conflict (in MNCs)"			
Description of indicators			
1. I do assignments that are apt to be accepted by one executive and not by others.			
2. I receive incompatible requests from two ore more executives.			
3. I work with two or more subsidiaries who operate quite differently.			
4. I receive assignments without adequate resources to complete it.			
5. I have to do assignments that have to be done differently.			
Information on scale "Role Conflict (in MNCs)"			
Descriptive Statistics		*Result of Exploratory Factor Analysis*	
Cronbach's alpha:	0.53	Total variance explained:	–*

*Not available

References

***Gupta, A. K./Govindarajan, V./Malhotra, A.* (1999): Feedback-Seeking Behavior within Multinational Corporations, in: Strategic Management Journal, Vol. 20, pp. 205-222.**

Rizzo, J. R./House, R. J./Lirtzman, S. I. (1970): Role Conflict and Ambiguity in Complex Organizations, in: Administrative Science Quarterly, Vol. 15, pp. 150-163.

185. Role Involvement

Scale Description

The scale measures the extent to which a manager participated in the „shaping“ of his or her role, including involvement in strategy formulation and later interactions with superiors to determine the exact nature of the role.

Origin

Developed by Noble and Mokwa (1999).

Samples

The survey-based study conducted by Noble and Mokwa (1999) involved samples from two firms: One firm was a large, multi state, financial services organization. Subjects were managers with extensive responsibilities for the implementation of marketing strategies. The other firm was a market share leader in the packaged goods industry. In this company, participants were regional sales managers with full responsibility for a geographic area, including discretionary budgets for promotions and responsibility for implementing corporate promotional strategies. The sample consisted of 254 managers in the financial services company and 534 managers in the packaged goods industry. Usable responses were 161 from the financial service company (63% response rate) and 325 from the other company (61% response rate). The total of 486 usable responses represents an overall 62% response rate.

Scale Indicators and Reliability / Validity Parameters

Scale: from 1 (strongly agree) to 5 (strongly disagree)

Information on individual indicators regarding "Role Involvement"			
Description of indicators	*Item to Total-Correlation*	*Indicator-Reliability*	*t statistic*
1. My superiors and I worked together to decide exactly what I would do to help implement the strategy.	–*	0.565	5.15
2. The first I heard of this promotion was when I was told to implement it. (R)	–*	0.509	4.86
3. During the implementation of the strategy, I felt I could approach my superiors if I wanted to suggest changes in my responsibilities.	–*	0.644	5.50

Information on scale "Role Involvement"			
Descriptive Statistics		*Result of Exploratory Factor Analysis*	
Cronbach's alpha:	0.59	Total variance explained:	–*

*Not available

References

Noble, C. H./Mokwa, M. P. **(1999): Implementing Marketing Strategies: Developing and Testing a Managerial Theory, in: Journal of Marketing, Vol. 63, pp. 57-73.**

186. Role Performance

Scale Description

The scale measures the degree to which a manager achieves the goals and objectives of a particular role and facilitates the overall success of the implementation effort.

Origin

Developed by Noble and Mokwa (1999).

Samples

The survey-based study conducted by Noble and Mokwa (1999) involved samples from two firms: One firm was a large, multi state, financial services organization. Subjects were managers with extensive responsibilities for the implementation of marketing strategies. The other firm was a market share leader in the packaged goods industry. In this company, participants were regional sales managers with full responsibility for a geographic area, including discretionary budgets for promotions and responsibility for implementing corporate promotional strategies. The sample consisted of 254 managers in the financial services company and 534 managers in the packaged goods industry. Usable responses were 161 from the financial service company (63% response rate) and 325 from the other company (61% response rate). The total of 486 usable responses represents an overall 62% response rate.

Scale Indicators and Reliability / Validity Parameters

Scale: from 1 (strongly agree) to 5 (strongly disagree)

Information on individual indicators regarding "Role Performance"			
Description of indicators	*Item to Total-Correlation*	*Indicator-Reliability*	*t statistic*
1. My superiors would say I performed extremely well on the strategy.	–*	0.517	5.15
2. This was not one of my better implementation efforts. (R)	–*	0.494	5.00
3. My overall performance in implementing the strategy was outstanding.	–*	0.842	6.59

Information on scale "Role Performance"			
Descriptive Statistics		*Result of Exploratory Factor Analysis*	
Cronbach's alpha:	0.63	Total variance explained:	–*

*Not available

References

Noble, C. H./Mokwa, M. P. **(1999): Implementing Marketing Strategies: Developing and Testing a Managerial Theory, in: Journal of Marketing, Vol. 63, pp. 57-73.**

187. Role Significance

Scale Description

The scale measures the extent to which a role is perceived to be critical to the success of the overall implementation effort.

Origin

Developed by Aiken and Hage (1965); adapted by Noble and Mokwa (1999).

Samples

The survey-based study conducted by Noble and Mokwa (1999) involved samples from two firms: One firm was a large, multi state, financial services organization. Subjects were managers with extensive responsibilities for the implementation of marketing strategies. The other firm was a market share leader in the packaged goods industry. In this company, participants were regional sales managers with full responsibility for a geographic area, including discretionary budgets for promotions and responsibility for implementing corporate promotional strategies. The sample consisted of 254 managers in the financial services company and 534 managers in the packaged goods industry. Usable responses were 161 from the financial service company (63% response rate) and 325 from the other company (61% response rate). The total of 486 usable responses represents an overall 62% response rate.

Scale Indicators and Reliability / Validity Parameters

Scale: from 1 (strongly agree) to 5 (strongly disagree)

Information on individual indicators regarding "Role Significance"			
Description of indicators	*Item to Total-Correlation*	*Indicator-Reliability*	*t statistic*
1. My responsibilities in implementing this strategy were not that significant. (R)	–*	0.718	8.89
2. I played a relatively minor role in this strategy. (R)	–*	0.940	11.50
3. I was one of the key members of the implementation team on this strategy.	–*	0.577	7.18

Information on scale "Role Significance"			
Descriptive Statistics		*Result of Exploratory Factor Analysis*	
Cronbach's alpha:	0.78	Total variance explained:	–*

*Not available

References

Noble, C. H./Mokwa, M. P. **(1999): Implementing Marketing Strategies: Developing and Testing a Managerial Theory, in: Journal of Marketing, Vol. 63, pp. 57-73.**

Aiken, M./Hage, J. (1965): Organizational Alienations: A Comparative Analysis, in: American Sociological Review, Vol. 31, pp. 497-507.

188. Salesperson Dependence upon Firm

Scale Description

The measure assesses the benefits a salesperson derives from the firm that cannot readily be derived elsewhere.

Origin

Based on Emerson (1962). Frazier (1983) notes it is logical that benefits and irreplaceability go together because the greater the benefit level, the more rare the benefit level is likely to be.

Samples

Anderson and Robertson (1995) model dependence and exit barriers using perceptual data gathered directly from 208 salespeople of several cooperating firms that supplied names and addresses of a cross section of their salespeople. Surveys were sent by the researchers to home addresses and solicited cooperation in exchange for an executive summary of results. These 208 responses represent 49.5% of the 420 brokers sampled and are the basis for measure development and for modeling dependence and perceptions of the hazards of selling house brands.

Comments

Anderson and Robertson (1995) reported a mean of 4.00 and a standard deviation of 1.05.

Scale Indicators and Reliability / Validity Parameters

Scale: from 1 (strongly disagree) to 7 (strongly agree)

Information on individual indicators regarding "Salesperson Dependence upon Firm"			
Description of indicators			
1. The firm is a place where I can make a lot of money.			
2. My firm's support makes me a much more effective broker.			
3. At another firm, I'd have to work harder to make the same money as I do now.			
4. Few firms would offer me the advantages I get from being with this firm.			
5. I wouldn't be as effective a broker in another firm as I am here.			
6. I'd be worse off if I changed jobs right now.			
7. I would take a pay cut if I worked somewhere else.			
8. I could get a better job tomorrow if I wanted to look. (R)			
9. Other brokerage firms are good places to work, but here is best.			
Information on scale "Salesperson Dependence upon Firm"			
Cronbach's alpha:	0.83	Total variance explained:	–*

*Not available

References

***Anderson, E./Robertson, T. S.* (1995): Inducing Multiline Salespeople to Adopt House Brands, in: Journal of Marketing, Vol. 59, pp. 16-31.**

Emerson, R. M. (1962): Power-Dependence Relations, in: American Sociological Review, Vol. 27, pp. 31-41.

Frazier, G. L. (1983): On the Measurement of Interfirm Power in Channels of Distribution, in: Journal of Marketing Research, Vol. 20, pp. 158-166.

189. Satisfaction with Economic Performance [Zufriedenheit mit dem wirtschaftlichen Erfolg]

Scale Description

The scale measures the management teams´ assessment of the company's performance in terms of overall performance, e.g. financial goals or achievement of milestones.

Origin

The scale was newly developed by Spieker (2004).

Samples

Survey data were collected by questionnaire, administered via internet to 353 managers of German start-up companies. A total of 145 usable questionnaires (41.1%) were returned.

Scale Indicators and Reliability / Validity Parameters

Scale: from 1 (definitely false) to 7 (definitely true)

Information on individual indicators regarding "Satisfaction with Economic Performance [Zufriedenheit mit dem wirtschaftlichen Erfolg]"			
Description of indicators	*Item to Total-Correlation*	*Indicator-Reliability*	*t statistic*
1. Wir sind mit dem finanziellen Ergebnis unseres Unternehmens zufrieden.	0.88	0.68	14.70
2. Die wirtschaftliche Entwicklung unseres Unternehmens entspricht unseren anfangs gehegten Erwartungen.	0.88	0.75	15.19
3. Wir haben in der Vergangenheit alle gesetzten Meilensteine erreicht.	0.88	0.63	14.45
4. Unsere Prognosen über die wirtschaftliche Entwicklung unseres Unternehmens waren in der Vergangenheit zu optimistisch. (R)	0.74	0.61	14.28
5. Wir sind über die wirtschaftliche Entwicklung unseres Unternehmens enttäuscht. (R)	0.77	0.67	14.75

Information on scale "Satisfaction with Economic Performance [Zufriedenheit mit dem wirtschaftlichen Erfolg]"			
Descriptive Statistics		*Result of Exploratory Factor Analysis*	
Cronbach's alpha:	0.94	Total variance explained:	0.78
Results of Confirmatory Factor Analysis			
χ^2-Value (Degrees of Freedom):	0.30 (5)	χ^2-Value/Degrees of Freedom:	0.06
p Value:	0.02	RMSEA:	0.00
SRMR:	–*	CFI:	1.00
GFI:	1.00	AGFI:	1.00
Factor reliability:	0.94	Average variance explained:	0.61

*Not available

References

Spieker, M. **(2004): Entscheidungen in Gründerteams. Determinanten – Parameter – Erfolgsauswirkungen, Wiesbaden 2004, pp. 255-256.**

190. Satisfaction (with Controlling Department) [Zufriedenheit mit Controlling-Abteilung]

Scale Description

The scale measures the manager's level of overall satisfaction concerning the performance of the controlling department.

Origin

The scale was newly developed by Spillecke (2006) based on the American Customer Satisfaction Index (ACSI) as described in Krafft (1999).

Samples

Survey data were collected by questionnaire, administered via e-mail to 3,312 German managers of companies with at least 200 employees. The companies were from different industrial sectors. A total of 415 usable questionnaires (12.5%) were returned.

Scale Indicators and Reliability / Validity Parameters

Scale: from 1 (definitely false) to 5 (definitely true)

Information on individual indicators regarding "Satisfaction (with Controlling Department) [Zufriedenheit mit Controlling-Abteilung]"			
Description of indicators	*Item to Total-Correlation*	*Indicator-Reliability*	*t statistic*
1. Mit unserem Controlling bin ich insgesamt sehr zufrieden.	0.81	0.74	–*
2. Unser Controlling hat meine Erwartungen immer zur vollsten Zufriedenheit erfüllt.	0.87	0.88	25.20
3. Unser Controlling kommt meiner Idealvorstellung von einer perfekten Controllingabteilung sehr nahe.	0.82	0.74	22.94
Information on scale "Satisfaction (with Controlling Department) [Zufriedenheit mit Controlling-Abteilung]"			
Descriptive Statistics		*Result of Exploratory Factor Analysis*	
Cronbach's alpha:	0.91	Total variance explained:	0.79
Results of Confirmatory Factor Analysis			
Factor reliability:	0.92	Average variance explained:	0.79

*Not feasible

References

***Spillecke, D.* (2006): Interne Kundenorientierung des Controllerbereichs. Messung – Erfolgsauswirkungen – Determinanten, Wiesbaden 2006, pp. 146-149.**

Krafft, M. (2000): Der Kunde im Fokus: Kundennähe, Kundenzufriedenheit, Kundenbindung – und Kundenwert?, in: Die Betriebswirtschaft, Vol. 59, pp. 511-530.

191. Satisfaction (with Measurement System)

Scale Description

The scale measures a firm's satisfaction with its measurement system.

Origin

The scale was developed by Ittner et al. (2003).

Samples

A random sample of 600 US financial services firms was solicited to participate in the survey. A marketing research firm telephoned senior executives from each of these firms to request participation. Those agreeing to participate were sent a survey or guided to a web site containing the questionnaire. Executives from 140 firms (23.3%) completed usable surveys.

Comments

Ittner et al. (2003) report a scale mean of 3.42.

Scale Indicators and Reliability / Validity Parameters

Scale:

Item no. 1: from 1 (has not met expectations) to 6 (exceeded expectations)

Item no. 2: from 1 (not at all ideal) to 6 (very close to ideal)

Item no. 3: from 1 (not at all satisfied) to 6 (completely satisfied)

Information on individual indicators regarding "Satisfaction (with Measurement System)"			
Description of indicators			
1. How well does the system meet your expectations?			
2. How well does the system compare to your concept of an „ideal" system?			
3. How is your overall satisfaction with the system?			
Information on scale "Satisfaction (with Measurement System)"			
Descriptive Statistics		*Result of Exploratory Factor Analysis*	
Cronbach's alpha:	0.91	Total variance explained:	–*

*Not available

References

Ittner, C. D./Larcker, D. F./Randall, T. **(2003): Performance Implications of Strategic Performance Measurement in Financial Services Firms, in: Accounting, Organizations and Society, Vol. 28, pp. 715-741.**

192. Scope of Information [Informationsbreite]

Scale Description

The scale measures to which extent strategic information is provided by the reporting system.

Origin

Developed by Eckey and Schäffer (2006).

Samples

Eckey and Schäffer (2006) collected data using a survey questionnaire sent to a total of 51 group controlling departments of management holdings listed in the German Prime Standard. The sample of companies represented a variety of industries. 37 usable responses were received, yielding a response rate of 72.5%.

Comments

Eckey and Schäffer (2006) reported a mean of 4.68 and standard deviation of 1.45 on a theoretical range of 1-7.

Scale Indicators and Reliability / Validity Parameters

Scale: from 1 (strongly disagree) to 7 (strongly agree)

Information on individual indicators regarding "Scope of Information [Informationsbreite]"			
Description of indicators	*Item to Total-Correlation*	*Indicator-Reliability*	*t statistic*
1. Unser Reporting enthält nicht-finanzielle Kennzahlen (z.B. Marktanteile, Kundenzufriedenheit) etc. als Ergänzung zu finanziellen Daten.	0.78	0.64	5.29
2. Das Berichtswesen enthält Kenngrößen, die die wesentlichen Erfolgstreiber der Tochtergesellschaft abbilden.	0.76	0.68	5.79
3. Nicht-finanzielle Informationen geben ein umfassendes Bild der strategischen Positionierung der Tochtergesellschaft wider.	0.63	0.48	4.53
4. Frühindikatoren (z.B. ein drastischer prognostizierter Auftragsrückgang aufgrund der Kündigung eines wichtigen Kunden) deuten auf mögliche Gefährdungspotenziale hin.	0.72	0.72	5.94
5. Unser Berichtswesen enthält ausschließlich finanzielle Größen. (R)	0.79	0.61	5.24

Information on scale "Scope of Information [Informationsbreite]"			
Descriptive Statistics		*Result of Exploratory Factor Analysis*	
Cronbach's alpha:	0.89	Total variance explained:	0.70
Results of Confirmatory Factor Analysis			
χ^2-Value (Degrees of Freedom):	0.26 (3)	χ^2-Value/Degrees of Freedom:	0.09
p-value:	0.97	RMSEA:	0.00
NFI:	0.99	NNFI:	1.07
SRMR:	0.01	CFI:	1.00
GFI:	1.00	AGFI:	0.99
Factor reliability:	0.89	Average variance explained:	0.63

References

Eckey, M./Schäffer, U. (2006): Kontrolle von Mehrheitsbeteiligungen in börsennotierten Management-Holdings, in: Zeitschrift für Planung & Unternehmenssteuerung, Vol. 17, pp. 251-280.

193. Selection (in the Context of Business Networks) [Selektion im Kontext von Unternehmensnetzwerken]

Scale Description

The scale measures the degree of formalization in selecting partners for business networks.

Origin

The scale was first used by Möller (2006).

Samples

Survey data were collected by questionnaire, administered to business unit leaders or responsible controllers of 5,717 German companies. A total of 102 questionnaires (1.9%) were returned.

Scale Indicators and Reliability / Validity Parameters

Scale: from 1 (definitely false) to 5 (definitely true)

Information on individual indicators regarding "Selection (in the Context of Business Networks) [Selektion im Kontext von Unternehmensnetzwerken]"			
Description of indicators	*Item to Total-Correlation*	*Indicator-Reliability*	*t statistic*
1. Das Vorgehen der Partnerauswahl ist standardisiert	0.50	0.37	–*
2. Der Ablauf der Auswahl ist umfassend schriftlich dokumentiert.	0.58	0.78	5.54
3. Der Ablauf der Auswahl wird konsequent eingehalten.	0.62	0.60	5.78

Information on scale "Selection (in the Context of Business Networks) [Selektion im Kontext von Unternehmensnetzwerken]"			
Descriptive Statistics		*Result of Exploratory Factor Analysis*	
Cronbach's alpha:	0.75	Total variance explained:	0.51
Results of Confirmatory Factor Analysis			
Factor reliability:	0.80	Average variance explained:	0.58

*Not feasible

References

Möller, K. (2006): Unternehmensnetzwerke und Erfolg – eine empirische Analyse von Einfluss- und Gestaltungsfaktoren, in: Zeitschrift für betriebswirtschaftliche Forschung (zfbf), Vol. 58, pp. 1051-1076.

194. Self-Reflection [Selbstreflexion]

Scale Description

The scale measures the extent to which management teams are over-confident, e.g. by suppressing thoughts of the company's possible failure.

Origin

The scale was newly developed by Spieker (2004).

Samples

Survey data were collected by questionnaire, administered via internet to 353 managers of German start-up companies. A total of 145 usable questionnaires (41.1%) were returned.

Scale Indicators and Reliability / Validity Parameters

Scale: from 1 (definitely false) to 7 (definitely true)

Information on individual indicators regarding "Self-Reflection [Selbstreflexion]"			
Description of indicators	*Item to Total-Correlation*	*Indicator-Reliability*	*t statistic*
1. Wir sind uns sicher, dass wir die uns gesteckten Ziele erreichen.	0.80	0.76	15.61
2. Es gibt wohl kaum ein Team, das unsere Arbeit besser bewältigen könnte, als wir.	0.81	0.76	15.62
3. Egal was passiert, unser Team wird es schon meistern.	0.82	0.73	15.67
4. Wir stellen unsere Fähigkeiten/Kompetenzen selten in Zweifel.	0.73	0.66	15.16
5. Wir lassen es nicht zu, dass einzelne Teammitglieder am Erfolg unseres Unternehmens zweifeln.	0.56	0.43	11.32

Information on scale "Self-Reflection [Selbstreflexion]"			
Descriptive Statistics		*Result of Exploratory Factor Analysis*	
Cronbach's alpha:	0.87	Total variance explained:	0.71
Results of Confirmatory Factor Analysis			
χ^2-Value (Degrees of Freedom):	2.73 (5)	χ^2-Value/Degrees of Freedom:	0.55
p Value:	0.00	RMSEA:	0.00
SRMR:	–*	CFI:	1.00
GFI:	0.99	AGFI:	0.99
Factor reliability:	0.92	Average variance explained:	0.69

*Not available

References

Spieker, M. **(2004): Entscheidungen in Gründerteams. Determinanten – Parameter – Erfolgsauswirkungen, Wiesbaden 2004, pp. 247-248.**

195. Senior Management Support in Strategy Implementation

Scale Description

The scale measures the degree of senior management support in strategy implementation. Senior management support is generally associated with resource allocations.

Origin

Developed by Noble and Mokwa (1999).

Samples

The survey-based study conducted by Noble and Mokwa (1999) involved samples from two firms: One firm was a large, multi state, financial services organization. Subjects were managers with extensive responsibilities for the implementation of marketing strategies. The other firm was a market share leader in the packaged goods industry. In this company, participants were regional sales managers with full responsibility for a geographic area, including discretionary budgets for promotions and responsibility for implementing corporate promotional strategies. The sample consisted of 254 managers in the financial services company and 534 managers in the packaged goods industry. Usable responses were 161 from the financial service company (63% response rate) and 325 from the other company (61% response rate). The total of 486 usable responses represents an overall 62% response rate.

Scale Indicators and Reliability / Validity Parameters

Scale: from 1 (strongly agree) to 5 (strongly disagree)

Information on individual indicators regarding "Senior Management Support in Strategy Implementation"			
Description of indicators	*Item to Total-Correlation*	*Indicator-Reliability*	*t statistic*
1. It was clear that senior management wanted this strategy to be a success.	–*	0.756	10.39
2. I didn't feel upper management placed a great deal of significance on this strategy. (R)	–*	0.703	9.45
3. I felt that this strategy was strongly supported by senior management.	–*	0.838	11.96
4. Senior management didn't seem to care much about this strategy. (R)	–*	0.755	10.38

Information on scale "Senior Management Support in Strategy Implementation"			
Descriptive Statistics		*Result of Exploratory Factor Analysis*	
Cronbach's alpha:	0.85	Total variance explained:	–*

*Not available

References

Noble, C. H./Mokwa, M. P. **(1999): Implementing Marketing Strategies: Developing and Testing a Managerial Theory, in: Journal of Marketing, Vol. 63, pp. 57-73.**

196. Shared Vision (in MNCs)

Scale Description

The scale measures the level of shared visions between two parties.

Origin

Based on Nohria and Ghoshal (1994); Tsai and Ghoshal (1998) and Simonin (1999) to measure, respectively, „normative integration", „shared values", and „organizational distance".

Samples

Barner-Rasmussen (2003) collected data through structured face-to-face interviews with 89 top managers of Finnish subsidiaries of foreign MNCs. The participating firms were picked from a list of the 150 largest foreign-owned subsidiaries in Finland, resulting in a sample of 30 US-owned, 32 Scandinavian-owned, and 27 European-owned units. Their parent companies' annual turnover ranged from US$34 million to 183,000 million and operated in between three and 190 countries.

Scale Indicators and Reliability / Validity Parameters

Scale: from 1 (not at all) to 7 (very much)

Information on individual indicators regarding "Shared Vision (in MNCs)"			
Description of indicators			
1. The business practices and operational mechanisms of the two units are very similar.			
2. The organizational culture and management style is very coherent and similar across the two units.			
3. Your unit shares the same ambitions with the unit in question.			
4. Together with the other unit, you have a shares understanding of doing business.			
Information on scale "Shared Vision (in MNCs)"			
Descriptive Statistics		*Result of Exploratory Factor Analysis*	
Cronbach's alpha:	0.78	Total variance explained:	–*

*Not available

References

***Barner-Rasmussen, W.* (2003): Determinants of the Feedback-Seeking Behaviour of Subsidiary Top Managers in Multinational Corporations, in: International Business Review, Vol. 12, pp. 41-60.**

Nohria, N./Ghoshal, S. (1994): Differentiated Fit and Shared Values: Alternatives for Managing Headquarters-Subsidiary Relations, in: Strategic Management Journal, Vol. 15, pp. 491-502.

Simonin, B. L. (1999): Transfer of Marketing Know-How in International Strategic Alliances: An Empirical Investigation of the Role and Antecedents of Knowledge Ambiguity, in: Journal of International Business Studies, Vol. 30, pp. 463-490.

Tsai, W./Ghoshal, S. (1998): Social Capital and Value Creation: The Role of Intrafirm Networks, in: Academy of Management Journal, Vol. 41, pp. 464-476.

197. Standard Tightness

Scale Description

The scale measures the degree of standard tightness as the difference between two constructs – resources needed (as perceived by a respondent to accomplish a job) and resources available (to accomplish the job as perceived by a respondent).

Origin

Developed by Shields et al. (2000).

Samples

480 questionnaires were distributed to automobile design engineers. Of 480 questionnaires distributed, 415 (86%) were returned. However, only 358 (74%) were usable because 46 respondents' self-reported job titles were not design engineers and 11 had missing data. These 358 usable subjects had a mean of 11.2 (SD=7.3, range=1-33) years of employment with the company and a mean of 7.8 (SD=6.1, range=0-32) years of experience in their current job assignment.

Comments

Shields et al. (2000) reported a scale mean of 32.37 and a standard deviation of 4.65 on an actual (theoretical) range of 19-48 (4-52).

Scale Indicators and Reliability / Validity Parameters

Scale: from 1 (no resources) to 7 (an extremely large quantity of resources)

Information on individual indicators regarding "Standard Tightness"			
Description of indicators			
Please indicate the total amounts of each of the following resources you believed typically were required for you to achieve your performance standards on design assignments; *minus* Please indicate the total amounts of each of the following resources that typically were made available to you on design assignments.			
1. Your time at work.			
2. Design technology (e.g. CAD, CAM, CAE).			
3. Assistance from other employees of your company (e.g. time, skills, information).			
4. Assistance from external sources (e.g. consultants, suppliers, customers).			
Information on scale "Standard Tightness"			
Descriptive Statistics		*Result of Exploratory Factor Analysis*	
Cronbach's alpha:	0.67	Total variance explained:	–*

*Not available

References

***Shields, M. D./Deng, F. J./Kato, Y.* (2000): The Design and Effects of Control Systems: Tests of Direct-and Indirect-Effects Models, in: Accounting, Organizations and Society, Vol. 25, pp. 185-202.**

198. Standard-based Incentives

Scale Description

The scale measures the extent of standard-based incentives.

Origin

Shields et al. (2000) used a modified version of the three-item instrument from Shields and Young (1993).

Samples

480 questionnaires were distributed to automobile design engineers. Of 480 questionnaires distributed, 415 (86%) were returned. However, only 358 (74%) were usable because 46 respondents' self-reported job titles were not design engineers and 11 had missing data. These 358 usable subjects had a mean of 11.2 (SD=7.3, range=1-33) years of employment with the company and a mean of 7.8 (SD=6.1, range=0-32) years of experience in their current job assignment.

Comments

Shields et al. (2000) reported a scale mean of 3.37 and a standard deviation of 3.56 on an actual (theoretical) range of 3-21 (3-21).

Scale Indicators and Reliability / Validity Parameters

Scale: from 1 (extremely low) to 7 (extremely high)

Information on individual indicators regarding "Standard-based Incentives"			
Description of indicators			
1. The degree to which valued rewards to design engineers increase with increases in their measures performance.			
2. The degree to which design engineers' valued rewards are totally determined by measured performance relative to performance standards.			
3. Consider the design engineers whose performance relative to the performance standards are in the top 25% of all design engineers' performance. The extent to which these engineers receive larger valued rewards than do those engineers whose performance in relation to the standards are not in the top 25%.			
Information on scale "Standard-based Incentives"			
Descriptive Statistics		*Result of Exploratory Factor Analysis*	
Cronbach's alpha:	0.80	Total variance explained:	–*

*Not available

References

***Shields, M. D./Deng, F. J./Kato, Y.* (2000): The Design and Effects of Control Systems: Tests of Direct-and Indirect-Effects Models, in: Accounting, Organizations and Society, Vol. 25, pp. 185-202.**

Shields, M. D./Young, S. M. (1993): Antecedents and Consequences of Participative Budgeting: Evidence on the Effects of Asymmetrical Information, in: Journal of Management Accounting Research, Vol. 5, pp. 265-280.

199. Strategic Audits

Scale Description

The scale measures the frequency with which strategic audits of product and process technologies and product/service quality relative to competitors are used to monitor the organization's strategic position.

Origin

A major international management consulting firm developed the construct in 1991.

Samples

Ittner and Larcker (1997) examined the use and performance consequences of strategic control systems using survey data collected by a major international management consulting firm during 1991. The survey covered the automobile and computer industries in Canada, Germany, Japan, and the United States. All automobile assemblers and a random sample of their suppliers were invited to participate. A total of 249 organizations agreed to participate, representing an 85% response rate.

Comments

The scale emerged from a principal component analysis used to reduce the dimensionality of 36 questions from a survey assessing the extent to which organizations employ strategic control practices discussed in the quality literature.

Scale Indicators and Reliability / Validity Parameters

Scale: 1 (slight or not at all), 2 (secondary), 3 (major), 4 (primary)

Information on individual indicators regarding "Strategic Audits"			
Description of indicators			
1. How often are strategic audits of product technology used to monitor the position of your operation?			
2. How often are strategic audits of process technology used to monitor the position of your operation?			
3. How often are strategic audits of product/service quality used to monitor the position of your operation?			
Information on scale "Strategic Audits"			
Descriptive Statistics		*Result of Exploratory Factor Analysis*	
Cronbach's alpha:	0.69	Total variance explained:	–*

*Not available

References

Ittner, C. D./Larcker, D. F. **(1997): Quality Strategy, Strategic Control Systems, and Organizational Performance, in: Accounting, Organizations and Society, Vol. 22, pp. 293-314.**

200. Strategic Implementation Monitoring [Strategische Durchführungskontrolle]

Scale Description

The scale measures the degree to which the strategic course of the subsidiary should be changed in the light of past events by continuously questioning the basic direction of the strategy.

Origin

Developed by Eckey and Schäffer (2006) based on Schreyögg and Steinmann (1987).

Samples

Eckey and Schäffer (2006) collected data using a survey questionnaire sent to a total of 51 group controlling departments of management holdings listed in the German Prime Standard. The sample of companies represented a variety of industries. 37 usable responses were received, yielding a response rate of 72.5%.

Comments

Eckey and Schäffer (2006) reported a mean of 5.41 and standard deviation of 1.05 on a theoretical range of 1-7.

Scale Indicators and Reliability / Validity Parameters

Scale: from 1 (strongly disagree) to 7 (strongly agree)

Information on individual indicators regarding "Strategic Implementation Monitoring [Strategische Durchführungskontrolle]"			
Description of indicators	*Item to Total-Correlation*	*Indicator-Reliability*	*t statistic*
1. Wir überprüfen regelmäßig die Durchführung strategischer Maßnahmen bei der Tochtergesellschaft.	0.61	0.48	4.30
2. Wir überprüfen, ob die eingeschlagene Richtung der Strategierealisierung der Tochtergesellschaft im Hinblick auf das langfristige strategische Ziel akzeptabel ist.	0.68	0.62	4.95
3. Wir überprüfen bereits ergriffene Maßnahmen darauf, ob die eingeschlagene Richtung mit Blick auf das strategische Ziel geeignet ist.	0.69	0.66	5.09

Information on scale "Strategic Implementation Monitoring [Strategische Durchführungskontrolle]"			
Descriptive Statistics		*Result of Exploratory Factor Analysis*	
Cronbach's alpha:	0.81	Total variance explained:	0.72
Results of Confirmatory Factor Analysis			
Factor reliability:	0.81	Average variance explained:	0.59

References

Eckey, M./Schäffer, U. **(2006): Kontrolle von Mehrheitsbeteiligungen in börsennotierten Management-Holdings, in: Zeitschrift für Planung & Unternehmenssteuerung, Vol. 17, pp. 251-280.**

Schreyögg, G./Steinmann, H. (1987): Strategic Control: A new Perspective, in: Academy of Management Review, Vol. 12, pp. 91-103.

201. Strategic Surveillance [Strategische Überwachung]

Scale Description

The scale measures to which extent events inside or outside the subsidiary, which are likely threatening the course of strategic action, are monitored by the central controlling department.

Origin

Developed by Eckey and Schäffer (2006) based on a model from Schreyögg and Steinmann (1987).

Samples

Eckey and Schäffer (2006) collected data using a survey questionnaire sent to a total of 51 group controlling departments of management holdings listed in the German Prime Standard. The sample of companies represented a variety of industries. 37 usable responses were received, yielding a response rate of 72.5%.

Comments

Eckey and Schäffer (2006) reported a mean of 4.41 and standard deviation of 1.22 on a theoretical range of 1-7.

Scale Indicators and Reliability / Validity Parameters

Scale: from 1 (strongly disagree) to 7 (strongly agree)

Information on individual indicators regarding "Strategic Surveillance [Strategische Überwachung]"			
Description of indicators	*Item to Total-Correlation*	*Indicator-Reliability*	*t statistic*
1. Wir untersuchen das Umfeld der Tochtergesellschaft ungerichtet, um Risiken und Chancen aufzuspüren.	0.50	0.37	3.32
2. Wir versuchen regelmäßig, schwache Signale zu identifizieren, die uns Anhaltspunkte für mögliche Risiken und Chancen geben.	0.57	0.55	3.91
3. Im Rahmen unserer Tätigkeit analysieren wir die Umwelt unserer Tochtergesellschaft auf mögliche Chancen und Risiken.	0.55	0.48	3.69

Information on scale "Strategic Surveillance [Strategische Überwachung]"			
Descriptive Statistics		*Result of Exploratory Factor Analysis*	
Cronbach's alpha:	0.72	Total variance explained:	0.64
Results of Confirmatory Factor Analysis			
Factor reliability:	0.72	Average variance explained:	0.47

References

Eckey, M./Schäffer, U. (2006): Kontrolle von Mehrheitsbeteiligungen in börsennotierten Management-Holdings, in: Zeitschrift für Planung & Unternehmenssteuerung, Vol. 17, pp. 251-280.

Schreyögg, G./Steinmann, H. (1987): Strategic Control: A new Perspective, in: Academy of Management Review, Vol. 12, pp. 91-103.

202. Strategy Commitment

Scale Description

The scale measures the extent to which a manager comprehends and supports the goals and objectives of a marketing strategy.

Origin

Developed by Noble and Mokwa (1999).

Samples

The survey-based study conducted by Noble and Mokwa (1999) involved samples from two firms: One firm was a large, multi state, financial services organization. Subjects were managers with extensive responsibilities for the implementation of marketing strategies. The other firm was a market share leader in the packaged goods industry. In this company, participants were regional sales managers with full responsibility for a geographic area, including discretionary budgets for promotions and responsibility for implementing corporate promotional strategies. The sample consisted of 254 managers in the financial services company and 534 managers in the packaged goods industry. Usable responses were 161 from the financial service company (63% response rate) and 325 from the other company (61% response rate). The total of 486 usable responses represents an overall 62% responsc rate.

Scale Indicators and Reliability / Validity Parameters

Scale: from 1 (strongly agree) to 5 (strongly disagree)

Information on individual indicators regarding "Strategy Commitment"			
Description of indicators	*Item to Total-Correlation*	*Indicator-Reliability*	*t statistic*
1. I didn't think this strategy was in the best interests of the company. (R)	–*	0.672	–*
2. I thought the strategy was a great deal.	–*	0.876	–*
3. I can't say that I supported the strategy. (R)	–*	0.618	–*
4. I personally felt that the goals of the strategy were appropriate.	–*	0.602	–*
Information on scale "Strategy Commitment"			
Descriptive Statistics		*Result of Exploratory Factor Analysis*	
Cronbach's alpha:	0.78	Total variance explained:	–*

*Not available

References

***Noble, C. H./Mokwa, M. P.* (1999): Implementing Marketing Strategies: Developing and Testing a Managerial Theory, in: Journal of Marketing, Vol. 63, pp. 57-73.**

203. Subsidiary Role Overestimation

Scale Description

The scale measures the degree of subsidiary role overestimation by capturing the subsidiary role vis-à-vis other MNC units.

Origin

Developed by Birkinshaw et al. (2000).

Samples

Birkinshaw et al. (2000) collected data on a total of 100 HQ-subsidiary dyads. The MNCs operate in a wide variety of industries, though with an emphasis in manufacturing (hard materials, paper, power, retailing, transportation services and telecommunications). A total of 19 MNC divisions participated in the study, all but one were headquartered in Sweden. The sample of subsidiaries was selected through discussion with HQ managers in the 19 MNC divisions. Between 3 and 10 subsidiaries in each MNC division were selected.

Scale Indicators and Reliability / Validity Parameters

Scale: from 1 (not at all) to 5 (very high)

Information on individual indicators regarding "Subsidiary Role Overestimation"			
Description of indicators	*Item to Total-Correlation*	*Indicator-Reliability*	*t statistic*
To what extent is the subsidiary important to other divisional units concerning…			
1. their sales volume?	–*	0.87	8.01
2. their information about market activities?	–*	0.74	6.85
3. maintaining important relations to other corporate units?	–*	0.54	4.99
Information on scale "Subsidiary Role Overestimation"			
Descriptive Statistics		*Result of Exploratory Factor Analysis*	
Cronbach's alpha:	–*	Total variance explained:	–*

*Not available

References

Birkinshaw, J./Holm, U./Thilenius, P./Arvidsson, N. **(2000): Consequences of Perception Gaps in the Headquarters-Subsidiary Relationship, in: International Business Review, Vol. 9, pp. 321-344.**

204. Subsidiary Technology Embeddedness

Scale Description

The scale measures the degree of a subsidiary's capacity to absorb new technology.

Origin

Developed by Andersson et al. (2001).

Samples

Andersson et al. (2001) collected data from 98 subsidiaries belonging to 20 international divisions within 15 Swedish MNCs. The division headquarters were all located in Sweden. The majority of the subsidiaries were located in Europe and a few (five) in North America. The sample was chosen to represent a wide spectrum of Swedish industry and involves large and well-known companies in industries such as pulp and paper, telecommunications equipment, petrochemicals, power distribution, hard metal tools, saws and chains, gas applications, transportation, software, management training and industrial equipment.

Scale Indicators and Reliability / Validity Parameters

Scale: from 1 (not at all) to 5 (very much)

Information on individual indicators regarding "Subsidiary Technology Embeddedness"			
Description of indicators	*Item to Total-Correlation*	*Indicator-Reliability*	*t statistic*
1. To what extent is this counterpart important to subsidiary's product development?	–*	0.72	8.01
2. To what extent is this counterpart important to the subsidiary's production development?	–*	0.83	8.83
3. To what extent has the relationship with this counterpart caused adaptation to the subsidiary's product development?	–*	0.87	9.55
4. To what extent has the relationship with this counterpart caused adaptation to the subsidiary's production development?	–*	0.76	8.48

Information on scale "Subsidiary Technology Embeddedness"			
Descriptive Statistics		*Result of Exploratory Factor Analysis*	
Cronbach's alpha:	–*	Total variance explained:	–*

*Not available

References

Andersson, U./Forsgren, M./Pedersen, T. **(2001): Subsidiary Performance in Multinational Corporations: The Importance of Technology Embeddedness, in: International Business Review, Vol. 10, pp. 3-23.**

205. Supervisory Attention

Scale Description

The scale measures the attention the salesperson's immediate supervisor gives him or her. This attention has been shown to have the potential to influence the salesperson's behavior and create positive outcomes, such as elements of job satisfaction (Churchill Jr. et al. (1976)) and role clarification (Behrman and Perreault Jr. (1984)).

Origin

Developed by Anderson and Robertson (1995).

Samples

Anderson and Robertson (1995) model dependence and exit barriers using perceptual data gathered directly from 208 salespeople of several cooperating firms that supplied names and addresses of a cross section of their salespeople. Surveys were sent by the researchers to home addresses and solicited cooperation in exchange for an executive summary of results. These 208 responses represent 49.5% of the 420 brokers sampled and are the basis for measure development and for modeling dependence and perceptions of the hazards of selling house brands.

Comments

Anderson and Robertson (1995) reported a mean of 0.00 and a standard deviation of 0.66.

Scale Indicators and Reliability / Validity Parameters

Scale: from 1 (strongly disagree) to 7 (strongly agree)

Information on individual indicators regarding "Supervisory Attention"
Description of indicators
1. My branch manager is too busy selling to give me much time and attention. (R)
2. My branch manager basically leaves me alone to do my thing. (R)
3. My branch manager doesn't have much time to spend with any individual broker. (R)
4. My branch manager supervises too many brokers to give me much time. (R)
5. My branch manager is always available to meet with me.
6. My branch manager gets very involved in what I'm doing.
7. My branch manager has the time to meet with me.
8. I talk with my branch manager often.
9. As far as I'm concerned, my branch manager is invisible. (R)
10. In a typical week, how many hours do you spend talking with your branch manager (about any subject)? _______ hours per week.

Information on scale "Supervisory Attention"			
Descriptive Statistics		*Result of Exploratory Factor Analysis*	
Cronbach's alpha:	0.86	Total variance explained:	–*

*Not available

References

***Anderson, E./Robertson, T. S.* (1995): Inducing Multiline Salespeople to Adopt House Brands, in: Journal of Marketing, Vol. 59, pp. 16-31.**

Behrman, D. N./Perreault Jr., W. D. (1984): A Role Stress Model of the Performance and Satisfaction of Industrial Salespersons, in: Journal of Marketing, Vol. 48, pp. 9-21.

Churchill Jr., G. A./Ford, N. M./Walker Jr., O. C. (1976): Organizational Climate and Job Satisfaction in the Salesforce, in: Journal of Marketing Research, Vol. 13, pp. 323-332.

206. Symbolic Use (of Controlling Information) [Symbolische Nutzung von Controlling-Informationen]

Scale Description

The scale measures the extent to which managers use controlling information in the decision-making process for enforcing decisions once they have been made.

Origin

The scale was newly developed by Bauer (2002), adapting items from Karlshaus (2000).

Samples

Survey data were collected by questionnaire, administered via mail to 2,527 German companies. A total of 347 companies sent usable answers, yielding a 14.8% return rate.

Comments

The study used a dyadic design approach, where a manager and a controller of the same company were questioned. The data for this scale sole stem from the answers of the managers.

Scale Indicators and Reliability / Validity Parameters

Scale: from 1 (definitely false) to 7 (definitely true)

Information on individual indicators regarding "Symbolic Use (of Controlling Information) [Symbolische Nutzung von Controlling-Informationen]"			
Description of indicators	*Item to Total-Correlation*	*Indicator-Reliability*	*t statistic*
1. Die Informationen des Controlling helfen mir bei der Durchsetzung von Entscheidungen bei anderen Personen.	0.62	0.62	11.50
2. Die geeignete Interpretation der Informationen aus unserem Controlling erlaubt es mir, Entscheidungen zu beeinflussen.	0.68	0.89	11.50
3. Die Informationen aus unserem Controlling helfen mir bei der Begründung von bereits getroffenen Entscheidungen.	0.51	0.39	11.50

Information on scale "Symbolic Use (of Controlling Information) [Symbolische Nutzung von Controlling-Informationen]"			
Descriptive Statistics		*Result of Exploratory Factor Analysis*	
Cronbach's alpha:	0.78	Total variance explained:	0.70
Results of Confirmatory Factor Analysis			
Factor reliability:	0.84	Average variance explained:	0.64

References

***Bauer, M.* (2002): Controllership in Deutschland. Zur erfolgreichen Zusammenarbeit von Controllern und Managern, Wiesbaden 2002, pp. 208-209.**

Karlshaus, J. T. (2000): Die Nutzung von Kostenrechnungsinformationen im Marketing, Wiesbaden 2000.

207. Symbolic Use of Metrics [Symbolische Nutzung von Kennzahlen]

Scale Description

The scale measures the extent to which managers use metrics in the decision-making process for enforcing decisions once they have been made.

Origin

The scale was adopted by Sandt (2004) from Karlshaus (2000). A similar approach concerning accounting data was used by Hunold (2003).

Samples

The questionnaire was sent to 2,386 German upper level managers. 254 responses could be integrated into the analysis, yielding a response rate of 11.1%.

Scale Indicators and Reliability / Validity Parameters

Scale: from 1 (definitely false) to 5 (definitely true)

Information on individual indicators regarding "Symbolic Use of Metrics [Symbolische Nutzung von Kennzahlen]"			
Description of indicators	*Item to Total-Correlation*	*Indicator-Reliability*	*t statistic*
1. Die Kennzahlen helfen mir bei der Durchsetzung von Entscheidungen bei anderen Personen.	0.59	0.49	10.97
2. Die geeignete Interpretation der Kennzahlen erlaubt es mir, Entscheidungen zu beeinflussen.	0.69	0.83	10.97
3. Die Kennzahlen helfen mir bei der Begründung von bereits getroffenen Entscheidungen.	0.58	0.54	10.97

Information on scale "Symbolic Use of Metrics [Symbolische Nutzung von Kennzahlen]"			
Descriptive Statistics		*Result of Exploratory Factor Analysis*	
Cronbach's alpha:	0.78	Total variance explained:	0.70
Results of Confirmatory Factor Analysis			
Factor reliability:	0.83	Average variance explained:	0.62

References

Sandt, J. (2004): Management mit Kennzahlen und Kennzahlensystemen. Bestandsaufnahme, Determinanten und Erfolgswirkungen, Wiesbaden 2004, pp. 162-165.

Hunold, C. (2003): Kommunale Kostenrechnung. Gestaltung, Nutzung und Erfolgsfaktoren, Wiesbaden 2003.

Karlshaus, J. T. (2000): Die Nutzung von Kostenrechnungsinformationen im Marketing, Wiesbaden 2000.

208. Systems Complexity of Cost Accounting [Systemkomplexität der Kostenrechnung]

Scale Description

The scale measures the complexity of the accounting department's processes, e.g. the quantity of different calculation methods.

Origin

The scale was newly developed by Aust (1999). Frank (2000) used reverse-coded items exclusively in a related approach while Hunold (2003) used a similar scale again.

Samples

Survey data were collected by questionnaire administered to general managers as well as managers of accounting and marketing units from 1,163 German companies from the manufacturing industry which had more than 50 employees. A total of 105 usable triads of questionnaires (9%) were returned.

Scale Indicators and Reliability / Validity Parameters

Scale: from 1 (definitely false) to 5 (definitely true)

Information on individual indicators regarding "Systems Complexity of Cost Accounting [Systemkomplexität der Kostenrechnung]"			
Description of indicators	*Item to Total-Correlation*	*Indicator-Reliability*	*t statistic*
1. Die Anzahl der Kontierungsobjekte (wie Kostenstellen, Produkte oder Aufträge) ist bei uns sehr hoch.	0.50	0.57	4.82
2. Je nach Problemstellung rechnen wir mit unterschiedlichen Wertansätzen (z.B. Vollkosten und Teilkosten).	0.33	0.11	3.27
3. Die Anzahl der Verrechnungsbeziehungen in unserer Kostenrechnung ist sehr hoch.	0.60	0.91	6.01

Information on scale "Systems Complexity of Cost Accounting [Systemkomplexität der Kostenrechnung]"			
Descriptive Statistics		*Result of Exploratory Factor Analysis*	
Cronbach's alpha:	0.65	Total variance explained:	0.61
Results of Confirmatory Factor Analysis			
Factor reliability:	0.72	Average variance explained:	0.53

References

***Aust, R.* (1999): Kostenrechnung als unternehmensinterne Dienstleistung, Wiesbaden 1999, pp. 166-167.**

Frank, S. (2000): Erfolgreiche Gestaltung der Kostenrechnung: Determinanten und Wirkungen am Beispiel mittelständischer Unternehmen, Wiesbaden 2000.

Hunold, C. (2003): Kommunale Kostenrechnung. Gestaltung, Nutzung und Erfolgsfaktoren, Wiesbaden 2003.

209. Systems Dynamics of Cost Accounting [Systemdynamik der Kostenrechnung]

Scale Description

The scale measures the dynamics of the accounting department's processes, e.g. the regularity of modifications in the relationships of cost objects.

Origin

The scale was newly developed by Aust (1999).

Samples

Survey data were collected by questionnaire administered to general managers as well as managers of accounting and marketing units from 1,163 German companies from the manufacturing industry which had more than 50 employees. A total of 105 usable triads of questionnaires (9%) were returned.

Scale Indicators and Reliability / Validity Parameters

Scale: from 1 (definitely false) to 5 (definitely true)

Information on individual indicators regarding "Systems Dynamics of Cost Accounting [Systemdynamik der Kostenrechnung]"			
Description of indicators	*Item to Total-Correlation*	*Indicator-Reliability*	*t statistic*
1. Die Zurechnungsobjekte der Kostenrechnung (wie Kostenstellen, Produkte oder Aufträge) verändern sich häufig.	0.55	0.47	7.48
2. Die Verrechnungsbeziehungen zwischen den Zurechnungsobjekten variieren häufig.	0.68	0.92	9.90
3. Die Verrechnungssätze (z.B. Zuschlagssätze oder andere Kostensätze) verändern sich häufig.	0.44	0.31	5.99

Information on scale "Systems Dynamics of Cost Accounting [Systemdynamik der Kostenrechnung]"			
Descriptive Statistics		*Result of Exploratory Factor Analysis*	
Cronbach's alpha:	0.72	Total variance explained:	0.65
Results of Confirmatory Factor Analysis			
Factor reliability:	0.79	Average variance explained:	0.57

References

***Aust, R.* (1999): Kostenrechnung als unternehmensinterne Dienstleistung, Wiesbaden 1999, pp. 166-167.**

210. Task Coordination [Aufgabenkoordination]

Scale Description

The scale measures the extent to which management teams regularly perceive themselves as being in conflict concerning the allocation of task and responsibilities.

Origin

The scale was newly developed by Spieker (2004).

Samples

Survey data were collected by questionnaire, administered via internet to 353 managers of German start-up companies. A total of 145 usable questionnaires (41.1%) were returned.

Scale Indicators and Reliability / Validity Parameters

Scale: from 1 (definitely false) to 7 (definitely true)

Information on individual indicators regarding "Task Coordination [Aufgabenkoordination]"			
Description of indicators	*Item to Total-Correlation*	*Indicator-Reliability*	*t statistic*
1. Es kommt häufig zu Konflikten über die Rollen- und Aufgabenzuteilung im Team.	0.74	0.68	13.32
2. In unserem Team gibt es konkurrierende Interessen bezüglich der Aufgabenbereiche.	0.82	0.86	13.87
3. Es gibt häufig Konflikte darüber, ob Teammitglieder für bestimmte Entscheidungen lieber das Team hätten konsultieren sollen.	0.80	0.77	13.56
4. Einzelne Teammitglieder mischen sich ungefragt in die Aufgabenbereiche anderer ein.	0.71	0.62	13.00

Information on scale "Task Coordination [Aufgabenkoordination]"			
Descriptive Statistics		*Result of Exploratory Factor Analysis*	
Cronbach's alpha:	0.89	Total variance explained:	0.76
Results of Confirmatory Factor Analysis			
χ^2-Value (Degrees of Freedom):	0.17 (2)	χ^2-Value/Degrees of Freedom:	0.09
p Value:	0.00	RMSEA:	0.00
SRMR:	–*	CFI:	1.00
GFI:	0.99	AGFI:	0.99
Factor reliability:	0.92	Average variance explained:	0.73

*Not available

References

Spieker, M. **(2004): Entscheidungen in Gründerteams. Determinanten – Parameter – Erfolgsauswirkungen, Wiesbaden 2004, pp. 246-247.**

211. Task Significance

Scale Description

The scale measures the level of task significance (i.e. the set of activities that the team must perform to achieve the group's goal, see Goodman et al. (1987)) of ABC team members.

Origin

Developed by Anderson et al. (2002).

Samples

Data from 18 ABC projects in two automobile manufacturing firms and survey data from 89 individual ABC team members were collected.

Comments

Anderson et al. (2002) reported an item mean of 3.4 and a standard deviation of 0.81.

Scale Indicators and Reliability / Validity Parameters

Scale: from 1 (strongly disagree) to 5 (strongly agree)

Information on individual indicators regarding "Task Significance"			
Description of indicators			
1. A lot of people will be affected by how I do my job on ABC.			
2. The future of this plant will be affected by how well I do my job on ABC.			
3. Working on ABC gave me the opportunity to contribute something worthwhile to this plant.			
4. The work I did on ABC was extremely meaningful to me.			
5. My work on ABC had a visible effect to this plant.			
6. As I performed my tasks on ABC, I could see the contribution I was making.			
Information on scale "Task Significance"			
Descriptive Statistics		*Result of Exploratory Factor Analysis*	
Cronbach's alpha:	0.89	Total variance explained:	–*

*Not available

References

***Anderson, S./Hesford, J./Young, S. M.* (2002): Factors Influencing the Performance of Activity Based Costing Teams: A Field Study of ABC Model Development Time in the Automobile Industry, in: Accounting, Organizations and Society, Vol. 27, pp. 195-211.**

Goodman, P. S./Ravlin, E./Schminke, M. (1987): Understanding Teams in Organizations, in: Cummings, L./Staw, B. (Ed.): Research in Organizational Behavior, Greenwich, Conn. 1987, pp. 121-183.

212. Team Cohesion

Scale Description

The scale measures the degree of commitment of ABC members to the team task (Goodman et al., 1987).

Origin

Developed by Anderson et al. (2002).

Samples

Data from 18 ABC projects in two automobile manufacturing firms and survey data from 89 individual ABC team members were collected.

Comments

Anderson et al. (2002) reported an item mean 3.9 and a standard deviation of 0.81.

Scale Indicators and Reliability / Validity Parameters

Scale: from 1 (strongly disagree) to 5 (strongly agree)

Information on individual indicators regarding "Team Cohesion"			
Description of indicators			
1. When I was on the ABC team I felt I was really a part of the group.			
2. I looked forward to working with ABC team members each day.			
3. There was a strong feeling of camaraderie among ABC team members.			
Information on scale "Team Cohesion"			
Descriptive Statistics		*Result of Exploratory Factor Analysis*	
Cronbach's alpha:	0.80	Total variance explained:	–*

*Not available

References

***Anderson, S./Hesford, J./Young, S. M.* (2002): Factors Influencing the Performance of Activity Based Costing Teams: A Field Study of ABC Model Development Time in the Automobile Industry, in: Accounting, Organizations and Society, Vol. 27, pp. 195-211.**

Goodman, P. S./Ravlin, E./Schminke, M. (1987): Understanding Teams in Organizations, in: Cummings, L./Staw, B. (Ed.): Research in Organizational Behavior, Greenwich, Conn. 1987, pp. 121-183.

213. Technology Dynamics [Technologiedynamik]

Scale Description

The scale measures the extent to which managers think that technologies in their respective branch develop or change rapidly.

Origin

Schäffer/Steiners (2004) based their scale on items by Farrell (2000).

Samples

Survey data were collected by questionnaire, administered to business unit leaders of 3,500 German companies with 100 to 2,000 employees from the industrial sector. A total of 449 usable questionnaires (12.8%) were returned.

Scale Indicators and Reliability / Validity Parameters

Scale: from 1 (definitely false) to 5 (definitely true)

Information on individual indicators regarding "Technology Dynamics [Technologiedynamik]"			
Description of indicators	*Item to Total-Correlation*	*Indicator-Reliability*	*t statistic*
1. Die Technologie in unserer Branche ändert sich schnell.	0.60	0.43	14.65
2. Technologische Veränderungen bieten in unserer Branche große Möglichkeiten.	0.73	0.66	19.54
3. Viele Produkte in unserer Branche wurden durch bahnbrechende Änderungen ermöglicht.	0.73	0.66	19.39
4. Technologische Entwicklungen sind in unserer Branche eher unwesentlich. (R)	0.70	0.61	18.56

Information on scale "Technology Dynamics [Technologiedynamik]"			
Descriptive Statistics		*Result of Exploratory Factor Analysis*	
Cronbach's alpha:	0.85	Total variance explained:	0.69
Results of Confirmatory Factor Analysis			
χ^2-Value (Degrees of Freedom):	4.67 (2)	χ^2-Value/Degrees of Freedom:	2.33
p Value:	0.10	RMSEA:	0.6
NFI:	1.00	NNFI:	0.99
SRMR:	0.01	CFI:	1.0
GFI:	0.99	AGFI:	0.97
Factor reliability:	0.85	Average variance explained:	0.59

References

***Schäffer, U./Steiners, D.* (2004): Zur Nutzung von Controllinginformationen, in: Zeitschrift für Planung und Unternehmenssteuerung, Vol. 15, pp. 377-404.**

Farrell, M. A. (2000): Developing a Market-Oriented Learning Organisation, in: Australian Journal of Management, Vol. 25, pp. 201-223.

214. Timeliness of Information [Informationsaktualität]

Scale Description

The scale measures whether information is reported early in the process of budgetary control.

Origin

Künkele and Schäffer (2007) used one indicator of the 13-item scale of Karlshaus (2000) and three additional indicators measure timeliness of information. The instrument was developed by Karlshaus (2000) to measure the quality of accounting information and was initially conceived as having four dimensions: breadth, timeliness, reliability and understandability. In order to test the impact of these dimensions separately, the item relating to the dimension timeliness was extracted and related to budgetary control. Three additional indicators, which also describe the timeliness of data, were developed and added to build a scale with four indicators.

Samples

Survey data were collected by questionnaire, administered to business unit leaders and the responsible controllers of these business units of 1,120 German companies from 500 to 5,000 employees. The companies were from services and industrial sectors. A total of 140 usable pairs of questionnaires (12.5%) were returned.

Comments

The instrument of Karlshaus (2000) has been used recently by Schäffer and Steiners (2004). They concentrated on five indicators and found good reliability coefficients (Cronbach's alpha = 0.81).

Scale Indicators and Reliability / Validity Parameters

Scale: from 1 (definitely false) to 5 (definitely true)

Information on individual indicators regarding "Timeliness of Information [Informationsaktualität]"			
Description of indicators	*Item to Total-Correlation*	*Indicator-Reliability*	*t statistic*
1. Bei uns stehen die Kontrollberichte nach Abschluss der Budgetkontrolle in kürzester Zeit zur Verfügung.	0.81	0.88	18.78
2. Die Kontrollberichte sind in unserem Unternehmen stets top-aktuell.	0.77	0.75	16.82
3. Ich wünschte mir, dass die Kontrollberichte nach Abschluss der Budgetkontrolle schneller erstellt würden. (R)	0.67	0.46	12.41

Information on scale "Timeliness of Information [Informationsaktualität]"			
Descriptive Statistics		*Result of Exploratory Factor Analysis*	
Cronbach's alpha:	0.79	Total variance explained:	0.63
Results of Confirmatory Factor Analysis			
Factor reliability:	0.85	Average variance explained:	0.65

References

Künkele, J./Schäffer, U. (2007): Zur erfolgreichen Gestaltung der Budgetkontrolle, in: Die Betriebswirtschaft, Vol. 67, pp. 75-92.

Karlshaus, J. T. (2000): Die Nutzung von Kostenrechnungsinformationen im Marketing: Bestandsaufnahme, Determinanten und Erfolgsauswirkungen, Wiesbaden 2000.

Schäffer, U./Steiners, D. (2004): Zur Nutzung von Controllinginformationen, in: Zeitschrift für Planung und Unternehmenssteuerung, Vol. 15, pp. 377-404.

215. Time Pressure [Zeitdruck]

Scale Description

The scale measures the extent to which management teams regularly perceive themselves as being under time pressure in the decision-making process.

Origin

The scale was newly developed by Spieker (2004).

Samples

Survey data were collected by questionnaire, administered via internet to 353 managers of German start-up companies. A total of 145 usable questionnaires (41.1%) were returned.

Scale Indicators and Reliability / Validity Parameters

Scale: from 1 (definitely false) to 7 (definitely true)

Information on individual indicators regarding "Time Pressure [Zeitdruck]"			
Description of indicators	*Item to Total-Correlation*	*Indicator-Reliability*	*t statistic*
1. Es gelingt uns, bei wichtigen Entscheidungen den Druck des Tagesgeschäfts auszuklammern. (R)	0.53	0.39	9.59
2. Wir beraten wichtige Entscheidungen zeitlich getrennt vom Tagesgeschäft. (R)	0.57	0.38	9.46
3. Wichtige Teamentscheidungen werden durch das Tagesgeschäft behindert.	0.76	0.77	11.02
4. Wichtige Entscheidungen sind durch Stress und hohen Zeitdruck gekennzeichnet.	0.75	0.81	11.09

Information on scale "Time Pressure [Zeitdruck]"			
Descriptive Statistics		*Result of Exploratory Factor Analysis*	
Cronbach's alpha:	0.82	Total variance explained:	0.66
Results of Confirmatory Factor Analysis			
χ^2-Value (Degrees of Freedom):	1.89 (2)	χ^2-Value/Degrees of Freedom:	0.95
p Value:	0.33	RMSEA:	0.00
SRMR:	–*	CFI:	1.00
GFI:	0.99	AGFI:	0.98
Factor reliability:	0.84	Average variance explained:	0.58

*Not available

References

Spieker, M. **(2004): Entscheidungen in Gründerteams. Determinanten – Parameter – Erfolgsauswirkungen, Wiesbaden 2004, pp. 245-246.**

216. Tolerance for Uncertainty [Ungewissheitstoleranz]

Scale Description

The scale measures the extent to which managers perceive uncertain situations either as challenge or threat.

Origin

Schäffer/Steiners (2004) based their scale on Dalbert (1999).

Samples

Survey data were collected by questionnaire, administered to business unit leaders of 3,500 German companies with 100 to 2,000 employees from the industrial sector. A total of 449 usable questionnaires (12.8%) were returned.

Comment

The scale initially consisted of 8 items. 4 items had to be eliminated due to a lack of Indicator-Reliability.

Scale Indicators and Reliability / Validity Parameters

Scale: from 1 (definitely false) to 5 (definitely true)

Information on individual indicators regarding "Tolerance for Uncertainty [Ungewissheitstoleranz]"			
Description of indicators	*Item to Total-Correlation*	*Indicator-Reliability*	*t statistic*
1. Ich mag es, wenn unverhofft Überraschungen auftreten.	0.56	0.46	13.67
2. Ich warte geradezu darauf, dass etwas Aufregendes passiert.	0.53	0.41	12.84
3. Wenn es um mich herum alles so richtig drunter und drüber geht, fühle ich mich so richtig wohl.	0.55	0.45	13.45
4. Ich weiß gerne, was auf mich zukommt. (R)	0.50	0.35	11.78

Information on scale "Tolerance for Uncertainty [Ungewissheitstoleranz]"			
Descriptive Statistics		*Result of Exploratory Factor Analysis*	
Cronbach's alpha:	0.74	Total variance explained:	0.56
Results of Confirmatory Factor Analysis			
χ^2-Value (Degrees of Freedom):	5.83 (2)	χ^2-Value/Degrees of Freedom:	2.92
p Value:	0.05	RMSEA:	0.07
NFI:	0.99	NNFI:	0.98
SRMR:	0.02	CFI:	0.99
GFI:	0.99	AGFI:	0.97
Factor reliability:	0.74	Average variance explained:	0.42

References

***Schäffer, U./Steiners, D.* (2004): Zur Nutzung von Controllinginformationen, in: Zeitschrift für Planung und Unternehmenssteuerung, Vol. 15, pp. 377-404.**

Dalbert, C. (1999): Die Ungewissheitstoleranzskala: Skaleneigenschaften und Validierungsbefunde, in: Hallesche Berichte zur Pädagogischen Psychologie, Vol. 1, Halle 1999.

217. Trust in Controlling Department [Vertrauen in das Controlling]

Scale Description

The scale measures the manager´s level of trust in the controlling department.

Origin

The scale was newly developed by Spillecke (2006) based on the scales of Doney/Cannon (1997) and Werner (1997).

Samples

Survey data were collected by questionnaire, administered via e-mail to 3,312 German managers of companies with at least 200 employees. The companies were from different industrial sectors. A total of 415 usable questionnaires (12.5%) were returned.

Comment

The scale initially consisted of 7 items of which 4 address the aspect of credibility and 3 the aspect of friendliness. 3 items had to be eliminated due to a lack of Item-to-Total Correlation.

Scale Indicators and Reliability / Validity Parameters

Scale: from 1 (definitely false) to 5 (definitely true)

Information on individual indicators on scale "Trust in Controlling Department [Vertrauen in das Controlling]"			
Description of indicators	*Item to Total-Correlation*	*Indicator-Reliability*	*t statistic*
1. Ich habe das Gefühl, dass unser Controlling die Interessen meiner Geschäftseinheit/Abteilung sehr gut vertritt.	0.61	0.43	–*
2. Unser Controlling ist bei auftretenden Problemen immer ehrlich zu mir.	0.72	0.61	13.39
3. Ich bin davon überzeugt, dass unser Controlling sein möglichstes tut, um auftretende Probleme zu beseitigen.	0.75	0.69	14.03
4. Unser Controlling ist ein absolut vertrauenswürdiger Partner.	0.79	0.80	14.56

Information on scale "Trust in Controlling Department [Vertrauen in das Controlling]"			
Descriptive Statistics		*Result of Exploratory Factor Analysis*	
Cronbach's alpha:	0.87	Total variance explained:	0.63
Results of Confirmatory Factor Analysis			
χ^2-Value (Degrees of Freedom):	1.48 (2)	χ^2-Value/Degrees of Freedom:	0.74
p Value:	0.48	RMSEA:	0.00
SRMR:	–*	CFI:	0.99
GFI:	1.00	AGFI:	0.99
Factor reliability:	0.87	Average variance explained:	0.62

*Not feasible

References

Spillecke, D. **(2006): Interne Kundenorientierung des Controllerbereichs. Messung – Erfolgsauswirkungen – Determinanten, Wiesbaden 2006, pp. 149-154.**

Doney, P./Cannon, J. P. (1999): An Examination of the Nature of Trust in Buyer-Seller Relationships, in: Journal of Marketing, Vol. 61, pp. 35-51.

Werner, H. (1997): Relationales Beschaffungsverhalten: Ausprägungen und Determinanten, Wiesbaden 1997.

218. Trust in MAS Information [Vertrauen in Controlling-Informationen]

Scale Description

The scale measures to what extent a user trusts in controlling information.

Origin

Schäffer/Steiners (2004) used indicators developed by Karlshaus (2000). A similar approach concerning accountants was used by Hunold (2003).

Samples

Survey data were collected by questionnaire, administered to business unit leaders of 3,500 German companies with 100 to 2,000 employees from the industrial sector. A total of 449 usable questionnaires (12.8%) were returned.

Scale Indicators and Reliability / Validity Parameters

Scale: from 1 (definitely false) to 5 (definitely true)

Information on individual indicators regarding "Trust in MAS Information [Vertrauen in Control-ling-Informationen]"			
Description of indicators	*Item to Total-Correlation*	*Indicator-Reliability*	*t statistic*
1. Ich vertraue darauf, dass mir richtige Informationen geliefert werden.	0.56	0.36	13.32
2. Die Informationslieferanten sind vertrauenswürdig.	0.79	0.81	23.37
3. Ich denke, dass die Informationslieferanten kompetent sind.	0.77	0.81	23.24
4. Ich kann mich darauf verlassen, dass die Zusagen der Informationslieferanten eingehalten werden.	0.65	0.51	16.86

Information on scale "Trust in MAS Information [Vertrauen in Controlling-Informationen]"			
Descriptive Statistics		*Result of Exploratory Factor Analysis*	
Cronbach's alpha:	0.84	Total variance explained:	0.70
Results of Confirmatory Factor Analysis			
χ^2-Value (Degrees of Freedom):	5.65 (2)	χ^2-Value/Degrees of Freedom:	2.83
p Value:	0.06	RMSEA:	0.06
NFI:	0.99	NNFI:	0.99
SRMR:	0.01	CFI:	1.0
GFI:	0.99	AGFI:	0.97
Factor reliability:	0.86	Average variance explained:	0.62

References

***Schäffer, U./Steiners, D.* (2004): Zur Nutzung von Controllinginformationen, in: Zeitschrift für Planung und Unternehmenssteuerung, Vol. 15, pp. 377-404.**

Hunold, C. (2003): Kommunale Kostenrechnung. Gestaltung, Nutzung und Erfolgsfaktoren, Wiesbaden 2003.

Karlshaus, J. T. (2000): Die Nutzung von Kostenrechnungsinformationen im Marketing, Wiesbaden 2000.

219. Trust in MNCs

Scale Description

The scale measures the degree of trust in MNCs, characterized by both openness and an absence of formal checks, procedures and controls.

Origin

Developed by Barner-Rasmussen (2003) based on previous research (e.g. Das and Teng (1998); Kanter (1994); Mishra (1996); Whitener et al. (1998)).

Samples

Barner-Rasmussen (2003) collected data through structured face-to-face interviews with 89 top managers of Finnish subsidiaries of foreign MNCs. The participating firms were picked from a list of the 150 largest foreign-owned subsidiaries in Finland, resulting in a sample of 30 US-owned, 32 Scandinavian-owned, and 27 European-owned units. Their parent companies' annual turnover ranged from US$34 million to 183,000 million and operated in between three and 190 countries.

Scale Indicators and Reliability / Validity Parameters

Scale: from 1 (very formal/not open) to 7 (very informal/very open)

Information on individual indicators regarding "Trust in MNCs"			
Description of indicators			
Please grade the atmosphere of the following forms of intracorporate interaction			
1. interunit trips and visits.			
2. corporate interunit committees, teams, and task forces.			
3. training involving participants from several units.			
4. other corporate activities such as meetings and conferences.			
Information on scale "Trust in MNCs"			
Descriptive Statistics		*Result of Exploratory Factor Analysis*	
Cronbach's alpha:	0.87	Total variance explained:	–*

*Not available

References

Barner-Rasmussen, W. **(2003): Determinants of the Feedback-Seeking Behaviour of Subsidiary Top Managers in Multinational Corporations, in: International Business Review, Vol. 12, pp. 41-60.**

Das, T. K./Teng, B.-S. (1998): Between Trust and Control: Developing Confidence in Partner Cooperation in Alliances, in: Academy of Management Review, Vol. 23, pp. 491-512.

Kanter, R. M. (1994): Collaborative Advantage: The Art of Alliances, in: Harvard Business Review, Vol. 72, pp. 96-108.

Mishra, A. K. (1996): Organizational Responses to Crises: The Centrality of Trust, in: Kramer, R. M./Tyler, T. R. (Ed.): Trust in Organizations: Frontiers of Theory and Research, Thousand Oaks, Calif. 1996, pp. 261-287.

Whitener, E. M./Brodt, S. E./Korsgaard, M. A./Werner, J. M. (1998): Managers as Initiators of Trust: An Exchange Relationship Framework for Understanding Managerial Trustworthy Behavior, in: Academy of Management Review, Vol. 23, pp. 513-530.

220. Trust within Management Teams [Vertrauen in Management Teams]

Scale Description

The scale measures management teams' general attitude towards using the services of non-company people or groups in the decision-making process.

Origin

The scale was newly developed by Spieker (2004) adopting items from Mayer/ Davis/Schoormann (1995) and Simons/Peterson (2000).

Samples

Survey data were collected by questionnaire, administered via internet to 353 managers of German start-up companies. A total of 145 usable questionnaires (41.1%) were returned.

Scale Indicators and Reliability / Validity Parameters

Scale: from 1 (definitely false) to 7 (definitely true)

Information on individual indicators regarding "Trust within Management Teams [Vertrauen in Management Teams]"			
Description of indicators	*Item to Total-Correlation*	*Indicator-Reliability*	*t statistic*
1. Die Zusammenarbeit im Team ist durch gegenseitiges Vertrauen geprägt.	0.89	0.92	18.93
2. Wir können darauf vertrauen, dass jeder Einzelne seinen Aufgaben gewachsen ist.	0.80	0.73	17.70
3. Wichtige Zahlen/Sachverhalte behält jeder lieber erstmal für sich; man weiß ja nie, was die anderen damit machen. (R)	0.87	0.82	18.30
4. Vorsicht und gegenseitiges Misstrauen sind bei uns verbreitet. (R)	0.91	0.94	19.08
5. Der Mangel an Vertrauen hat in der Vergangenheit zu Konflikten zwischen Teammitgliedern geführt. (R)	0.83	0.78	17.97

Information on scale "Trust within Management Teams [Vertrauen in Management Teams]"			
Descriptive Statistics		*Result of Exploratory Factor Analysis*	
Cronbach's alpha:	0.95	Total variance explained:	0.83
Results of Confirmatory Factor Analysis			
χ^2-Value (Degrees of Freedom):	1.54 (5)	χ^2-Value/Degrees of Freedom:	0.31
p Value:	0.00	RMSEA:	0.00
SRMR:	–*	CFI:	1.00
GFI:	0.99	AGFI:	0.99
Factor reliability:	0.96	Average variance explained:	0.84

*Not available

References

***Spieker, M.* (2004): Entscheidungen in Gründerteams. Determinanten – Parameter – Erfolgsauswirkungen, Wiesbaden 2004, pp. 243-244.**

Mayer, R. C./Davis, J. H./Schoormann, F. D. (1995): An Integrative Model of Organizational Trust, in: Academy of Management Review, Vol. 20, pp. 709-734.

Simons, T. L./Peterson, R. S. (2000): Task Conflict and Relationship Conflict in Top Management Teams: The Pivotal Role of Intragroup Trust, in: Journal of Applied Psychology, Vol. 85, pp. 102-111.

221. Turnover Intentions

Scale Description

The scale measures the degree of turnover intentions by focusing on „thinking about leaving the firm“ and „the probability of looking for another job“ with a five point Likert scale.

Origin

Developed by Viator (2001).

Samples

Viator (2001) collected data through a mail survey of 3,000 CPAs in large public accounting firms. A mailing list was obtained from the American Institute of CPAs, with support provided by the institute's academic relations division.

A total of 903 surveys were returned, representing a 30% response rate. 13 responses were deleted for coding errors or incomplete surveys. Of the remaining 890 responses, other participants excluded from this study were 25 who had left public accounting, 27 who were employed by either regional of local public firms, and 44 who were partners/directors in large firms. The remaining 794 participants were included in the study.

Comments

Other accounting studies have used different measures of employee turnover intentions (Aranya and Ferris (1984); Aranya et al. (1982); Dillard and Ferris (1979); Harrell and Stahl (1984); Harrell et al. (1986); Senatra (1980)). In the current study, the turnover intentions scale was constructed from two questionnaire items adopted from prior studies.

Scale Indicators and Reliability / Validity Parameters

Scale: from 1 (strongly disagree) to 5 (strongly agree)

Information on individual indicators regarding "Turnover Intentions"			
Description of indicators			
1. I often think about leaving my public accounting firm.			
2. I will probably look for a job outside of this firm within the next 3 years.			
Information on scale "Turnover Intentions"			
Descriptive Statistics		*Result of Exploratory Factor Analysis*	
Cronbach's alpha:	0.85	Total variance explained:	–*

*Not available

References

***Viator, R. E.* (2001): The Association of Formal and Informal Public Accounting Mentoring with Role Stress and Related Job Outcomes, in: Accounting, Organizations and Society, Vol. 26, pp. 73-93.**

Aranya, N./Ferris, K. R. (1984): A Reexamination of Accountants' Organizational-Professional Conflict, in: The Accounting Review, Vol. 59, pp. 1-15.

Aranya, N./Lachman, R./Amernic, J. (1982): Accountants' Job Satisfaction: A Path Analysis, in: Accounting, Organizations and Society, Vol. 7, pp. 201-215.

Dillard, J. F./Ferris, K. R. (1979): Sources of Professional Staff Turnover in Public Accounting Firms: Some Further Evidence, in: Accounting, Organizations and Society, Vol. 4, pp. 179-186.

Harrell, A./Chewning, E./Taylor, M. (1986): Organizational-Professional Conflict and the Job Satisfaction and Turnover Intentions of Internal Auditors, in: Auditing, Vol. 5, pp. 109-121.

Harrell, A. M./Stahl, M. J. (1984): McClelland's Trichotomy of Needs Theory and the Job Satisfaction and Work Performance of CPA Firm Professionals, in: Accounting, Organizations and Society, Vol. 9, pp. 241-252.

Senatra, P. T. (1980): Role Conflict, Role Ambiguity, and Organizational Climate in a Public Accounting Firm, in: The Accounting Review, Vol. 55, pp. 594-603.

222. Use of Capital Market – Information Function [Nutzung der Informationsfunktion des Kapitalmarktes]

Scale Description

The scale measures the degree to which research reports of financial analysts are used by the central controlling department to supplement internally generated information in order to be informed about the subsidiary. The scale comprises three dimensions: information relating to competitors, current developments within the industry of the subsidiary as well as strengths and weaknesses of the subsidiary compared to the competitors.

Origin

Developed by Eckey and Schäffer (2006).

Samples

Eckey and Schäffer (2006) collected data using a survey questionnaire sent to a total of 51 group controlling departments of management holdings listed in the German Prime Standard. The sample of companies represented a variety of industries. 37 usable responses were received, yielding a response rate of 72.5%.

Comments

Eckey and Schäffer (2006) reported a mean of 4.40 and standard deviation of 1.51 on a theoretical range of 1-7.

Scale Indicators and Reliability / Validity Parameters

Scale: from 1 (strongly disagree) to 7 (strongly agree)

Information on individual indicators regarding "Use of Capital Market – Information Function [Nutzung der Informationsfunktion des Kapitalmarktes]"			
Description of indicators	*Item to Total-Correlation*	*Indicator-Reliability*	*t statistic*
1. Wir nutzen Berichte von Finanzanalysten („Research Reports"), um uns über finanzielle Informationen von Konkurrenten zu informieren.	0.82	0.67	5.93
2. Über finanzielle Informationen in Research Reports informieren wir uns über die aktuellen Branchenentwicklungen, in denen die Tochtergesellschaft tätig ist.	0.87	0.79	6.71
3. Über die in Research Reports enthaltenen finanziellen Informationen informieren wir uns über Stärken und Schwächen der Tochtergesellschaft relativ zu den Konkurrenten.	0.70	0.45	4.51
4. Wir nutzen die in Research Reports enthaltenen finanziellen Informationen nicht für interne Zwecke. (R)	0.88	0.79	6.76
5. Wir nutzen die in Research Reports enthaltenen finanziellen/nicht-finanziellen Informationen als Ergänz-ung zu den intern generierten Informationen.	0.84	0.67	5.96
6. Wir nutzen Berichte von Finanzanalysten („Research Reports"), um uns über nicht-finanzielle Informationen von Konkurrenten zu informieren.	0.81	0.64	5.76

7. Über nicht-finanzielle Informationen in Research Reports informieren wir uns über die aktuellen Branchenentwicklungen, in denen die Tochtergesellschaft tätig ist.	0.90	0.85	7.12
8. Über die in Research Reports enthaltenen nicht-finanziellen Informationen informieren wir uns über Stärken und Schwächen der Tochtergesellschaft relativ zu den Konkurrenten.	0.78	0.56	5.25
9. Wir nutzen die in Research Reports enthaltenen nicht-finanziellen Informationen nicht für interne Zwecke. (R)	0.90	0.85	7.19
10. Wir nutzen die in Research Reports enthaltenen nicht-finanziellen Informationen als Ergänzung zu den intern generierten Informationen.	0.81	0.69	6.04

Information on scale "Use of Capital Market – Information Function [Nutzung der Informationsfunktion des Kapitalmarktes]"			
Descriptive Statistics		*Result of Exploratory Factor Analysis*	
Cronbach's alpha:	0.96	Total variance explained:	0.75
Results of Confirmatory Factor Analysis			
χ^2-Value (Degrees of Freedom):	25.11 (27)	χ^2-Value/Degrees of Freedom:	0.93
p-value:	0.57	RMSEA:	0.00
NFI:	0.96	NNFI:	0.99
SRMR:	0.03	CFI:	1.00
GFI:	0.88	AGFI:	0.75
Factor reliability:	0.96	Average variance explained:	0.70

References

Eckey, M./Schäffer, U. **(2006): Kontrolle von Mehrheitsbeteiligungen in börsennotierten Management-Holdings, in: Zeitschrift für Planung & Unternehmenssteuerung, Vol. 17, pp. 251-280.**

223. Use of Equity Capital Market – Monitoring Function [Nutzung der Kontrollfunktion des Kapitalmarktes]

Scale Description

The scale measures the degree to which research reports and discussions with financial analysts are used by the central controlling department for the direction of the subsidiary by considering corrective action called for by the analysts of the stock market.

Origin

Developed by Eckey and Schäffer (2006).

Samples

Eckey and Schäffer (2006) collected data using a survey questionnaire sent to a total of 51 group controlling departments of management holdings listed in the German Prime Standard. The sample of companies represented a variety of industries. 37 usable responses were received, yielding a response rate of 72.5%.

Scale Indicators and Reliability / Validity Parameters

Scale: from 1 (strongly disagree) to 7 (strongly agree)

Information on individual indicators regarding "Use of Equity Capital Market – Monitoring Function [Nutzung der Kontrollfunktion des Kapitalmarktes]"			
Description of indicators	*Item to Total-Correlation*	*Indicator-Reliability*	*t statistic*
1. Wir berücksichtigen von den Analysten des Aktienmarktes geforderte Korrekturmaßnahmen bei der Tochtergesellschaft im Rahmen der operativen Kontrolle.	0.75	0.71	5.80
2. Im Rahmen der strategischen Kontrolle berücksichtigen wir die Berichte („Research Reports") der Analysten des Aktienmarktes zur Ausrichtung der Tochtergesellschaft.	0.60	0.40	4.04
3. Wir berücksichtigen von den Analysten des Aktienmarktes geforderte Korrekturmaßnahmen bei der Tochtergesellschaft im Rahmen der strategischen Kontrolle.	0.84	1.00	7.38

Information on scale "Use of Equity Capital Market – Monitoring Function [Nutzung der Kontrollfunktion des Kapitalmarktes]"			
Descriptive Statistics		*Result of Exploratory Factor Analysis*	
Cronbach's alpha:	0.86	Total variance explained:	0.78
Results of Confirmatory Factor Analysis			
Factor reliability:	0.87	Average variance explained:	0.70

References

***Eckey, M./Schäffer, U.* (2006): Kontrolle von Mehrheitsbeteiligungen in börsennotierten Management-Holdings, in: Zeitschrift für Planung & Unternehmenssteuerung, Vol. 17, pp. 251-280.**

224. Use of Measurement Alignment Techniques

Scale Description

The scale describes the use of several techniques that are claimed to improve the alignment between performance measurement systems and the firm's organizational objectives. These techniques include the balanced scorecard process, economic value measurement, and causal business models.

Origin

Ittner et al. (2003) developed the construct based on Krumwiede (1998).

Samples

A random sample of 600 US financial services firms was solicited to participate in the survey. A marketing research firm telephoned senior executives from each of these firms to request participation. Those agreeing to participate were sent a survey or guided to a web site containing the questionnaire. Executives from 140 firms (23.3%) completed usable surveys.

Scale Indicators and Reliability / Validity Parameters

Scale: from 1 (not considered) to 6 (used extensively)

Information on individual indicators regarding "Use of Measurement Alignment Techniques"
Description of indicators
1. Implementation of balanced scorecards measures
2. Implementation economic value measures (e.g., economic value added or cash flow return on investment)
3. Extent of formal reliance on a „business model" or „theory of business" that causally links performance drivers to performance outcomes

Information on scale "Use of Measurement Alignment Techniques"			
Descriptive Statistics		*Result of Exploratory Factor Analysis*	
Cronbach's alpha:	–*	Total variance explained:	–*

*Not available

References

***Ittner, C. D./Larcker, D. F./Randall, T.* (2003): Performance Implications of Strategic Performance Measurement in Financial Services Firms, in: Accounting, Organizations and Society, Vol. 28, pp. 715-741.**

Krumwiede, K. R. (1998): The Implementation Stages of Activity-Based Costing and the Impact of Contextual and Organizational Factors, in: Journal of Management Accounting Research, Vol. 10, pp. 239-277.

225. User Involvement

Scale Description

The scale measures manager's involvement in the process of generating and adapting the output of the accounting department.

Origin

The scale was adopted by Aust (1999) from Moorman/Deshpandé/Zaltman (1993). An enhanced version of the scale was used by Hunold (2003).

Samples

The questionnaire was sent to 2,386 German upper level managers. 254 responses could be integrated into the analysis, yielding a response rate of 11.1%.

Scale Indicators and Reliability / Validity Parameters

Scale: from 1 (definitely false) to 5 (definitely true)

Information on individual indicators regarding "User Involvement"			
Description of indicators	*Item to Total-Correlation*	*Indicator-Reliability*	*t statistic*
1. Meine Vorstellungen werden beim Entwurf und bei der Veränderung der Kostenrechnung und ihrer Produkte erfragt.	0.85	–*	–*
2. Beim Entwurf und der Veränderung der Kostenrechnung und ihrer Produkte werden meine Vorstellungen berücksichtigt.	0.85	–*	–*

Information on scale "User Involvement"			
Descriptive Statistics		*Result of Exploratory Factor Analysis*	
Cronbach's alpha:	0.92	Total variance explained:	0.93

*Not feasible

References

***Aust, R.* (1999): Kostenrechnung als unternehmensinterne Dienstleistung, Wiesbaden 1999, pp. 163-164.**

Hunold, C. (2003): Kommunale Kostenrechnung. Gestaltung, Nutzung und Erfolgsfaktoren, Wiesbaden 2003.

Moorman, C./Deshpandé, R./Zaltman, G. (1993): Factors affecting Trust in Market Research Relationships, in: Journal of Marketing, Vol. 57, pp. 81-101.

226. User Know-how

Scale Description

The scale measures the extent, to which managers perceive themselves as capable of understanding and utilizing the metrics used to monitor their business unit.

Origin

The scale was adopted by Sandt (2004) from Frank (2000). A similar operationalization was used by Schäffer/Steiners (2004).

Samples

The questionnaire was sent to 2,386 German upper level managers. 254 responses could be integrated into the analysis, yielding a response rate of 11.1%.

Scale Indicators and Reliability / Validity Parameters

Scale: from 1 (definitely false) to 5 (definitely true)

Information on individual indicators regarding "User Know-how"			
Description of indicators	*Item to Total-Correlation*	*Indicator-Reliability*	*t statistic*
1. Die Berechnungsmethodik ist mir sehr gut bekannt.	0.75	0.72	20.35
2. Ich muß nicht lange über die Bedeutung nachdenken.	0.69	0.59	19.24
3. Ich frage mich oft, was hinter den Kennzahlen steckt. (R)	0.57	0.50	18.16
4. Der Aussagegehalt der Kennzahlen ist mir klar.	0.76	0.75	20.49
5. Ich kann die Kennzahlen ohne weiteres einem Dritten erklären.	0,82	0,84	21,04

Information on scale "User Know-how"			
Descriptive Statistics		*Result of Exploratory Factor Analysis*	
Cronbach's alpha:	0.67	Total variance explained:	0.87
Results of Confirmatory Factor Analysis			
χ^2-Value (Degrees of Freedom):	1.64 (2)	χ^2-Value/Degrees of Freedom:	0.82
p Value:	0.90	RMSEA:	0.00
SRMR:	–*	CFI:	0.99
GFI:	1.00	AGFI:	1.00
Factor reliability:	0.91	Average variance explained:	0.68

*Not available

References

Sandt, J. (2004): Management mit Kennzahlen und Kennzahlensystemen. Bestandsaufnahme, Determinanten und Erfolgswirkungen, Wiesbaden 2004, pp. 136-137.

Frank, S. (2000): Erfolgreiche Gestaltung der Kostenrechnung: Determinanten und Wirkungen am Beispiel mittelständischer Unternehmen, Wiesbaden 2000.

Schäffer, U./Steiners, D. (2004): Zur Nutzung von Controllinginformationen, in: Zeitschrift für Planung und Unternehmenssteuerung, Vol. 15, pp. 377-404.

227. Vertical Coordination [Vertikale Koordination]

Scale Description

The scale measures the extent to which the strategic planning process is managed by a central planning unit as opposed to being managed in the functional units.

Origin

The scale was newly developed by Willauer as part of a doctoral research project. Results were published in Weber/Schäffer/Willauer (2003).

Samples

Survey data were collected by questionnaire, administered to managers of planning departments of 4,186 German companies from the industrial sector. A total of 298 usable questionnaires (7.1%) were returned.

Scale Indicators and Reliability / Validity Parameters

Scale: from 1 (definitely false) to 7 (definitely true)

Information on individual indicators regarding "Vertical Coordination [Vertikale Koordination]"			
Description of indicators	*Item to Total-Correlation*	*Indicator-Reliability*	*t statistic*
1. Die Konzernplanung setzt bei uns die Eckpunkte für die strategische/langfristige Planung unserer Geschäftseinheit.	0.86	0.82	21.93
2. Ziele und Maßnahmen der strategischen/langfristigen Planung unserer Geschäftseinheit sind auf die Ziele und Maßnahmen der Konzernplanung ausgerichtet.	0.87	0.87	22.19
3. Die Konzernplanung setzt bei uns die Eckpunkte für die operative Planung unserer Geschäftseinheit.	0.84	0.81	21.87
4. Ziele und Maßnahmen der operativen Planung unserer Geschäftseinheit sind auf die Ziele und Maßnahmen der Konzernplanung ausgerichtet.	0.86	0.85	22.08

Information on scale "Vertical Coordination [Vertikale Koordination]"			
Descriptive Statistics		*Result of Exploratory Factor Analysis*	
Cronbach's alpha:	0.94	Total variance explained:	0.85
Results of Confirmatory Factor Analysis			
χ^2-Value (Degrees of Freedom):	2.45(2)	χ^2-Value/Degrees of Freedom:	1.23
p Value:	0.29	RMSEA:	0.03
SRMR:	–*	CFI:	1.00
GFI:	1.00	AGFI:	0.99
Factor reliability:	0.95	Average variance explained:	0.84

*Not available

References

Weber, J./Schäffer, U./Willauer, B. **(2003): Skalenübersicht, in: Weber, J./Kunz, J. (Ed.): Empirische Controllingforschung: Begründung, Beispiele, Ergebnisse, Wiesbaden 2003, pp. 385-467.**

228. Utilization Intensity [Nutzungsintensität]

Scale Description

The scale measures how regularly accounting information is asked for and used by treasurers of communes.

Origin

The scale was newly developed by Hunold (2003) based on an approach of Schewe (1979).

Samples

Survey data were collected by questionnaire administered to treasurers and accountants of 1,520 German municipalities as part of a dyadic research design. A total of 201 usable dyads (13.22%) were returned.

Scale Indicators and Reliability / Validity Parameters

Scale: from 1 (definitely false) to 7 (definitely true)

Information on individual indicators regarding "Utilization Intensity [Nutzungsintensität]"			
Description of indicators	*Item to Total-Correlation*	*Indicator-Reliability*	*t statistic*
1. Ich lasse mir häufig Kostenrechnungsinformationen zukommen.	0.84	0.84	13.61
2. Neben regelmäßigen Standardberichten frage ich bei Entscheidungen oftmals um weitere spezifische Kostenrechnungsinformationen.	0.80	0.74	13.61
3. Insgesamt benutze ich die Kostenrechnungsinformationen intensiv.	0.87	0.91	13.61

Information on scale "Utilization Intensity [Nutzungsintensität]"			
Descriptive Statistics		*Result of Exploratory Factor Analysis*	
Cronbach's alpha:	0.92	Total variance explained:	0.586
Results of Confirmatory Factor Analysis			
Factor reliability:	0.94	Average variance explained:	0.83

References

***Hunold, C.* (2003): Kommunale Kostenrechnung. Gestaltung, Nutzung und Erfolgsfaktoren, Wiesbaden 2003, pp. 181-182.**

Schewe, C. D. (1976): The Management Information System User, An exploratory Behavioral Analysis, in: Academy of Management Journal, Vol. 19, pp. 577-590.

229. Weak-Point Analysis and Measures Development [Schwachstellenanalyse und Maßnahmenentwicklung]

Scale Description

The scale indicates manager's perception of the controlling staff's involvement and scope of activities in the process of analyzing weak-points and generating appropriate counter-measures.

Origin

The scale was newly developed by Bauer (2002).

Samples

Survey data were collected by questionnaire, administered via mail to 2,527 German companies. A total of 347 companies sent usable answers, yielding a 14.8% return rate.

Comments

The study used a dyadic design approach, where a manager and a controller of the same company were questioned. The data for this scale sole stem from the answers of the managers.

Scale Indicators and Reliability / Validity Parameters

Scale: from 1 (definitely false) to 7 (definitely true)

Information on individual indicators regarding "Weak-Point Analysis and Measures Development [Schwachstellenanalyse und Maßnahmenentwicklung]"			
Description of indicators	*Item to Total-Correlation*	*Indicator-Reliability*	*t statistic*
1. Unser Controller sucht systematisch nach möglichen Schwachstellen im Geschäft.	0.73	0.68	25.9
2. Hinweise auf Schwachstellen koppelt er stets mit einer Analyse der Ursachen.	0.79	0.79	26.6
3. Der Controller entwickelt Maßnahmen zur Beseitigung der Schwachstellen mit.	0.71	0.58	25.1
4. Die Bewertung der Wirkung von Maßnahmen übernimmt unser Controller.	0.72	0.59	25.1

Information on scale "Weak-Point Analysis and Measures Development [Schwachstellen-analyse und Maßnahmenentwicklung]"			
Descriptive Statistics		*Result of Exploratory Factor Analysis*	
Cronbach's alpha:	0.88	Total variance explained:	0.73
Results of Confirmatory Factor Analysis			
χ^2-Value (Degrees of Freedom):	5.85 (2)	χ^2-Value/Degrees of Freedom:	2.93
p Value:	0.05	RMSEA:	0.06
NFI:	1.00	NNFI:	–*
GFI:	1.00	AGFI:	0.99
Factor reliability:	0.89	Average variance explained:	0.66

*Not available

References

Bauer, M. **(2002): Controllership in Deutschland. Zur erfolgreichen Zusammenarbeit von Controllern und Managern, Wiesbaden 2002, pp. 195-196.**

230. Workload Equity

Scale Description
The scale measures the degree of workload equity.

Origin
Developed by Quirin et al. (2001).

Samples
Data was collected using a survey questionnaire sent to a total of 240 managers from a cross-section of 15 large U.S. companies. The sample of companies represented a variety of industries. Of the 240 surveys distributed, respondents returned a total 105 usable surveys for a response rate of 44%.

Comments
Quirin et al. (2001) reported a scale mean of 22.89 and a standard deviation of 6.54 on a range of 5-35.

Scale Indicators and Reliability / Validity Parameters
Scale: from 1 (strongly disagree) to 7 (strongly agree)

Information on individual indicators regarding "Workload Equity"			
Description of indicators			
I feel my workload is equitable when compared to:			
1. Others in this company at my job level.			
2. What other employers are asking employees at my job level.			
3. What the company told me I would do when I accepted this position.			
4. What others below me in the company are asked to do.			
5. What my superior is asked to do.			
Information on scale "Workload Equity"			
Descriptive Statistics		*Result of Exploratory Factor Analysis*	
Cronbach's alpha:	0.92	Total variance explained:	–*

*Not available

References
***Quirin, J. J./Donnelly, D. P./O'Bryan, D.* (2001): Antecedents of Organizational Commitment: The Role of Perception of Equity, in: Advances in Accounting Behavioral Research, Vol. 4, pp. 261-280.**

MIX
Papier aus verantwortungsvollen Quellen
Paper from responsible sources
FSC® C105338

If you have any concerns about our products,
you can contact us on
ProductSafety@springernature.com

In case Publisher is established outside the EU,
the EU authorized representative is:
Springer Nature Customer Service Center GmbH
Europaplatz 3, 69115 Heidelberg, Germany

Printed by Libri Plureos GmbH
in Hamburg, Germany